To the people connected with creating the new shopping environment, may this book serve as an inspiration for continuous enhancement of this important phase of our daily living.

New Dimensions in Shopping Centers and Stores

Library of Congress Cataloging in Publication Data

Redstone, Louis G
    New dimensions in shopping centers and stores.

    1. Shopping centers.   I. Title.
NA6218.R43   711'.552   73-4021
ISBN 0-07-051368-6

*The editors for this book were William G. Salo, Jr.,
Lydia Maiorca Driscoll, and Robert E. Curtis,
the design and layout was done by Naomi Auerbach,
and its production was supervised by Teresa F. Leaden.
It was set in Optima by York Graphic Services, Inc.*

*It was printed by Halliday Lithograph Corporation and
bound by The Book Press.*

Contents

PART FOUR *Store Interiors* 231

PART FIVE *Reconversion and Preservation* 275

In the formative years of shopping centers, the developer/landlord often operated on instinct and logic to develop what he considered to be a strong, viable center, only to find that his reliance on empiricism frequently produced long-term commitments marked by weakness and potential errors.

Louis Redstone's book assumes a special importance during the present transition period, when social, ecological, and economic factors compel the developer to take a fresh look ahead. No longer can planning be hit-or-miss. Today's technology and knowledge, combined with the experience of close to a quarter century of shopping center development, is available to assist at every turn in studying the feasibility of our new projects.

This book gives today's developer an opportunity to review his thinking in a variety of new and productive channels. The ideas he can bring to bear to update existing centers are particularly helpful, for they will not only strengthen present centers but also help ensure the success of future operations.

For the new-center developer, the book provides an effective checklist that outlines in detail the procedures to follow, from site acquisition to final construction and operation, in creating a new retailing complex.

Architects and store designers will benefit from the generously illustrated review of some of the better-designed centers and stores of the last few years as well as of new concepts now in the planning stages, including a discussion of special design features and solutions to problems encountered in construction.

The references to the emergence of the center as the springboard for the new town, encompassing all the necessary facilities for well-rounded living, are particularly timely in the light of current industry thinking.

The author's stress on the importance of esthetics, including generous use of art, fountains, graphics, and landscaping as essential to the total concept, is in keeping with today's concept of transforming shopping centers into community centers in the broadest sense.

The shopping center industry is proud to have one of its respected professionals present a book that accurately reflects the past, present, and future of this fascinating business.

Foreword
by KENNETH TUCKER
President of International Council of Shopping Centers

The main purpose of this book is to focus the attention of architects, designers, and developers on new concepts in shopping center design and to stimulate their imaginations with examples that are either already completed or on the drafting boards. This material includes new trends in the design of regional centers; new approaches in store design; the reconversion of existing, uneconomic old buildings; and the preservation, wherever possible, of the historic character of worthwhile structures which could be converted to functional and profitable uses. I will deal briefly with the important subject of the development of completely new towns, where the shopping center will emerge as an integral part of the town's cultural and recreational character as well as its economic life.

A special section of the book will be devoted to the analysis of new procedures of planning, from the initial schematic stages to the final completion of the project. This section will include building systems, construction management and bidding methods, scheduling of construction operations through the critical path method, and quality control of all phases of the project.

The important elements of maintenance and operation, security, burglar protection systems, fire protection, and handling of public assemblies and demonstrations are given special attention.

The subject of shopping centers is so complex and encompasses so many different disciplines that it would be difficult to cover all its aspects in a single volume. However, I do hope that this book will be of help and interest to the profession and the general public. If its contents will lead to a better understanding of and improved solutions to the problems of shopping center design, it will indeed be a great satisfaction to me.

Louis G. Redstone

Preface

Acknowledgments

Since the preparation of this material involved so many specialized fields, I am indebted to a great extent to members of my staff and experts in the various disciplines for their help in creating a comprehensive presentation on the subject of shopping centers. I wish to thank the following members of my staff: Bernard Colton, AIA, for material on leasing; Dominic Merucci, PE, on lighting systems; Leo G. Shea, AIA, CSI, on construction implementation; and Henry Vallar, PE, on mechanical systems. My thanks and appreciation also go to the following consultants: Harold Black, market analyst and planner, for his assistance in the market and economic study; Earl Heenan, president of the Detroit Mortgage and Realty Company, and Daniel Redstone, president of Mid-America Properties, for financial studies; Robert G. Faber, city councilman and planning commissioner of Ann Arbor, Michigan, for his analysis of the social factors in planning commercial units; Wesley O. Mewer, formerly security superintendent with the J. L. Hudson Co. and presently security director of A.C.E., Inc., of Redford, Michigan; Lloyd Reid, PE, traffic engineering consultant of Reid, Cool & Michalski, Inc., for traffic study; Ralph Stephenson, PE, technical management consultant of Detroit for critical path material; and Joseph C. White, president of Syncon, for the data illustrating a completed systems center. I am especially indebted to the AIA state chapters and to the Canadian chapters of the Royal Institute of Architects, which brought me up to date on the recent shopping centers in their locales. To the architects of Germany, Australia, and Switzerland and to the editors of the many professional magazines and periodicals, not only of the United States and Canada but also of Japan, I am deeply indebted for their helpful cooperation. I thank the many architects, developers, and designers who so generously supplied me with excellent graphic materials and photographs as well as descriptive data. Other experts and consultants whose names are not mentioned here are acknowledged in the text itself. This includes statements on management problems, sociopolitical factors, special lighting systems, etc.

A special word of appreciation goes to my secretarial assistant Mrs. Gloria Barnabo Tonelli, and above all to my wife, Ruth, whose assistance and enthusiasm made this a stimulating and enjoyable experience.

Louis G. Redstone

Throughout the world, shopping for goods and services, acquiring these either by exchange of money or goods, always has been and still is an important part of the daily life of the family. Shopping methods and habits are varied and contrasting from one part of the world to another as well as from the city to village or farm areas. As varied as these may seem, however, upon comparing the outdoor, one-day market in the hinterland of Ecuador or the small hole-in-the-wall type of shop in the narrow market streets of the old section of Jerusalem to the very contemporary and elaborate shopping centers springing up in large numbers throughout the North American continent and other parts of the world, the underlying and basic desire in all these settings is to create a pleasant environment—not only for the purpose of buying goods and services but also to satisfy a social need. The human being seeks communication with others. In the primitive market, where people walk often many miles from far outlying, isolated areas carrying their produce and goods, the social aspect probably is the most important part of the person's experience. It becomes a festive day, and the market assumes the role of cummunity get-together and is a pleasurable culmination of the week's work.

Introduction

Port-au-Prince, Haiti.

Near Quito, Ecuador.

Addis Ababa, Ethiopia.

La Paz, Bolivia.

ABOVE: *The Old City of Jerusalem.*
BELOW: *The Old City of Nazareth.*

This important social aspect of the marketplace gradually lost its role when the rural patterns gave way to the sophistication and subsequent detachment characteristic of city life. In large cities, commercial centers were created in what we call central business districts. These were close to the administrative and recreational facilities, forming the dynamics of city life patterns.

In the smaller cities, for the most part, the commercial areas were and still are limited to the one and only "main street." This system worked quite well until the advent of the automobile. Where previously people had arrived by streetcar or bus, they now preferred to use their own cars. (For an idea of the number of cars the bus replaces, see chart.) It didn't take very long for the people to become increasingly unhappy about the problem of finding a parking space, paying for that privilege, and then walking some distance to their final destination. Despite the proliferation of private surface parking lots and the addition of a number of underground public parking facilities, the need for more parking spaces was still great. The merchants, on their part, saw their business volume slowly diminishing and made various efforts to attract people downtown to shop. In some instances, streets were blocked off from car traffic, minibuses were provided for a minimum charge, storefronts were remodeled, canopies were provided for weather protection, and special promotions of sales were planned by the downtown merchants' association.

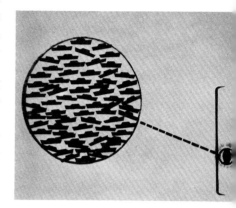

These solutions, however, were of the "Band-aid" type and did not get to the root of the problem. The movement of the population to the suburbs continued to accelerate. The inadequate improvements were too little and too late to make any difference to those about to join the exodus to the suburbs. It was only natural for the movement of the population to the suburbs to bring an immediate demand for shopping facilities. Because all the shopping would be done by those living within a radius of several miles of the new facilities, free parking was one of the first prerequisites for their success.

In brief, suburban commercial development started in the late forties in the form of small neighborhood centers consisting of a supermarket, a drugstore, and a few service stores. This was shortly followed by the so-called strip-center concept, which consisted of an unbroken line of sixteen to twenty stores with adequate parking in front. Most of these strip centers had a protective canopy across the length of the strip. The early fifties saw the beginning of the regional shopping center. This type of center usually was based on one or two major department stores which served as "anchors" at each end of a group of thirty to fifty specialty shops. With a few exceptions, these early regional centers had open, landscaped malls.

The sixties brought a new trend in shopping center development, introducing the closed-mall concept. These also were planned with two or three major department stores as the main attraction but with enclosed courts and arcades interconnecting with fifty to eighty specialty shops and service stores. The possibility of shopping in a controlled climate is probably one of the greatest factors in giving this type of center an added advantage for customer attraction.

Investment in the shopping center industry has shown, in the main, a good financial return, and we may expect, with the rapid growth of population, a continuing demand for more shopping facilities. In the decade of the seventies, it is estimated that there will be between two and three thousand new and remodeled center complexes planned and built. In Canada, rate of growth is expected to parallel that of the United States. Stan Witkin, vice president of development for the Fairview Corporation, Ltd., confirmed that "the new center complexes will need the expertise of many disciplines. These include economists, sociologists, financiers, architects, engineers, lawyers, experts in transportation and merchandise, environmental planners, and trained administrators to coordinate the various aspects of the centers' commercial and community activities."

The seventies will see radical changes in the design of centers. A beginning is already being made in the building of two- and three-level centers which have as their main attraction three to five department (anchor) stores. This concept is a forerunner of new small satellite towns, whose centers will include many of the amenities that the towns will require, i.e., recreation, offices, civic and governmental facilities, and even church quarters. The surrounding residential areas will be master planned to tie-in with such centers.

The economics of the sixties and early seventies, when ample and inexpensive farmland was available, favored the planning of vast areas of surface asphalt parking. This created an unsightly gap between the center and the residential areas. Such space in the future will be utilized in a more productive way; that is, it will be filled with additional commercial facilities, professional office buildings, multilevel parking structures, use of the land for sports, parkways, etc.

Another phase of development activity in the seventies will be the conversion of the open-type mall center of the fifties and sixties to the completely enclosed center. This will appear mostly in those parts of the country where weather conditions make the enclosed mall a shoppers' attraction. Still another building activity will take place in the expansion and remodeling of the many existing enclosed centers which must be updated, in order to create new attractions to compete with the more recently built centers. The necessity for such remodeling and updating will apply not only to the centers but to individual stores as well, whether these are located in the centers or in downtown areas.

Parallel with the development of large regional centers and new town centers, there will be a trend of replacing the small neighborhood shops with mini-mall centers. The mini-mall is envisioned as an enclosed 80,000 to 150,000 square foot mall containing approximately twenty stores and boutiques, with the largest store having an area between 18,000 to 25,000 square feet. This smaller-type mall will also provide an opportunity for a number of black developers to enter this field and to become experienced in the planning, building, and administration of centers.

The effort to create a better center is being stimulated by the recent trend whereby the developers, architects, and contractors form a joint venture. Such teams, working closely with the community leaders and public authorities, will no doubt achieve better results in fulfilling aesthetic as well as functional requirements. The long-range concept factor which this type of planning should incorporate would make the project more remunerative because of its much more lasting quality.

Environmental and ecological factors will be of prime concern to the developers and planners of all future centers. Such elements as the preservation of existing natural land attractions, additional parkways, pedestrian safety and comfort, improvements in disposal of waste materials, etc., must be given increased attention and consideration.

We cannot emphasize enough the importance of the above-mentioned factors. The shopping activity which has always been and still is a major part of family life warrants the best efforts of our architects, designers, and developers. This team is challenged to create an environment which, in addition to the functional uses, would combine pleasurable and aesthetic experiences for the shopper.

PART ONE

Suburban Shopping Centers

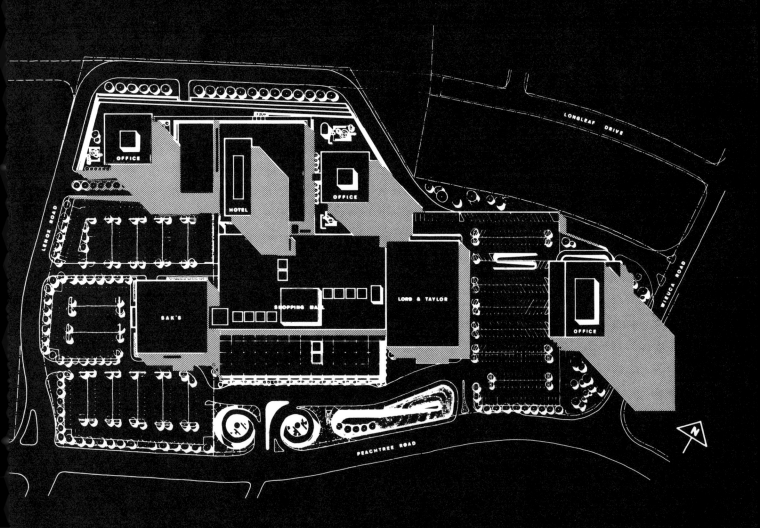

BASIC CONSIDERATIONS IN SHOPPING CENTER DEVELOPMENT

The following digest is presented in broad terms, encompassing vital steps in the procedures of developing a shopping center. Detailed studies have been published by many connected with this field. My purpose is to highlight those changes that are currently taking place at an astonishingly rapid tempo.

Whether you are a private entrepreneur developing land for the first time or whether you have had previous experience with shopping centers, there are basic steps that have to be taken to accomplish the final goal of building a viable commercial center.

Site Acquisition

The first step is the *site acquisition*. In some instances, the developer already owns the site or needs only contiguous parcels of land to round out for a desirable area or shape. The additional parcels of land can be negotiated through a local broker who would be discreet in keeping private the knowledge of ownership and purpose. In order to keep information confidential, the purchase of land is usually made in the name of the broker.

Some developers will assemble tracts of land which in their opinion are suitable for future development. They acquire these parcels either outright through brokers, or they get options for a lengthy period until necessary studies (outlined below) can be made and major tenants secured. The option period may vary from six to eighteen months.

One of the most important things that must be done before acquiring a site is to obtain a thorough knowledge of the utilities available. Also, the soil must be tested at a number of random locations on site. The utilities to be checked should include sanitary sewers, storm sewers or drains, gas mains, water mains, and electric power. It is necessary to obtain a map of all existing utilities from the city and county engineer's office. Should sanitary facilities, sewers, water mains, or any other utilities have to be brought in from the nearest source, the cost of such work should be ascertained.

Regarding the soil conditions, a number of borings to the depth of 40 feet in the projected building area and a number to the depth of 10 to 15 feet in the other areas (parking, landscaping, small adjacent buildings, etc.) are imperative. The results may be completely satisfactory for normal foundation work and basement construction. On the other hand, the tests may show a high water level and poor soil conditions, making the cost of foundation and basement construction prohibitive. In some cases, however, the additional costs of solving the above problems may be justified by the economic advantages which the specific site offers.

Other cost factors to be considered by the developer in connection with site acquisition are the legal requirements of the public authorities for highway widening and center approaches. Preliminary estimates for these improvements should be obtained from these authorities.

It is also important to check for the possible existence of easements assigned to electric, telephone, and other utility companies. In many cases, these easements will interfere with the proper setting of the main buildings unless costly arrangements are made to reroute them. Throughout the period of determining the above-mentioned factors, it is imperative that the services of an architect, a traffic consultant, and a real estate attorney be retained.

Other criteria for site selection which the developer should consider are housing growth and the number of potential future shoppers, community attitudes of local government officials and merchants, adequate fire protection, regional traffic patterns, topography, site, zoning, and cost of land. The site must be large enough to accommodate the projected buying needs of the area. This must be determined by feasibility studies which should include economic, traffic and projected population growth, which are discussed in the following section.

The recent development programs of new towns, initiated by large industrial corporations and national companies, suggest another approach to site determination. Here, the commercial center is only one part, although a most important part, of the total *master plan*. Integrated into this plan are the residential, recreational, and educational facilities. Here, the private developer may have an opportunity to acquire the site designated for the commercial center to be built within the guidelines of the master plan.

Although most of the background information will be available to him through the studies made by the prime developer, it will still be necessary to analyze and evaluate the economic viability of the commercial center before the final decision is made.

Market and Economic Study

Whether the site is already owned or under option, the next important step would be to have a *market and economic study*. This study is important to the developer, and it is also a necessary tool for presenting the project to the department stores and other tenants as well as to the financial institutions, the local zoning boards, and the municipality. The economic market analysis, in general, should include the following:

1. Accessibility and nearness to existing major regional highways
2. Proximity of other trade tributaries to the proposed center
3. Analysis of future population trends and income projections within radius of 1 to 6 miles
4. Analysis of total expenditures per capita within radius of 1 to 6 miles
5. Survey of driving time from site, calculated for intervals of five minutes, ten minutes, and forty-five minutes, as related to the distances from the center
6. Study of types of major and specialty stores most needed in this area
7. Analysis of the effect on the projected center of the existing discount department stores and retail stores serving the area
8. Analysis of sales-volume potential foreseeable over a ten-year period
9. Determination that no other major shopping center is being planned within the primary trade area of the proposed center

A shopping center is first and foremost an economic entity. Whatever social, cultural, or political impact a shopping development might have on its community, its essential purpose is economic. What is the profit potential at this site? Will a shopping center here make money? It is the job of market analysis to provide as precise an answer to that question as possible.

A market study must define the total amount of spendable income available within the prospective market area. (The "market area," very simply, is that geographical area which can reasonably be expected to provide customers for the proposed shopping center.) If we know the number of families and average family income within the market area, then we can easily determine the total income available to the proposed site. This is the base figure from which all the calculations and conclusions of the market study are derived.

We then have to determine typical spending patterns (e.g., what percent of family income is spent on what commodities?); how much demand there might be for a given commodity; how many square feet of retail space there ought to be for each kind of retail store; how these last two figures will have to be corrected for the existence of competing retail outlets within or near the market area, and so on.

The statistics for this part of the market study come primarily from two sources: the U.S. Bureau of the Census and the U.S. Bureau of Labor Statistics.

The census provides data on family size and age distribution, the number of families within a given market area, the income of the families, own/rent ratios, and so on. These (and other) data are accumulated and summarized in the census in a number of ways (census tract, block, metropolitan area, county, etc.), so that the analyst can look at the site from a number of points of view—with different-powered lenses, so to speak—and can accumulate small-area information for the area under study.

The Bureau of Labor Statistics provides valuable data on regional spending habits—what the typical family with a given income tends to spend its money on. These statistics, combined with figures from the census, can provide a relatively accurate overview of the area under study—that is, if the area happens to be under study sometime close to a census year. The census data, however accurate they may be at the time of the survey, are generally two years old (if the computer is used) or more than four years old by the time they are published and available. Any market study of this type can therefore give us only a general kind of analysis. However, an experienced analyst can refine this data by using common-sense judgment and utilizing any relevant information wherever he can find it. This includes evaluation of building permits, local and regional planning surveys, recent population estimates and sales tax data by counties, etc.

He has a feeling for the special attitudes and habits of the consumer in this region. He can recommend from his experience what kinds of stores will be successful in this center, what kinds of stores will tend to complement each other's sales. He can also analyze, in general, the traffic-flow patterns and general requirements.

However helpful this study is, it can be improved greatly by making a more exact survey of the area involved. This analysis is based on a random-sample survey of the area and is a much more expensive process. It would require a random selection of families within the general market area and a questionnaire that is later tabulated and summarized. The accuracy and reliability of these findings will expedite the decisions, thereby saving valuable time and effort.

Market analysis is of importance not only to the developer but also to any of the interested parties who have large financial stakes in the shopping center. Among these are the financial institutions that provide mortgages and the local government, which is often called upon to make large investments in the construction of new sewers, roads, water service, fire protection, and other public services. Last but not least, the individual retailers who are the tenants in this development and who extend themselves to make a substantial financial investment are very much interested in this type of economic report.

To double check the various findings before final site selections are made, whether for individual stores or for centers, developers are relying more and more on the use of the computer. Because three to five years may pass from the time of site selection to the opening of the center, the proper input of all available data should provide the developer with a fairly accurate projection for a number of years following the opening.

In terms of physical planning, the market analysis helps the architect to prepare the initial schematic drawings. It assists him in determining the sizes and types of stores and in projecting future expansion. Based on the market analysis, the architect's schematic drawings, and the cost estimates, the developer is given a thorough insight into the potential for a successful venture.

Traffic Studies

The traffic engineering consultant plays an important role in the development of the regional shopping center. From the time of inception to the time that the center is open for business (and frequently even after that), recommendations of the traffic engineering consultant can mean the difference between a thriving and successful enterprise and one that is marginal. After all, if the customer encounters a lot of difficulty getting to, in, out, or home from the center, he or she may very well decide to shop elsewhere in the future.

The traffic engineering consultant is part of a team which includes the developer, the market analyst, the architect, and the civil engineer. As indicated earlier, he is involved from the beginning to the end in five different but related capacities:

1. Choosing the site
2. Design of the exterior road system and connections, and negotiations with concerned county and state highway authorities
3. Design of the interior parking and circulation facilities
4. Traffic-control signs and markings
5. Follow-up

In choosing the site for a regional shopping center, the developer relies on the traffic engineering consultant for answers to several pertinent questions. In order to answer these questions, the consultant ascertains the relationship of a prospective site to the market area. Then he must determine whether there are any immediate traffic problems in the vicinity of the site. He must evaluate the existing road system, taking into consideration known plans for improvements of the highways; he must determine probable road improvements; and, finally, he must alert his client to any apparent unsolvable deficiencies that would make the regional center difficult or impossible to operate.

In some instances regional shopping centers were not built because of the negative findings of the traffic consultant. In one particular case, access to one of two arterials was not economically feasible. Without this access, a great number of turning movements would have to take place at an already overburdened intersection.

After the developer has decided to proceed with the shopping center, he usually acquires the land (subject to rezoning, which is frequently necessary). Quite often the local governmental unit is most anxious to have the regional shopping center because of its tax base, so that there is seldom any difficulty in obtaining rezoning. When opposition to rezoning does appear, the traffic consultant can be of great assistance in presenting the case.

After the site has been selected and necessary approvals have been obtained, the traffic engineering consultant determines the roadway requirements of the center. Here the report of the market analyst assumes great importance. If no market analysis is available, then the traffic engineering consultant must add an economic survey to his services by analyzing the population data and the locations of competing centers. Assignments of potential customers from within the market area are then made. These assignments are weighted by their distances from the center and their locations relative to competing centers. From this step, routings to the site from their locations within the market area are determined. A traffic flow diagram is prepared to show the distribution of the traffic that would be generated by the center over the thoroughfare system. As a rule, the average center will generate about forty daily trips per thousand square feet of gross leaseable area—twenty inbound and twenty outbound.

Using data obtained from established centers, traffic volumes for three critical periods are determined. These include the hour during which the thoroughfares are heavily traveled by people going from their places of employment to their homes, usually 5 to 6 P.M., when the center will usually generate 2 trips per thousand square feet each way; the hour when most people travel from their homes to the center, usually 7 to 8 P.M., when there will usually be 2.5 to 3 trips per thousand in and 2 trips per thousand out; and the hour nearest the closing time of the center, usually 8:30 to 9:30 P.M., when there will be about 1.5 trips per thousand in and 3 trips per thousand out. Estimates of traffic that would be generated by the center are added to traffic counts conducted on the existing thoroughfare system to determine the total traffic load to which the streets would be subjected during the three critical hours.

An appraisal is then made of the ability of the roadway system to absorb the anticipated increases in traffic volumes. The next step in the procedure is the formulation of specific recommendations to resolve problems that are found. Often, these problems require widening of intersections and roadways adjacent to the center. Very often it is necessary for the developers to persuade the governmental agencies responsible for the roads to widen them. Sometimes it is necessary for the shopping center developer to provide incentives, either by donation of right-of-way or by financially contributing to the cost of the project. Frequently, such costs amount to the price of one lane of pavement in addition to payment for the driveway approaches to the site. Considerable negotiation with official agencies may be necessary to secure agreements and approvals for such projects.

Having determined external roadway requirements, the traffic consultant then must establish the location of the driveways. The starting point usually is the preliminary site plan prepared by the architect. In determining the location of the driveways, it is important to keep in mind the following factors:

1. Location in relation to buildings on the site.
2. Location in relation to other driveways. As a rule, to minimize difficulties on external roadways a spacing of at least 300 feet between major driveways of the center should be the objective. Further, the spacing between driveways should be such that efficient use (for parking) can be made of the space on the site between drives. The actual number of driveways needed will vary from

center to center. As a general rule, it is better to have too many driveways than too few, so that each will function efficiently. Such factors as driveway volumes, grades, sight limitation, other driveways and streets, signal controls, property not in the development, and prohibited movements all enter into the picture.

3. Location of driveways with respect to existing and known future developments that are or would be located across the street from the subject center.

4. Relation to signalized intersections. Every effort should be made to avoid driveway locations so close to signals as to create unwanted problems. It may be desirable to plan for immediate or future traffic-signal control at a driveway. Hence, the driveway should be as close as possible to the logical point for signalization within the progressive signal system.

5. Location in relation to intersecting streets. The design of each driveway must also be considered individually. Quite often, a driveway on which all possible movements into and out of a site are permitted will cause problems. Left-turn traffic entering the drive may interfere with left-turn traffic leaving the drive. In many cases it is best to prohibit one of these left-turn movements. Where such prohibition is made at one driveway, motorists should be permitted to make the left turn at another driveway. Through this method, it is possible to have several different movements into and out of the site, utilizing a common gap in the through traffic on the external roadway. Wherever a driveway movement is to be prohibited, the driveway should be divided and so designed as to physically discourage the prohibited movement. Where both left and right turns are allowed out of the same driveway or where a drive is to be signalized, the driveway should have at least two outbound lanes, one for each movement.

In the design of the driveway it is desirable to keep the first opening to it at least 100 feet within the shopping center site's property line, so that traffic can flow into the center without immediately encountering side friction. If present, such side friction would cause vehicles to queue on the external highway to the detriment of through traffic that is unrelated to the center. Keeping the first opening away from the property line also provides a reservoir for the storage of cars departing from the center and promotes more efficient use of available gaps in the traffic stream on the abutting highway.

Interior Design

The traffic engineering consultant is deeply involved in the interior areas of the center. Insofar as they are practicable, the following principles should be observed in the design of interior facilities:

1. Parking arrangements should be expressly for the convenience of the shopping center patron, with the greatest supply of parking spaces most easily accessible from the heaviest approach direction. In doing this it is best to locate the customers by direction and to follow through from their street of approach to their parking lot and into the store. The parking should not necessarily be designed to be opposite the entrances to the center, but rather the entrances should be designed to conveniently fit the customer parking.

2. It should be possible for the motorist to drive from one part of the site to another without having to use any part of the exterior roadway system. If possible, there should be a continuous peripheral roadway around the entire site.

3. The design of the interior should encourage the motorist to use the peripheral road for access to the parking areas at all times.

4. Traffic immediately adjacent to the main building of the center should be held to a minimum to eliminate hazardous conflicts with pedestrians walking from parking spaces to stores and vice versa.

5. Parking stalls should be oriented at angles other than 90 degrees to aisles and should be delineated by double striping. Motorists find it much easier to maneuver into and out of angle parking stalls and cause less interference to traffic in parking area aisles. Double striping promotes better positioning of cars within the parking space and makes it easier for occupants to enter or leave their cars. It also minimizes car damage.

6. Insofar as possible, the parking aisles should be perpendicular to buildings so that customers can walk along aisles rather than between cars to reach the shopping area.

Traffic Signing

Once the design of the center has been finalized, a signing plan is prepared. Involved in this plan are both informational and control signs. As a rule, within the site, "Yield" signs are preferred to "Stop" signs to establish right-of-way without requiring unnecessary and arbitrary stops when potential conflicts are low in magnitude. In addition to the "Yield" and "Stop" signs, locations of "No Parking or Standing" signs are also included in the signing plan. In this respect it should be noted that for fire protection purposes and in order to avoid congestion and interference with pedestrian movement, parking or standing adjacent to the central buildings should not be permitted. Stopping to allow a driver to drop off or pick up a passenger should be allowed, of course. It is also important to include in the signing plan informational signs advising motorists of restrictions in movements at exits to external streets, so that the motorist is not trapped into making an unwanted maneuver or trip when he leaves the peripheral road.

The role of the traffic engineer does not end with the completion of the design of the center. When the center opens, he should check out traffic operations at the site to determine if there are any problems which need correction. Among such problems may very well be the need to install signs which did not seem necessary at the time the signing plan was prepared or the need to correct installations which were improperly made or omitted. Generally, the best policy is to ask the shopping center manager to keep the consultant posted on problems within the site so that necessary corrections can be made quickly. Naturally, the experience gained by surveillance of the site and exposure to operational problems helps the traffic engineer to avoid similar problems in the design of future centers.

Leasing

Developer organizations run the gamut from total in-house professional capability to the one-man operation which engages outside leasing expertise. In any case, the architect, whether he is a member of the developer organization or retained as architect-engineer for a particular project, can perform major services in both the preparation of the shopping center lease and in consultation during lease negotiations.

From the architect's standpoint, the lease can be divided into two major sections: one, the operating section which concerns itself primarily with lease term, rent, sales, taxes, use, maintenance, and promotion, while section two dedicates itself to the site plan, tenant space location, design, and construction.

Although the architect-engineer's primary involvement lies in the latter section, he should be thoroughly versed in all phases in order to integrate the many-faceted elements of the lease agreement. The objective, of course, is to produce trouble-free lease documents. There are many instances when the architect's experience is required and called upon. In cases where the owner chooses to assume the responsibility for the provision of heating, cooling, and electrical services to each tenant space, it is necessary for the architect-engineer to project operating, installation, and maintenance costs for both common area and tenant spaces, so that a per-square-foot cost can be apportioned to each tenant. In addition, certain tenancies such as restaurants and beauty shops require the provision of greater cooling and electrical capacities, and formulas must be developed that will enable these tenants to pay their fair shares of the operational and utility costs.

The architect should also be consulted in those lease areas which call for tenant's furnishing of drawings, specifications, and information relating to the finishing of a particular tenant space. Time limits for submittal of design and engineering drawings, as well as procedures for approval and implementation, should be set by the architect. Methods of coordinating tenant work with general construction activities should at this point be established. A schedule of design and construction activities which encompasses both landlord and tenant responsibilities and culminates in an opening date is most desirable, since this provides specific completion dates for the various phases and pinpoints responsibilities.

As noted earlier, section two of the lease document dedicates itself to the actual construction of the project and the resulting physical spaces. This section can be outlined to contain the following information in the form of exhibit drawings and descriptive data.

Exhibit A—A total site plan indicating property lines, major streets, parking lot, building location, and anticipated future expansion.

Exhibit B—A location plan which indicates the tenant space within the total building complex.

Exhibit C—A tenant-space layout indicating all columns within the demised premises, utility services, storefront line, service door, and dimensions of the space. Also, a cross section and longitudinal section of the demised premises should be shown.

Exhibit D—A complete description "landlord's work." This exhibit should clearly define all items of construction that the landlord will provide within the demised premises as well as a material schedule of finishing of malls, courts, service areas, public rest rooms, parking lots, landscaping, etc.

Exhibit E—A general description of the work which the tenant is responsible for is titled "tenant's work." This statement is primarily directed toward defining the fact that all work not provided by the landlord shall be accomplished by the tenant at the tenant's own expense.

Exhibit F—Design criteria—a detailed description of the design and construction criteria for all design, engineering, and construction to be done on the project. This exhibit is directed toward setting guidelines for all those involved in the project: tenants, architects, engineers, and contractors. This document should be very carefully prepared and made a part of all construction contracts on the project.

The foregoing exhibits are basic to all shopping center leases and can be expanded to include turn-key and partial turn-key approaches. The term *turn-key* is used when the developer provides the tenant with a completed interior and storefront based on the tenant's specifications. The landlord may also elect to provide the tenant with no more than the essential "shell" or store enclosure, bringing all utilities just inside the tenant's premises. The landlord then will give the tenant a cash allowance for finishing the storefront and all the interiors. Total allowance per square foot is based on unit cost of main items such as linear foot of storefront, ceilings, floors, and mechanical and electrical installations. The tenant has the option to engage his own architect and contractor and have his individual design used. However, the tenant in such instances would have to pay the difference between the actual cost of his own design and the cost allowed by the landlord.

When landlord and tenant are seated at the negotiating table and each is committing himself to a five-, ten-, or fifteen-year lease, all areas—rent, location, economics, legal implications, construction, and operations—must be carefully and expeditiously evaluated. Serious thought should be given to having the attorney, accountant, and architect part of such a meeting, which could result in more expert evaluation of each point in question and lead to a more rapid lease resolution.

One successful method in shopping center developments is the preparation of a graph approach to tenant improvement cost. Such a tool is of great help to lease negotiations and several typical examples of such cost graphs appear on pages 12 and 13. Note that in the case of the heating and cooling graphs two types of costs have been plotted, one for a normal retail use and the other for a restaurant or heat-generating type of business, which generally increases cooling loads. At the bottom line is the unit cost per square foot, while the vertical line indicates floor area. The graph indicates that if a tenant is contemplating a 5,000-square-foot restaurant, the estimated cost for heating and cooling of such a space will approximate $4.82 per square foot or a total cost of $24,100. This same approach can be utilized for all areas of tenant improvements such as storefronts, floors, ceilings, electrical distribution, sprinklers, etc.

It is quite evident that a commercial development, the success of which is dependent primarily on dollar return for dollar invested, requires the availability of this information during negotiations for the setting of an equitable rental rate. This input is invaluable, especially when applied to many tenants in large centers.

Shopping Center Financing

Shopping Center as Security for Loans

In recent years, the shopping center has become a popular vehicle for long-term investment. Properly planned, it is a sound investment with a relatively low risk factor. This is because, in most cases, construction is not started until several leases have been executed with strong-credit tenants and the financing has been arranged. Such preleasing to strong-credit tenants will accomplish two major objectives in effecting a low-risk investment. First, the presence of well-known tenants will attract other tenants to the center, thereby providing a high level

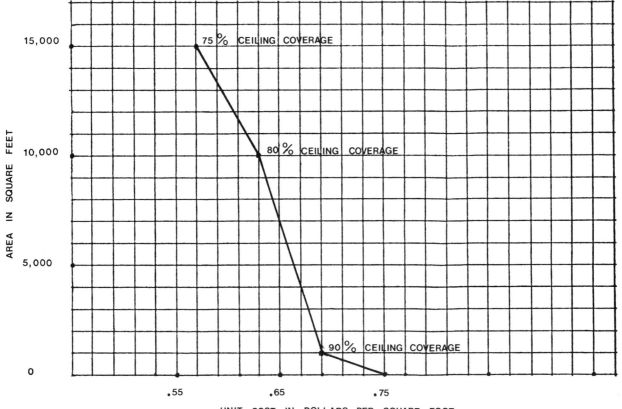

Estimated cost of tenant improvements: grid-type ceilings.

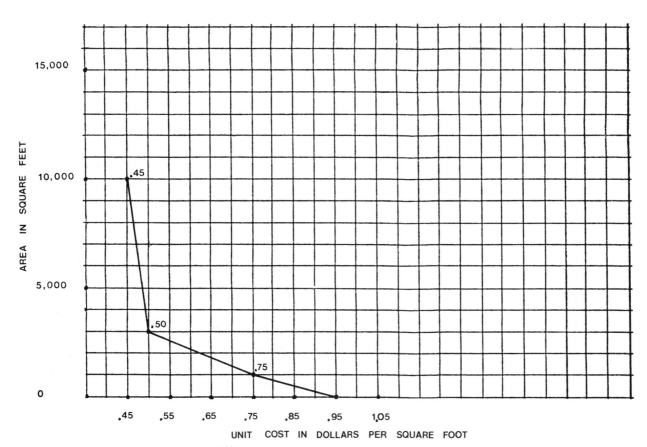

Estimated cost of tenant improvements: sprinklers.

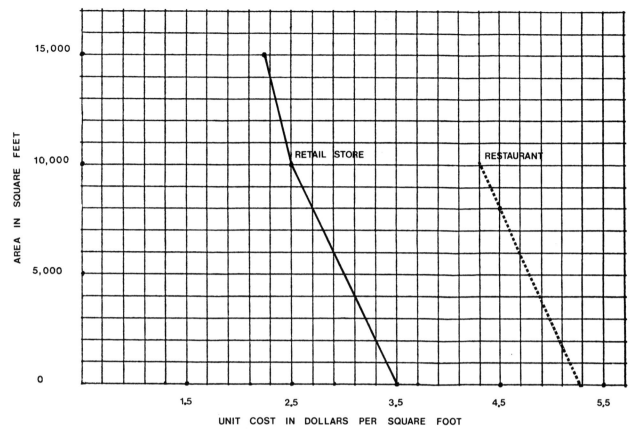

Estimated cost of tenant improvements: heating and cooling.

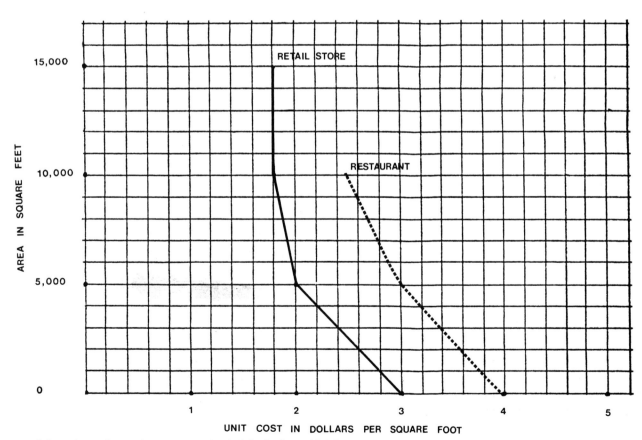

Estimated cost of tenant improvements: electrical distribution and lighting.

of occupancy; and, second, a substantial amount of the money necessary to cover debt service and operating expenses is obtained from reliable sources of income. Preleasing also enables the developer to negotiate the best terms possible for long-term financing, since the development is no longer a speculative enterprise.

Assuming the developer is sufficiently experienced or engages leasing experts to lease space at the highest possible market rents, on a net basis, with reasonable percentage rental provisions, the resulting economic value is often in excess of the cost of the development. As mortgage lenders base their loans on economic value rather than cost, developers are frequently able to restrict equity to the original cost of land. Therefore the cash flow or net income on such minimal equity produces a favorable return on the investment. It is possible to achieve the same result without writing leases on a net basis, but in such instances it is necessary to include in the leases a formula requiring tenants to pay escalated rentals for any increases in operating or fixed (real estate taxes and insurance) expenses. The latter method of leasing, however, is giving way to the more popular net lease approach and is considered less desirable.

Another attractive feature of investment in shopping centers is the fact that the investor is provided a hedge against inflation. This is accomplished by the earlier mentioned percentage or overage rental provisions in the leases. In such cases, the tenants agree to pay at least a guaranteed minimum annual rental and their pro rata share of expenses, but they also agree to pay a percentage of their annual sales or a percentage of sales in excess of an agreed upon annual gross amount. Percentage or overage rental agreements must be based on realistic figures in order to have any worth and provide the desired protection against inflation. There are a number of publications which provide schedules showing typical percentage rents for each type of retail store as well as schedules showing the current range and average sales per square foot of store area for each type of use. A study and understanding of these tables is necessary to structure percentage or overage rentals. As an example, if sales for a given type of retail store average $60 per square foot, an overage provision would have little worth if overage rents did not commence until after the tenant achieved sales of $100 per square foot. For this reason, it is, as earlier stated, necessary to have or obtain professional judgment before attempting to negotiate any leases.

Long-term Financing

In today's economy, financing has become a critical element in determining whether or not to proceed with a project. The developer must be able to anticipate, within reason, the availability and cost of financing. To do this, the developer should have preliminary meetings with his mortgage banker. A competent mortgage banker will be able to analyze a project's economics and will work with a developer to put together a project that can be sold in today's mortgage market.

In order to obtain a long-term mortgage commitment, the developer must assemble a mortgage package for the long-term lender. This will include schematic drawings, an outline of specifications, an itemization of projected costs, and a pro forma income statement. The pro forma will include a leasing plan with rental estimates from which the gross income estimate is determined. The package also will include copies of the signed leases from the tenant(s), if any, along with financial statements on the tenants, the developer, and any other investors. If no leases have been executed, a specimen copy of the lease intended for use should be enclosed.

Helpful, but not absolutely required as part of the mortgage package, is a feasibility study. (See page 4 on Market and Economic Study and page 6 on Traffic Studies.) The individual receiving the mortgage application may not be familiar with the characteristics of the area in which the site is located, and a good feasibility study will help this individual get a "feel" for the project. Many developers prepare feasibility studies early in a project's life, and it is a simple matter to include a copy in the mortgage package. A good feasibility study will include an analysis of present and projected data on population, economics, tax structures, etc., of the area where the center is to be located as well as surrounding areas. Road systems and availability of utilities as well as the locations of existing and proposed centers should be reviewed. Most data can be assembled easily from census studies, highway departments, and various governmental agencies. A good starting point is the local planning agency, as most of the necessary data is available there.

If the center to be developed has no major tenant, any commitment given will be based on the value and location of the real estate involved and the developer's integrity and financial worth. In this case, the developer probably will be required to sign personally for the mortgage loan until a percentage (usually 80 to 85 percent) of the center is leased.

Standby Commitments Pending Long-term Commitments

On occasion, a developer will secure a standby commitment—a long-term commitment which neither the lender nor the developer contemplate executing. A standby commitment is bankable just like a normal long-term mortgage commitment, and the developer can use it to obtain his short-term financing. The purpose of a standby commitment is to allow the developer to negotiate a long-term mortgage at a future date. A developer may desire to wait to obtain his long-term mortgage either because he feels that the mortgage market will be more favorable at some future time or because he feels that once his center is leased and operating, he will be in a better position to negotiate a long-term mortgage.

A standby commitment will cost the developer considerably more than a normal long-term commitment, and the developer must weigh the extra cost of a standby commitment against the possible savings that may be generated by waiting until a future date to obtain a long-term mortgage. Standby commitments are usually obtained from real estate investment trusts or from investment subsidiaries of major corporations that are actively involved in real estate financing.

Construction Financing

With a permanent or a standby commitment, the developer can proceed to obtain his short-term or interim financing. Sources of interim construction funds are commercial banks, savings and loan associations, and real estate investment trusts. A short-term construction mortgage loan is nothing more than a commercial loan allowing a developer to create a finished product with its value based on leases in full force and effect, and when this has been accomplished the interim loan is replaced by the permanent financing. As in all commercial loans, the developer's ability, knowledge, and financial integrity are important factors influencing the lender's decision on whether or not to grant the construction loan. The developer will be required to submit not only his financial statements but also statements from tenants and the contractors to the interim lender. It is important that the developer submit a good set of plans and specifications from a reliable architectural firm, preferably a member of the American Institute of Architects. This will permit the short-term lender to develop a good cost appraisal and it will also reflect strongly on the developer's integrity. Items to be included are soil core samples (are there any unusual soil conditions?), a complete survey showing all utilities, a complete interior plan of all malls and public areas, and a complete site plan.

Contracts relating to the project should also be included in the submission. These would include the owner-architect agreement, owner-contractor agreement, etc. Copies of any ground leases must be submitted, and, as in the long-term mortgage package, copies of all signed tenant leases should be included.

A complete projection of costs is a critical requirement. Expose all costs. The lender is familiar with similar projects and is very experienced in analyzing statements. The lender will look for the inclusion of interim financing charges, legal fees, and architectural and engineering costs. The construction lender wants to be sure that the amount of the loan is adequate to complete the project. The lender does not want to be put in a position where he might have to lend out more than the permanent commitment or even more than what, in his mind, is a prudent amount.

Sources of interim construction funds are commercial banks, savings and loan associations, and real estate investment trusts.

Property Insurance

Insurance companies and building code authorities view building construction in entirely different ways: building authorities are primarily concerned with public safety, while insurance companies, considering this aspect, tend to emphasize possible damage to the insured structure.

The building authority's concern with public safety centers upon a structure's ability to withstand the ravages of a fire over a period of time. Therefore, fire ratings are always given in hours. Theoretically at least, a two-hour rating on a portion of a structure or assembly means that that portion will stand up in a fire without appreciable effect for a period of two hours, allowing for the evacuation of people over that period of time. A good example of the building authority philosophy is the fact that, by code, building areas having acceptable insurance are allowed to increase in size as building construction becomes more fire-resistant. In addition, allowable floor areas generally may be increased by 100 percent with the introduction of a sprinkler system. Codes further allow for the increase of the distance of travel to an exit within a building having a sprinkler system. Since building codes are uniformly requiring sprinklers, their installation in centers is a must to protect the public, the building, and store contents.

The developer is advised to consult early in the building design phase with his insurance counsel, so that certain basic recommendations of the insurance rating bureaus can be included in the documents as they progress. These include recommendations concerning sprinkler systems, protected structural steel, use of fire walls to divide malls and store buildings into areas of recommended size, use of fire-resistant partitions between stores, use of noncombustible building materials generally and ceiling materials specifically, proper roof coverings securely attached to the structure, use of automatic roof vents activated by smoke or similar detection systems, and many others. Specific project recommendations can result from a detailed review of partially completed drawings by the insurance rating agency arranged through an insurance counsel, and early advice in this area can reduce premiums substantially when the building is occupied.

Development of liability insurance requirements for the contractor should result from recommendations by the insurance counsel, and it is normal practice to receive evidence of adequate professional liability coverage from the architect and his consultants.

During construction, normal property insurance coverage, usually provided by the developer, would include provision of a basic fire and casualty insurance policy with extended coverage as well as endorsements covering vandalism and malicious mischief. Often a broader form of coverage called *all risk* is recommended by the insurance counsel, based upon possible exposure; but coverage is normally based on the total insurable value of the project (excluding foundations, underground work, etc.)—that is, it is based on the *completed value.*

Since tenant improvements fixed to the structure become the landlord's property after inclusion within the building, the developer should take special precautions to see that this work is included within the scope of the fire insurance policy when tenant work commences.

Other forms of property insurance are available, including loss due to sprinkler leakage, steam boiler and machinery insurance, insurance to building contents or covering loss of use, etc., depending on exposure that might be present.

The developer's insurance counsel will be invaluable in helping to prepare final approvals of the completed project and complete definition of risks. He will also determine appropriate degree of coinsurance, allowing the developer to seek from reputable insurance companies that will provide maximum coverage at a minimum premium cost.

DESIGN AND CONSTRUCTION

General Design Considerations

In the early design of shopping centers, the architect tried to translate the most essential needs of the developer in a minimal way—the strip center and slight variations of these minimal arrangements are still in evidence. In the next phase, we see the cluster centers which allowed the architect more freedom in grouping the individual buildings. Cluster planning also gave the shopper a variety of experiences in walking through different areas, experiences made more interesting by landscaping, art, and seating arrangements. In other words, cluster planning produced a more pleasant environment. The covered shopping center was a response to new demands for shoppers' comfort and climate control the year 'round. All these centers still remained isolated from their surroundings by huge asphalt-covered areas providing parking space for thousands of cars.

There is no doubt in anybody's mind that the environment around present suburban centers must be drastically changed. There are a great number recently

Woodfield Mall, a three-department-store center, has provisions for a fourth department store. The three-level mall is linked together by ramps, escalators, and stairs accented with sculpture, pools, and landscaped areas. The developers are Woodfield Associates.

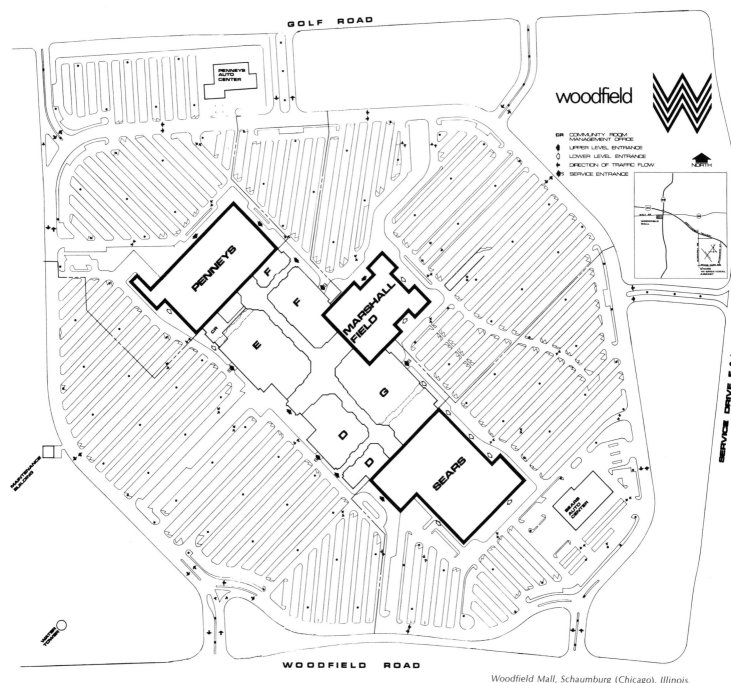

GOLF ROAD

PENNEYS AUTO CENTER

woodfield

CR COMMUNITY ROOM MANAGEMENT OFFICE
UPPER LEVEL ENTRANCE
LOWER LEVEL ENTRANCE
DIRECTION OF TRAFFIC FLOW
SERVICE ENTRANCE

NORTH

PENNEYS

F
F
E
CR
G
D
D

MARSHALL FIELD

SEARS

SEARS AUTO CENTER

MAINTENANCE BUILDING

WATER TOWER

WOODFIELD ROAD

SERVICE DRIVE F.A.I. 90

Woodfield Mall, Schaumburg (Chicago), Illinois. Site plan. (Architects: for the mall—Jickling & Lyman; for Sears—Larsen-Wulff & Associates; for J. C. Penney—Charles Luckman Associates; for Marshall Field—Loebl, Schlossman, Bennett & Dart.)

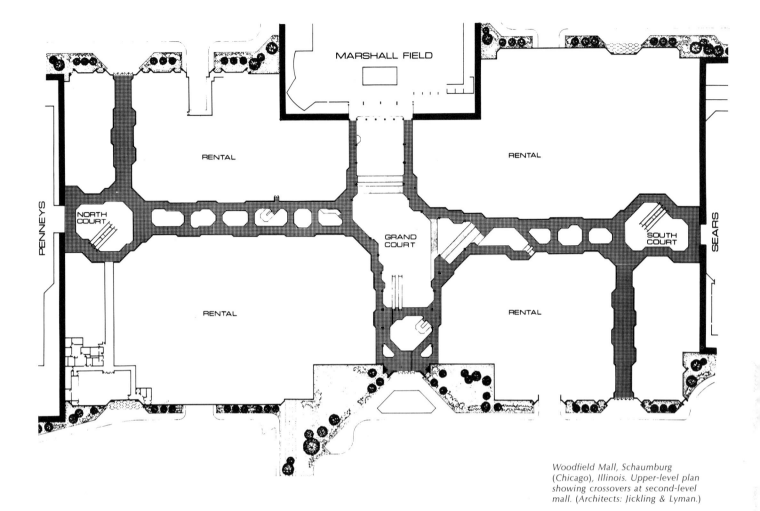

Woodfield Mall, Schaumburg (Chicago), Illinois. Upper-level plan showing crossovers at second-level mall. (Architects: Jickling & Lyman.)

completed and others in the planning stages which follow and blindly repeat the sterile patterns of the asphalt parking fields. Plans still on the drafting boards should be studied for more imaginative solutions, provided that owner, architect, and financier can broaden their vision of future potential.

In my presentation of design considerations, I will start with examples of various plan configurations as well as special adaptations to the topography of the site. This presentation will be followed by examples of parking solutions. I emphasize the parking solution because this is the shopper's first contact with the center facilities. It may condition the shopper for a positive and pleasant experience or put him in an irritated mood. I will then discuss exterior design elements and, following this, there will be a presentation of interior courts and malls. This discussion will include materials, lighting, climate and comfort control, artwork, graphics, and signing.

Plan Configurations

The desire on the part of the developer to place as many and various facilities and services in one area as possible has led to the planning of the two- or three-level centers. Whether they are planning one-level or multilevel centers, the architects are creating a variety of imaginative schemes all intended to shorten the distance which the shopper would need to walk from one department store to another. Some of these schemes are illustrated on pages 18–25.

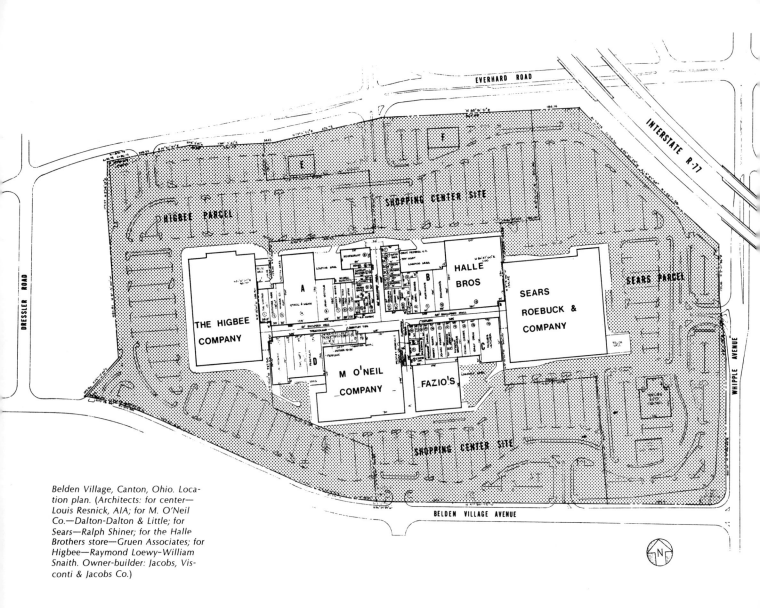

Belden Village, Canton, Ohio. Location plan. (Architects: for center—Louis Resnick, AIA; for M. O'Neil Co.—Dalton-Dalton & Little; for Sears—Ralph Shiner; for the Halle Brothers store—Gruen Associates; for Higbee—Raymond Loewy–William Snaith. Owner-builder: Jacobs, Visconti & Jacobs Co.)

Woodbridge Center, Woodbridge, New Jersey. Location plan. (Architects: Daverman Associates, Inc.)

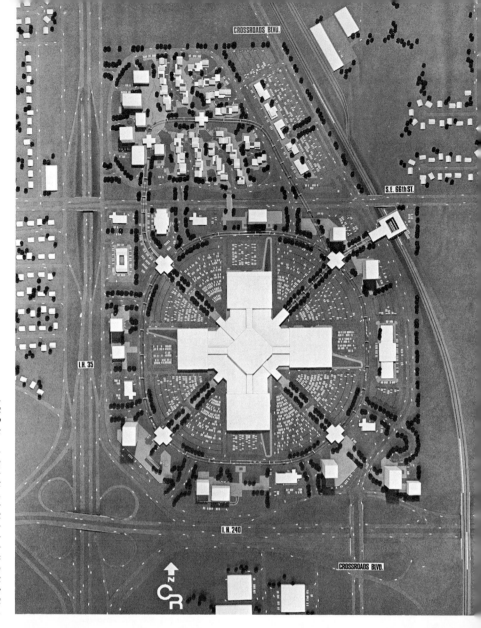

RIGHT: *Crossroads Center, Oklahoma City, Oklahoma. Development model showing the short distances from central court to all four department stores. (Architects: Omniplan Architects Harrell & Hamilton.)*

BELOW: *Town East Shopping Center, Mesquite, Texas. Aerial view (model) showing the concept plan. (Architects: Omniplan Architects Harrell & Hamilton.) The Town East Shopping Center is located in Mesquite, Texas, near Dallas. The two-level mall complex is anchored by three major department stores—Sears, Titche's (Allied), and Sanger-Harris (Federated). With three major retailers sited in the center, a three-pointed design was decided upon. The major shops occupy the points of a truncated Y, with the smaller shops opening on malls that form the bars of the Y. At the center of the Y is a triangular public court, emphasizing the center's main feature.*

SIDNEY H. MORRIS & ASSOCIATES
ARCHITECTS & ENGINEERS · 134 N. LA SALLE ST. · CHICAGO 2, ILLINOIS

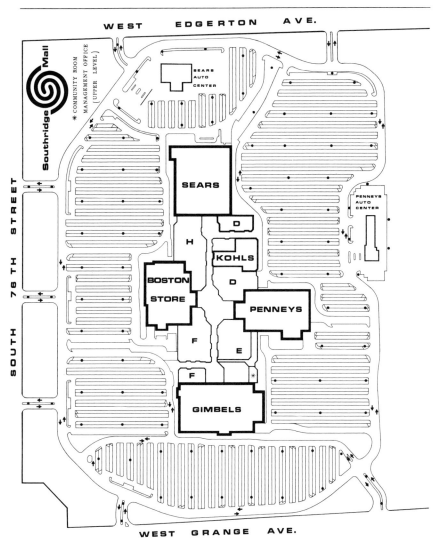

WEST EDGERTON AVE.

Southridge Mall

* COMMUNITY ROOM
MANAGEMENT OFFICE
(UPPER LEVEL)

SEARS
AUTO
CENTER

PENNEYS
AUTO
CENTER

SEARS

BOSTON STORE

KOHLS

H

D

D

PENNEYS

F

E

F

GIMBELS

SOUTH 76TH STREET

WEST GRANGE AVE.

ABOVE: *Sharpstown, Houston, Texas. Aerial view. (Architects: Sidney H. Morris & Associates.)* LEFT: *Southridge Mall, Milwaukee, Wisconsin. Site plan. (Architects: for the mall— Wah Yee Associates; for J. C. Penney—Daverman Associates; for Boston Store—Baxter, Hodell, Donnelly & Preston; for Gimbels—Abbott Merkt & Company, Inc.; for Sears— Neil & Wennlund.)*

York Mall, York, Pennsylvania. Site plan. (Architects: Evantash & Friedman Associates, Inc.) A unique arrangement to reduce the length of the mall nearly to half was used in this plan. The unusual feature is that the mall passes through and becomes the main aisle of a department store, Hochschild-Kohn, straddling the middle of the mall. The other two department stores—J. C. Penney and Montgomery Ward—anchor the ends. The plan also utilizes fully the narrow dimensions of the site.

Columbia Center, Kennewick, Washington. Site plan showing design for expansion. (Architects: John Graham & Company. Developers: Allied Stores Corp.) The impetus for building this center was the excellent access from the tri-city area of Richland, Pasco, and Kennewick. The center is within fifteen minutes' driving time from all the cities. Because of the prospects of continued rapid population increase, the center is designed to accommodate a third department store and will eventually become "the downtown center" for all three cities.

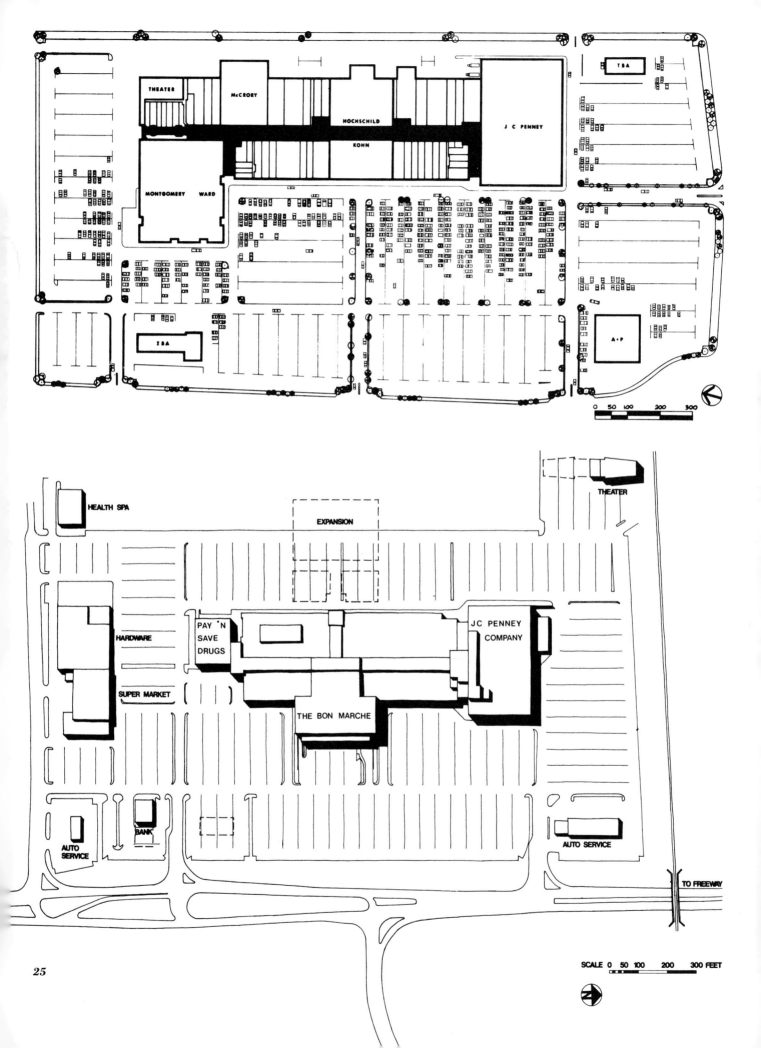

THEATER

McCRORY

HOCHSCHILD KOHN

J C PENNEY

MONTGOMERY WARD

T B A

A·P

0 50 100 200 300

HEALTH SPA

THEATER

EXPANSION

HARDWARE

PAY 'N SAVE DRUGS

JC PENNEY COMPANY

SUPER MARKET

THE BON MARCHE

AUTO SERVICE

BANK

AUTO SERVICE

TO FREEWAY

SCALE 0 50 100 200 300 FEET

Site Adaptation and Parking

Another consideration in evolving the shape of the plan is the topography of the site and the preservation of the existing character of the area. The planners and investors must take into account and utilize the natural topography and the potentials of the site and provide a flexible master plan to provide for fast-changing future needs. Too often, the site which has great differences in elevations, rolling ground, unusual tree specimens, etc., is bulldozed to create a level floor for a center and its parking.

The time is at hand when final decisions on the best utilization of a given site, preserving the natural attributes, will more and more depend on the land-planning authorities and community citizens' groups. More than ever before, citizens' awareness and concern for their overall environment in terms of green areas, traffic and safety, waste removal, noise control, clean air, etc., influence forward-looking policies and decisions made by the public authorities. In the case of the Del Monte Center, Monterey, California, the clusters of buildings of various heights and the sizes of the open areas are arranged so as to create the atmosphere of a hillside village (page 27).

Del Monte Center, Monterey, California. Site plan. (Architects: John Carl Warnecke & Associates. Landscape architects: Lawrence Halprin & Associates.)

La Cumbre Plaza, Santa Barbara, California. Exterior showing connecting bridge from street. An open-mall center designed in the early California style, which blends in with the surrounding area architecture. The topography of the site necessitated the construction of an overhead bridge which connects from the street to the center. Both first and second store levels of Robinson's store are accessible to adjacent parking areas. This arrangement was accomplished by soil balancing between high and low grades. (Architects: for center—Ainsworth & McClellan, Inc.; for Robinson's— William L. Pereira Associates; for Sears—Robert Clements & Associates. The owners are La Cumbre Associates.)

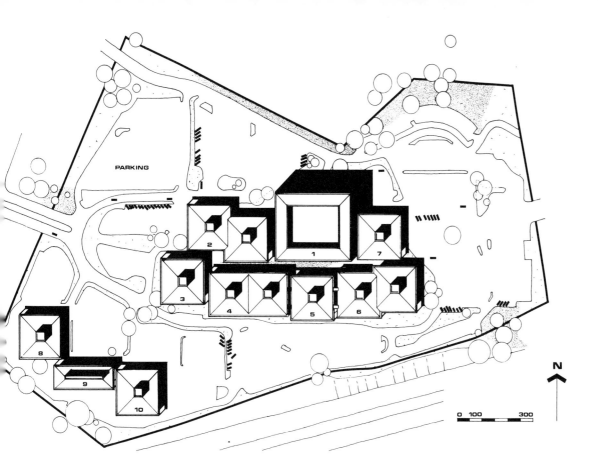

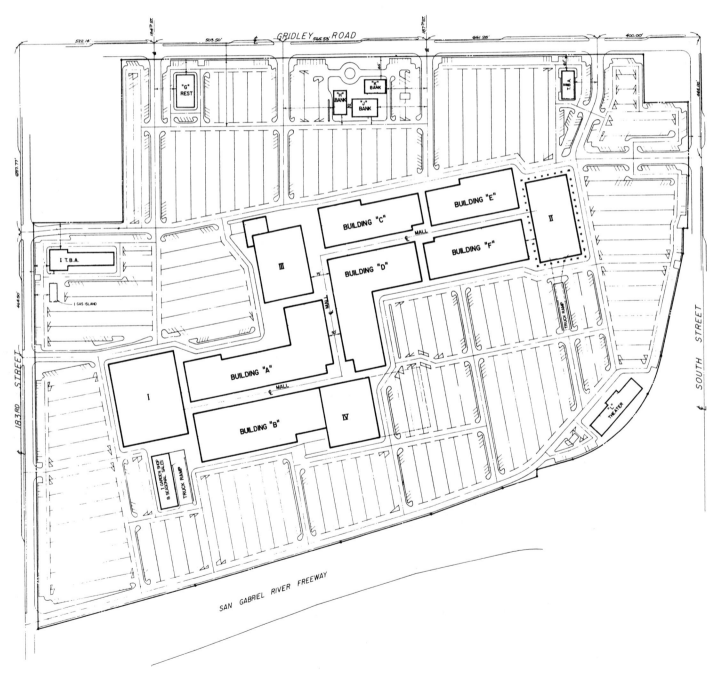

Los Cerritos, Cerritos, California. Site plan.
(Architects: Burke Kober Nicolais Archuleta.)

On the other hand, the imaginative use of site grading by creating landscaped embankments to screen the service areas was a factor in the shaping of the plan of the Parkway Plaza in El Cajon, California, as shown below.

The goal of humanizing the parking space was achieved in the North Park Center, Dallas, Texas, by breaking it into roomlike enclaves with trees and plantings, by the elimination of signs, and by simplification of lighting using only twenty-four 60-foot poles. Grade changes also help break down the expanse of 6,000 parking spaces laid out so that none is more than 350 feet from the mall entrance (page 30).

Another instance of shaping the site to meet the best functional uses of the plan is shown in the Mission Valley Center, San Diego, California. Due to

Parkway Plaza, El Cajon, California. Aerial view (perspective) showing large, sloped, landscaped embankments to screen service and delivery area. (Architects: Maxwell Starkman, AIA, & Associates. Owner-developers: E. W. Hahn Co. & Hobart, Division of Sears Company.)

Parkway Plaza, El Cajon, California. Entrance showing a close-up of landscaped embankment (perspective). (Architects: Maxwell Starkman, AIA, & Associates.)

North Park, Dallas, Texas. Exterior.
[Architects: Omniplan Architects
Harrell & Hamilton. Photographer:
ESTO (Ezra Stoller).]

North Park, Dallas, Texas. Site plan.
(Architects: Omniplan Architects
Harrell & Hamilton.)

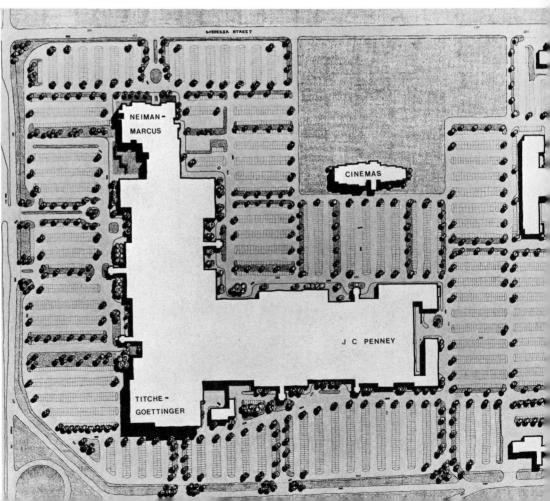

Beach, Florida. This four-department-store L-shaped regional center was developed by Leonard Faber Company, Inc. The roof-deck parking for 500 cars is accessible from two sides by means of two separate entry and exit ramps, one of which is located directly north of building A and the other directly east of building G. The building G ramp goes under a portion of the second-floor office space.

To give customers easy access to the ground-level stores, there is direct entry from the roof deck to each of the four department stores as well as a mall entrance which leads to a glass-enclosed elevator and a set of stairs. If customers come up the building G ramp and park in its vicinity, they can go through Penney's, Sears, or Jordan Marsh, or they may use the mall entrance which leads to the second-floor office area and restaurant. If customers come up the building A ramp and park in that vicinity, they can reach the ground-level stores by going into the Burdine's or Penney's stores (below and opposite).

Another interesting example of handling the roof parking is shown in Bankstown Square Center, Sydney, Australia. Space for 400 cars is reached by a concrete ramp adjacent to the building. Below the ramp is a department store parcel pickup and a plant nursery. On the southern side of the building there is a concrete deck-parking structure with covered access to the trading levels. A second parcel pickup, servicing one of the supermarkets, is located in this area (pages 34 and 35).

flooding conditions, the grading scheme provided for an "island" upon which the shopping center is built. This "island" is set in the saucerlike depression. One-way truck ramps lead to service concourses at the rear of the north and south specialty shop buildings. These truck ramps are screened from public view by a decorative masonry screen. All public access to the specialty shops is provided by means of moving ramps from the lower level to the mall level. An outstanding feature is the elevated "bridge" structure which connects both department stores and contains fifty specialty shops and chain stores. This bridge provides sheltered parking for 900 of the total of 5,000 cars that the center can accommodate, as shown below.

The average developer, in building the first phase (generally the commercial center), seeks out low-cost land. Inasmuch as the least expensive form of parking is surface parking, this has continued to be the most economically profitable form. When the cost of land becomes high, the developer will turn to other methods of car storage that allow him to utilize the land for additional profit-making buildings (i.e., additional shopping and commercial facilities and other amenities which could be incorporated—public swimming pools, tennis courts, skating rinks, outdoor theater, etc.). With the use of air structures, these facilities can be used all year around. Not only does this arrangement have the advantage of being aesthetically pleasing, but it has been found to be remunerative. The popularity of tennis and skating clubs is steadily increasing and membership initiation fees and transient users' fees are substantial profit items. The parking will then be largely accommodated by multideck structures, underground levels, and rooftop facilities, all integrated with the commercial center by overhead bridges and moving protected walks.

Roof-deck parking is well illustrated in the Pompano Fashion Square, Pompano

Mission Valley Shopping Center, San Diego, California. Aerial view. (Architects: Albert C. Martin & Associates. Associated Architects: Frank L. Hope & Associates. Owner-developer: The May Department Stores Company and Montgomery Ward & Co. Photographer: Jara Photo Service.)

An excellent example of incorporation of underground parking is Phipps Plaza, Atlanta, Georgia, which has two parking decks accommodating 715 cars, which are reached by means of helicoidal ramps (pages 36 and 37).

As for multideck parking, an example of good utilization of expensive land is the design of Kings Plaza in Brooklyn, New York. According to Fred Halden, senior associate of Emery Roth & Sons, the architects of the center, Kings Plaza was erected on a site of approximately 28 acres, one-third of which was under the waters of Mill Basin, a narrow tidal arm of Jamaica Bay. A rip-rap dike was constructed around the perimeter of this body of water along the property lines. The area between the then-existing shoreline and the new dike was filled with solidly compacted hydraulic fill. The land thus created at the southerly end of the property became the site of the (free) five-story split-level garage, the total capacity of which is somewhat less than 4,000 cars. Each of its full parking levels covers an area of almost 7 acres. Within the garage structure are housed a facility for local community meetings, the center's general offices, and a marina sales and service building. A 150-boat full-service marina facility is located south of the parking facility and is easily accessible from it. Direct access from the garage to both mall levels has been provided.

The store and mall facilities cover an area of approximately 450,000 square feet on each of two levels while the two anchor deparment stores (Alexander's

OPPOSITE PAGE: *Pompano Fashion Square, Pompano Beach, Florida. Aerial view of center (perspective). (Architects: John Graham & Company. Developer: Leonard L. Farber Company, Inc.)* LEFT: *Pompano Fashion Square, Pompano Beach, Florida. Entry and exit ramp for roof parking—building G. (Architects: John Graham & Company. Photographer: George Skadding Photo Associates.)*

This center, developed by Lend Lease Development Pty., Ltd., is located in the city of Bankstown, a western suburb of Sydney.

A roof parking area, with space for 400 cars, is approached by a concrete ramp adjacent to the building. Below the ramp is a department store parcel pickup and a plant nursery. On the southern side of the building is a concrete deck-parking structure with covered access to the trading levels. A second parcel pickup, servicing one of the supermarkets, is located in this area.

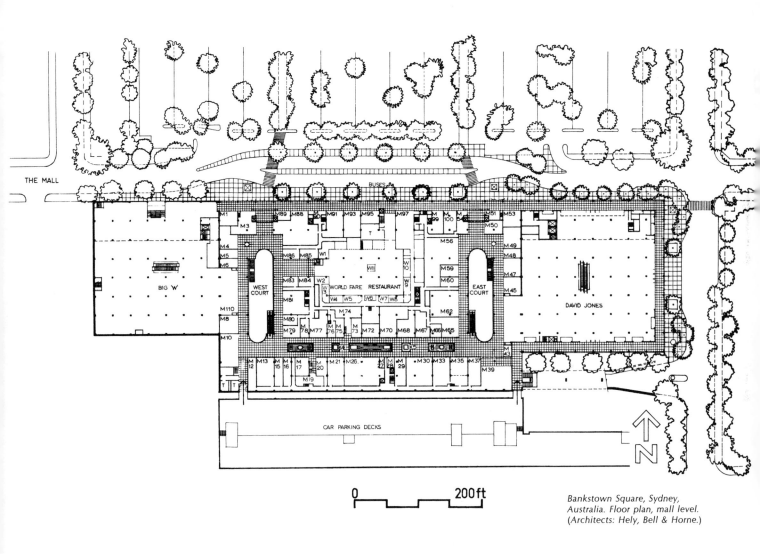

Bankstown Square, Sydney, Australia. Floor plan, mall level. (Architects: Hely, Bell & Horne.)

Bankstown Square, Sydney, Australia. Exterior showing car ramp. (Architects: Hely, Bell & Horne. Photographer: Ern McQuillan's Photographic Illustrators.)

SECTION THROUGH WESTERN COURT

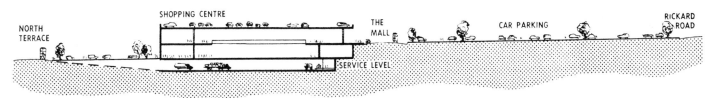

EAST-WEST SECTION THROUGH SHOPPING CENTRE

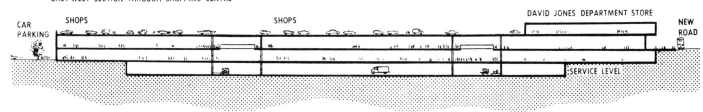

Bankstown Square, Sydney, Australia. Section through western court. (Architects: Hely, Bell & Horne.)

Phipps Plaza, Atlanta, Georgia. Site plan. (Architects: Finch Alexander Barnes Rothschild & Paschal. Photographer: Bryan-Young Photography.)

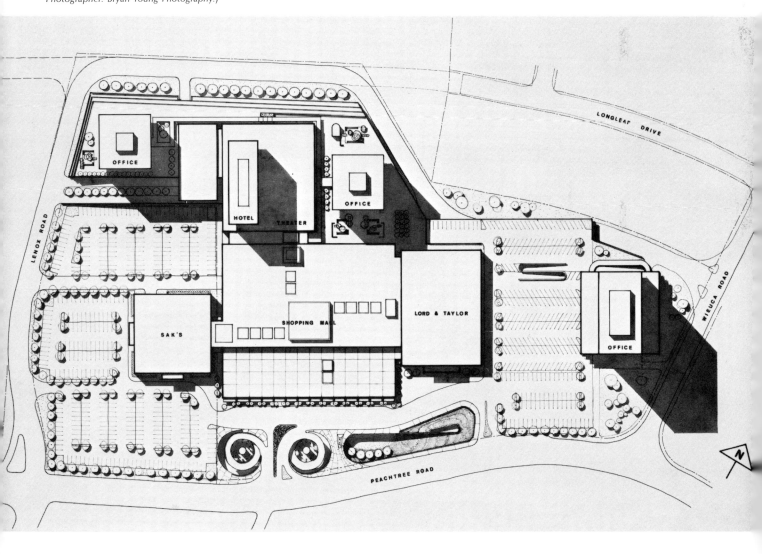

ABOVE: *Phipps Plaza, Atlanta, Georgia. Aerial view of site and center. (Architects: Finch Alexander Barnes Rothschild & Paschal. Photographer: Bryan-Young Photography.)* LEFT: *Phipps Plaza, Atlanta, Georgia. Ramp leading to underground parking area. (Architects: Finch Alexander Barnes Rothschild & Paschal. Photographer: Jack D. Mezrah Architectural Photography of Atlanta.*

and Macy's) rise another two stories of 80,000 square feet each above the shoppers' malls (see below).

Because of the close proximity of groundwater to grade and because of the difficulty of maneuvering great numbers of large trucks within a confined cellar area (with the resultant need to carry substantial numbers of building columns spaced on 28-foot centers on long-span girders), and also to avoid loss of the most valuable first-floor selling space, it was decided to locate all loading facilities on the roof, above the two-story shops and malls. The free, unobstructed area of this roof adds up to approximately 250,000 square feet, located at approximately the same level as the third floor of the department stores. Thus their receiving departments will be at the exact center of their buildings after the fifth-floor addition (for which the foundations and building columns have been designed) has been built.

There are a total of nineteen loading berths located at this level—six for each of the two department stores, two each for the three larger "satellite" store units, and one for the smaller unit of shops. Large-capacity freight elevators connect the loading docks with 8-foot-wide service passages at the rear of all satellite store units, while mechanical conveyor systems connect the department store receiving departments with all parts of their stores. The roof is reached by a two-way ramp with a gradient of about 5 percent, thus providing easy access to the loading facilities. In addition to the ease of maneuvering even long trailer trucks on the unobstructed and wide driving lanes on the roof, the large area available allows also for ample parking of vehicles waiting to be unloaded.

Kings Plaza, Brooklyn, New York. Aerial view of center showing the marina. (Architects: Emery Roth & Sons. Photographer: H. Bernstein.)

Although located in an urban setting, the 23 acres accommodate 1.1 million square feet of gross leasable area. The number of parking spaces is sufficient here because of the added advantage of intensive use of public transportation by nearly 50 percent of the shoppers. The same size site in a suburban area with surface parking and minimum public transportation would allow for gross leasable area of 150,000 square feet.

A basic element in any site and parking planning should be the provision for well-designed landscaped areas, which should add color and interest to the entire area. This should result in a more aesthetically pleasing environment, an added attraction for shoppers.

It would make good sense, even in the area where land is comparatively inexpensive and the temptation to use the surface parking is great, for developer and owner to take a long-range view of the future environmental needs of the growing population. In addition to the above considerations relating to types of plans and adaptation to site, it is the design concept of the entire complex which plays the dominant role in the image of the center.

In the development of the concepts, it is the role of the architect to be sensitively attuned to the requirements of new modes of living. As he proceeds with his planning, he needs to be aware not only of the physical requirements of the buildings and their functional use but also of the social ramifications in the community. Thus it is very important for the architect, the public authorities, and the developer to work closely from the very beginning.

Although the concept of the center as the core of a new town is already becoming viable, some time will pass before this concept is implemented on a large scale. However, for the present, much can be done to update the design approach of the contemporary shopping center.

Exterior and Interior Design Elements—
Creation of a Unified Entity

Exterior Design—Concept and Materials

Many of the recently enclosed centers have uninteresting exteriors. Solid shapes and monotonous unbroken surfaces predominate. In centers where each department store owner has insisted on his own choice of materials or colors, the result, due to variations of material, color, and texture, have often been a distracting hodgepodge.

One important element worth mentioning is the design of the service courts. These courts should meet only the actual functional requirements, should be placed in such locations where the number would be as few as possible, and should be designed so as not to detract from the main character of the building. The experience with underground service tunnels has proved that these are an expensive and less functional solution to servicing than surface courts. Examples of various solutions for servicing are illustrated in the plans shown in this chapter.

Architects are now trying to solve the problem of designing the exterior as a unified architectural entity, avoiding the fragmented character typical of many centers. The ideal way to achieve unified results is to have one architect plan or control the design of the whole center. In reality, however, where each major tenant chooses his own architect, it is imperative that all architects involved in a center plan the total design concept as a team. Complete cooperation and minor compromises will improve the character and image of the center immensely.

One way to achieve a unified design is by using one or two major materials throughout the complex of buildings. The use and choice of exterior materials should be carefully weighed. Main factors to consider are the waterproofing qualities, the ease of maintenance, the availability of selected materials, and the speed of assembling and erection.

Brick for exterior walls still remains an attractive material and, in most instances, the least expensive. The variety of ways in which it can be used is limitless. Exteriors can be made interesting by creating various patterns in brickwork (page 41).

The flexibility of brick, split brick, split masonry blocks, and split stone is conducive to creating sculptural building forms (pages 42 and 43).

Brick can also be used in a striking way in combination with precast concrete and cast stone (pages 44–48).

A material which has the advantage of time-saving construction is the precast-concrete wall panel. The precast system requires, however, that ample time be allowed for manufacturing and that the manufacturer be within a reasonable distance of the building site. Prefabrication of wall panels is also offered by the brick industry. The bricks are cemented together with a special adhesive and the whole panel is joined to the shell in the same manner as prefabricated concrete or stone slabs are attached. Lintels for doors and windows are prefabricated in the same way.

Another material which has come to the forefront because of its decorative quality is the new masonry grooved concrete block. When properly lined up, these blocks make for interesting exterior surfaces and tie in easily with poured-in-place concrete. In all cases where masonry is used, tests should be taken to ascertain the waterproofing qualities of the brick and mortar used (page 48).

One material that has been used ingeniously for exterior walls is colored ceramic paving tile. The Bullock's Northridge Fashion Center store uses this material in a dramatic pyramidal form (page 49).

In addition to the materials for exteriors mentioned above, metal panels— whether porcelain enameled steel, metal sheathing, aluminum, copper, or other metals being developed at this time—can be used to advantage to create attractive and permanent exteriors (page 50).

In regions where indigenous materials are abundant, these materials should be used. For example, in the northwestern states of Oregon and Washington and in the southeastern states of North Carolina and South Carolina, wood is used for much of the outside construction, but only when it has been properly treated for exposure to weather. With the new preservatives for wood being researched and guaranteed for years to come, wood can take its place among other permanent materials.

Exterior Design—Elements

The choice of materials and their proper use plays an important role in the total design concept and in establishing the image of the center.

It may be worthwhile to mention a number of varied approaches to the exterior design which may serve to attract the shopper. In some instances, placing display

Southcenter, Tukwila, Washington. Nordstrom Best, west elevation. White-painted brick on reinforced concrete frame. Brick arches used prestressed steel reinforcing to economically accomplish flat curve. (Architects: John Graham & Company. Photographer: Hugh N. Stratford.)

ABOVE LEFT: *Bonwit Teller, offices and stores, Eastchester, New York. Exterior view. (Architects: Copeland, Novak & Israel International.)* LEFT: *Genesee Valley Center, Flint, Michigan. Entrance showing patterns of brickwork. (Architects: Gruen Associates. Associated architects: Louis G. Redstone Associates, Inc. Photographer: Balthazar Korab.)*

Woodbridge Center, Woodbridge Township, New Jersey. Exterior of Abraham & Straus. The exposed reinforced-concrete frame with off-white split-face block contrasts with dark bronze anodized aluminum entrance. (Architects: for center—Daverman Associates, Inc.; for Abraham & Straus: Daniel Schwartzman & Assoc. Photographer: Otto Baitz.)

Fairview Mall Shopping Center, North York, Ontario, Canada. Parking area and entrance. (Architects: Bregman & Hamann. Design consultants: Gruen Associates. Photographer: Panda/Croydon Associates.)

BELOW, LEFT: Macy's, Smith Haven Mall, Smithtown, New York. Exterior of Macy's store. Exterior walls are of the same brick to unify the design. The striking use of rounded brick walls and towers enables Macy's to attract the attention of shoppers. Another interesting use of brickwork is in the concave wall which rises above the building and dominates the shopping center. (Architects: for mall—Copeland, Novak & Israel International; for Macy's—Abbott Merkt & Company, Inc. Photo by Gil Amiaga). BELOW, RIGHT: May Company, Esplanade Shopping Center, Oxnard, California. Exterior of May Company. (Architects: Ladd & Kelsey. Photographer: Wayne Thom.)

Eastridge Shopping Center, San Jose, California. Entrance. (Architect: Avner Naggar, AIA. Photographer: Joshua Freiwald.)

Fairview Pointe Claire Shopping Center, Point Claire, Quebec. Exterior of Eaton's department store. (Architects: Bregman & Hamann. Photographer: Panda Associates Photography.)

Fairview Pointe Claire Shopping Center, Pointe Claire, Quebec. Entrance to Simpson's department store. (Architects: Bregman & Hamann. Photographer: Panda Associates Photography.)

Diamond's Store, Tri-City Shopping Center, Mesa Tempe, Arizona. Exterior showing arched sun screens. (Architects: Copeland, Novak & Israel International. Photographer: Markow Photography.)

Fairview Mall Shopping Center, North York, Ontario, Canada. Exterior of Simpson's department store. (Architects: Bregman & Hamann. Design consultant for center: Gruen Associates. Photographer: Panda/Croydon Associates.)

LANDMARK SHOPPING CENTER
Alexandria, Virginia

ARCHITECTS: Abbott Merkt & Company, Inc.

It is not often that the design for a regional center including the major department stores is done by one architectural firm. The Landmark Center in Alexandria, Virginia, illustrates the benefits of such control. According to the architect "the basic elements used to unify the center were: carefully related masses, repetition of materials and colors, a sculptural treatment for the mall furniture that echoed some of the building decorations and motifs, and standards for graphics for the entire center."*

*Reprinted from *Stores,* December, 1966. Copyright 1966 by National Retail Merchants Assoc.

Woodward & Lothrop store, with mall area. (Photo by Gil Amiaga.)

Exterior of Hecht Company store. (Photo by Gil Amiaga.)

Greenbriar Shopping Center, Atlanta, Georgia. Parking area. (Architects: John Portman & Associates. Photographer: Alexandre Georges.)

Livonia Mall, Livonia, Michigan. Entrance to Crowley's showing brick and cast-in-place concrete. According to Jack Shenkman, former director of ICSC and developer of many regional shopping centers, the use of brickwork in combination with poured concrete provides flexibility in the design concept. It allows introduction of various shapes for which brick serves as an excellent background. Both of these materials are easily maintained. (Architects: Louis G. Redstone Associates, Inc. Photographer: Balthazar Korab.)

Genesee Valley Center, Flint, Michigan. Close-up of exterior. (Architects: Gruen Associates. Associated architects: Louis G. Redstone Associates, Inc. Photographer: Balthazar Korab.)

LEFT: *Gambles Delta Plaza, Escanaba, Michigan. Exterior of center is rough-textured concrete-block panels. (Architects: Thorsen & Thorshov, Inc.)*
BELOW: *Saks Fifth Avenue, Somerset Mall, Troy, Michigan. Exterior showing combination of precast concrete and split-face brick. (Architects: for Saks Fifth Avenue—Morganelli-Heumann & Associates; for center—Louis G. Redstone Associates, Inc.)*

Tyler Mall, Riverside, California. Entrance showing combined use of exterior stucco, split-face block, and scored concrete block. (Architects: Burke Kober Nicolais Archuleta. Photographer: Jordan Lagman.)

*Bullock's Northridge Fashion Center,
Northridge, California. Exterior is veneered with
earth-colored ceramic paving tiles, each 8" x
16". The sloped sides of the department store
create two free-form pyramidal volumes.
(Architects: Welton Becket & Associates.)*

Woodbridge Center, Woodbridge Township, New Jersey. Exterior of Ohrbach's building is of all-white metal sheathing 2" thick. Metal panels are curved at corners, top, and bottom over a base of dark reddish-brown split-face concrete brick. (Architects: for center—Daverman Associates, Inc.; for Ohrbach's—Copeland, Novak & Israel International. Photographer: Constance Hope Associates.)

Berkshire Mall, Reading, Pennsylvania. Exterior of LIT Brothers store, showing display windows. Coping is bronze-colored porcelain enamel. Material above windows is bronze color-anodized aluminum, with internally illuminated, plastic-faced "L." (Architects: Evantash & Friedman Associates, Inc.)

windows on the exterior walls of the buildings makes for more interest (pages 52 and 53).

The design of the main entries to the shopping malls and courts is of great importance. It should have an inviting quality and at the same time be imposing enough to draw the shopper's attention, so that he is led in with anticipation. In the daylight hours, this means an architectural concept of an exciting, three-dimensional quality which could take many forms: a colonnaded canopy, a center insignia tower, or a special wall design at the entry and landscaped areas which include not only interesting plantings, but also art and water forms (pages 54–57).

In the evening hours, the above elements have to accommodate special lighting effects and entrance signs. These signs should harmonize with the overall graphic lettering program for the entire center. Lighting standards in the parking area could also be designed to harmonize with the character of the exterior (pages 58 and 59).

As for the exterior signs for the individual tenant, these, if used at all, should be under strict control of architect and developer as to size, type, and location. One way to avoid constant friction with the tenant's demands for identification could be the placement of an outside directory with uniform lettering near the entrances. Because each major department store has its own logo and insists on its own public image and identity, it is difficult to coordinate the graphics. As previously pointed out, the problem of total coordination of the exterior of a center—including materials, signing, lighting, and graphics—becomes even more complicated when different architectural firms are commissioned for each of the various department stores and another architectural firm is retained for the mall proper.

Center Interiors

In the one-story enclosed mall with one or two department stores as well as in multistory centers with four or five department stores, the design of the arcades, malls, and courts should create a most inviting environment for the shopper. The elements of this new environment should provide such exciting interest that the shopper's first feeling is one of a satisfying emotional uplift.

Courts

The main court or courts should become the focal magnet of shoppers and visitors—an image they will carry with them and remember. Most of the recently completed regional centers and those now in the planning stages concentrate on excellence in the design of courts—on such various exciting features as glass space-frame domes, special lighting fixtures, sculptural fountains, landscaped areas, specially designed staircases, escalators, glass-enclosed elevators, and important art work. The design of the graphics—directional signs, banners, central symbols, and the choice of colors—also becomes an important element in the total impact on the shopper (pages 60–65). The very large centers that have a number of courts are more interesting if each court has its own individual character, shape, colors, and decor. The main court, in addition to serving as an exciting place for the shopper to sit, relax, and meet friends, could also be designed for functional and profitable uses. In order to provide for this flexibility, permanent installations (i.e., fountains, plantings, artwork) should be placed so as to allow for large open areas for special events—concerts, auto and boat (as well as other large equipment) displays, art shows, and community programs.

RIGHT: *Somerset Mall, Troy, Michigan. Entrance showing close-up of display windows. (Architects: Louis G. Redstone Associates, Inc. Photographer: Daniel Bartush.)* BELOW: *Somerset Mall, Troy, Michigan. Exterior view showing display windows. (Architects: Louis G. Redstone Associates, Inc. Photographer: Daniel Bartush.)*

Fairview Pointe Claire Shopping Center, Pointe Claire, Quebec. Exterior view of center showing awning display windows. (Architects: Bregman & Hamann. Photographer: Panda/Croydon Associates.)

Willowbrook Shopping Center, Wayne Township, New Jersey. Close-up of main entrance showing exterior canopied store treatment. (Architects: Welton Becket & Associates.)

Smith Haven Mall, Smithtown, New York.
Exterior view. (Architects: Copeland,
Novak & Israel International. Photographer:
Constance Hope Associates.)

Simpson's, Sherway Gardens, Sherway Plaza,
Toronto, Canada. West entrance. The
framing of the boxes is of aluminum with a
baked color finish, and the disks are
silk-screened on acrylic. People, abstract
trees, and pure abstracts are depicted on
the silk screens. There are a total of
seventeen designs, with varying color
combinations, used in the forty-three
boxes. The disks are illuminated by
fluorescent lighting.
The circular images can be interchanged
and advertising inserts can be substituted if
desired at a later date. (Architects: for
Sherway Gardens—James A. Murray &
Henry Fliess; for Simpson's—Searle
Wilbee Rowland. Photographer: Panda/
Croydon Associates.)

LEFT: *Fairview Mall Shopping Center, North York, Ontario, Canada. Entrance of The Bay. (Architects: Bregman & Hamann. Photographer: Roy Nichols.)* BELOW: *Abraham & Straus, Smith Haven, Smithtown, New York. Exterior, main facade. (Architects: for Abraham & Straus—Daniel Schwartzman & Assoc., Abbott Merkt & Company, Inc.; for center—Copeland, Novak & Israel International. Photographer: Ben Schnall.)*

RIGHT: *Montgomery Mall Shopping Center, Montgomery County, Maryland. Entrance to Hecht's department store.* (*Architects: John Graham & Company. Photographer: Louis Checkman.*) BELOW: *Willowbrook Shopping Center, Wayne Township, New Jersey. Entrance symbol.* (*Architects: Welton Becket & Associates. Photographer: Joseph Molitor.*) BELOW, RIGHT: *Perimeter Mall, Atlanta, Georgia. Close-up of main entrance showing the center insignia.* (*Architects: Katzman Associates, Inc.*)

ABOVE, LEFT: *Belden Village,
Canton, Ohio. Main entrance to
center mall. (Architect: Louis
Resnick, AIA. Sculptress: Joan
Robinson, styrofoam on
plywood. Textured frieze 54' x
10'; relief extension from 0" to
16". Photographer: Jack
Sterling.)* ABOVE: *Montgomery
Mall Shopping Center,
Montgomery County, Maryland.
Entrance. (Architects: John
Graham & Company.)* LEFT:
*Fashion Island, Irvine Ranch,
Newport Beach, California.
Plaza with pool. (Architects:
Welton Becket & Associates.
Landscape consultants:
Sasaki-Walker Associates, Inc.
Photographer: Marvin Rand.)*

Southcenter, Tukwila, Washington. View from north indicating variety of interior lighting recessed fixtures at Bon Marché and Nordstrom Best. (Architects: John Graham & Company. Photographer: Art Hupy. Photo used by special permission.)

Mission Valley Shopping Center, San Diego, California. Night view, exterior. (Architects: Albert C. Martin & Associates. Associated architects: Frank L. Hope & Associates. Photographer: Jara Photo Service.)

ABOVE: *Franklin Park Mall, Toledo, Ohio. Exterior view showing night lighting effect. (Architects: Daverman Associates, Inc.)*

LEFT: *Southcenter, Tukwila, Washington. North portico of Bon Marché. (Architects: John Graham & Company. Photographer: Art Hupy.)*

ABOVE. *Southland Center, Taylor, Michigan. Court. Architects: Gruen Associates. Associated architects: Louis G. Redstone Associates, Inc. Photographer: Balthazar Korab.* LEFT: *Perimeter Mall, Atlanta, Georgia. Interior of Court 4 showing court restaurant. (Architects: Katzman Associates, Inc.)*

Perimeter Mall, Atlanta, Georgia.
Interior of Court 2. (Architects:
Katzman Associates, Inc.)

Southland Center, Taylor,
Michigan. Court. (Architects:
Gruen Associates. Associated
architects: Louis G. Redstone
Associates, Inc. Artist for mural:
Elsie Crawford. Photographer:
Balthazar Korab.)

Mohawk Mall, Niskayuna, New York. Court showing the use of canvas and fieldstone. (Architects: Evantash & Friedman Associates, Inc. Photographer: Lawrence S. Williams, Inc.)

Franklin Park Mall, Toledo, Ohio. Court and fountain. (Architects: Daverman Associates, Inc.)

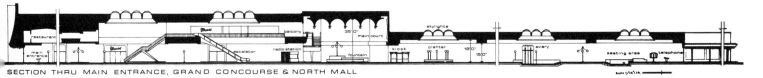

SECTION THRU MAIN ENTRANCE, GRAND CONCOURSE & NORTH MALL

Eastwood Mall, Niles, Ohio. Section.
(Architects: Andrew J. Burin Associates.)

Eastwood Mall, Niles, Ohio.
View of mall with fountains,
showing the vaulted ceilings
with the lighting installations.
(Architects: Andrew J. Burin
Associates.)

Genesee Valley Center, Flint, Michigan. Interior court showing sculpture in background by Harry Bertoia and sculpture in foreground by Sorel Etrog. (Architects: Gruen Associates. Associated architects: Louis G. Redstone Associates, Inc. Photographer: Balthazar Korab.)

Fairview Pointe Claire Shopping Center, Pointe Claire, Quebec. Mall area. (Architects: Bregman & Hamann. Photographer: Panda/ Croydon Associates.)

Highland Mall, Austin, Texas. Interior of Court 1. (Architects: Katzman Associates, Inc.; Curtis and Davis. Photographer: Alexandre Georges.)

Oakwood Shopping Center, New Orleans, Louisiana. Court area. The center is laid out in the form of a large plus sign, avoiding long-drawn-out corridors and reducing the walking distances between stores.

The interior focal point of the center is a tropical garden at the intersection of the mall passageways. A 50' multifaceted skylight of Plexiglas is centered above this hub. The domed skylight transmits ample light for plant growth yet is so constructed that it minimizes glare. This light control was achieved by using sheets of white translucent Plexiglas in the lower portions of the domed skylight and colorless sheets at the top. Light from the midday sun is permitted to shine directly down on the gardens, while midmorning and midafternoon sunlight is filtered by the white Plexiglas.

Four 25' skylights of the same material are spotted around the edges of the garden areas at the beginning of the mall passageways, serving as visual links between the malls and the center courtyard. The architects specified the acrylic plastic as the glazing for all skylights because of the material's strength, light weight, clarity, ease of handling, and durability. This breakage-resistant quality is important in the Gulf Coast region because of high winds and hurricanes.

RIGHT: *Woodbridge Center, Woodbridge Township, New Jersey. Court and 27'-high steel sculpture. (Architects: Daverman Associates, Inc. Sculptor: Alexander Calder. Photographer: Otto Baitz.)* BELOW: *York Mall, York, Pennsylvania. Court with fountain and flying-fish sculpture at the Hochschild-Kohn Department Store. (Architects: Evantash & Friedman Associates, Inc. Artist for fountain: Howard Geffert.)*

ABOVE: *Woodbridge Center, Woodbridge Township, New Jersey. Interior of main court. (Architects: Daverman Associates, Inc. Photographer: Otto Baitz.)* LEFT: *Echelon Mall, Echelon, Philadelphia, Pennsylvania. Court with fountain. (Architects: Francis G. Vitetta, AIA, with Day & Zimmerman Associates; for Strawbridge & Clothier store—Gruen Associates.)*

Woodfield Mall, Schaumburg (Chicago), Illinois. Court interior. (Architects: Jickling & Lyman.) The main feature of the Grand Court is an amphitheater and stage highlighted by an overhead Plexiglas space form. Another feature is a two-level pool connected by a waterfall. For the young at heart, there is a "behind-the-falls" aquarium.

The idea of providing amphitheater-type seating in the main court adds to the possibilities of arranging festive events for both the young and the older shopper. It also necessarily increases appreciably the size of the court.

Malls

Generally the design of the malls and arcades *leading* to main courts should strive for an intimate character and subdued atmosphere. The purpose is to have the shopper's eye attracted to the store displays. Also, from the overall design viewpoint, there is a change of pace for the shopper as he comes from a less elaborate area into a monumental court, which, in most cases, is planned as the highlight of the center (pages 66–68).

The traffic flow and ease of movement of the people from one major store to another is a prime consideration. Where the distance from one major store to another is long (over 700 feet), there are both physical and psychological reactions to the "tunnel" effect. One way to avoid these negative effects is by creating a break approximately midway—forming a Z-shape plan—usually at the court intersection. There the shopper has to make a short turn before he sees the other end of the center. Another way to make the visual impact more effective is by stepping back the storefronts starting from both ends of the mall, thus creating the largest area at the midpoint of the mall. There are other plans that will shorten distances for the shopper to all major destinations in the center. The "plus-sign" plan allows for four major department stores at the four ends with a minimum distance from the center.

A Y-shaped plan allows for a three-department-store arrangement and has advantages similar to those of the "plus" shape. There is no doubt that there are other shapes and ingenious combinations thereof which could help solve this problem.

The multistory center with its much increased shopping areas is another answer to the problem of greater customer convenience and minimum walking distance. Here the main mode of transportation is vertical—escalators, moving ramps, and stairways. The location of the vertical transportation must be seen from as many vantage points as possible. From the second and third floors, the surrounding gallery stores must have maximum view to and from the transportation points. To encourage shopping interest on both sides of the upper galleries, there should be connecting bridges to facilitate easy access and to give tempting views of the lower floor.

Additional attraction to vertical transportation is provided in many centers and stores by the use of glass-enclosed elevators. The ride itself is a pleasurable new experience for all age groups, and it orients the visitor to the surroundings. In the multistory center, the location of the vertical transportation could make the difference between a highly successful and a marginal center operation (pages 70–72).

The malls also can be planned—depending on the width and strategic location—for interesting and profitable uses. The introduction of well-designed kiosks adds another attraction for the shopper. The kiosks should help to create the gay and busy atmosphere of a marketplace. The range of kiosk use has been growing steadily and the design has been becoming more sophisticated. Uses include stands for greeting cards, candy, and toys; photo and camera equipment; flowers; hosiery; and many other varieties of goods. Special kiosks such as minibanks, coat-check service booths, and snack bars have been successfully used. To accommodate the installation of kiosks, the mall should be not less than 35 to 40 feet wide. The design of the kiosks should be such that, under operating conditions, the fixtures are low enough not to obstruct the view from one side of the mall to the other. The upper part of the fixtures should be either completely open during the business hours or glass-enclosed to provide a look-through advantage to the neighboring stores. Although in some cases there has been opposition to the installation of kiosks from tenants who cite competition, obstructed views of their own stores, and the side tracking of shoppers, there is a growing realization that the added activity also helps their own sales. For the developer, it provides an additional income source.

Materials

In choosing the materials for the interior malls and courts, functional consideration should go hand-in-hand with aesthetics. Here, floor materials and wall materials should be chosen for permanence and minimum maintenance.

Terrazzo floors (about 2 inches thick), when installed on a sand bed of a concrete floor, makes one of the most desirable installations. When cost is a limiting factor, a less expensive type of tile called Thinset terrazzo can be applied directly over finished concrete floor. In order to avoid cracks in unforeseen "field areas," the design should be organized in smaller units of interesting shapes. Thus, when cracks do occur, repairs can be made easily by replacing the affected sections. Interesting patterns in floor design can also be made up of the combination of terrazzo and quarry tile or paving bricks. However, the numerous joints of tile and brickwork often create maintenance problems.

ABOVE, LEFT: *Westland Shopping
Center, Westland, Michigan.
Court showing glass elevator.
(Architects: Gruen Associates,
Louis G. Redstone Associates,
Inc. Landscape architects:
Eichstedt & Grissom Associates.
Play sculpture by Samuel
Cashwan. Photographer:
Balthazar Korab.)*
ABOVE: *Woodbridge Center,
Woodbridge Township, New
Jersey. General view of mall.
(Architects: Daverman
Associates, Inc. Photographer:
Otto Baitz.)* LEFT: *The Fashion
Center, Paramus, New Jersey. An
interesting feature of this
two-department-store, one-level
mall is the roof parking for 360
cars. (The total parking space
provides for 2,400 cars.) The
main features of the interior
court are a large Plexiglas cupola
over a fountain and a decorative
spiral staircase leading to the
roof deck. (Architect: Lathrop
Douglass, FAIA.)*

Southridge Mall, Greendale (Milwaukee), Wisconsin. Mall area with plantings and aviary. (Architects: Wah Yee Associates.) The two-level, five-department-store regional center is owned and developed by Southridge Company.

"The main feature in the plan of this mall are six large see-through openings between the first and second levels, connected by bridges 8 to 10 feet wide. In addition there is vertical transportation provided by an elevator, three pairs of escalators, and four carpeted stairways."

"In order to minimize the effect of the 800 ft. length of the mall, several design features were used: Changes in elevations, especially in the grand court where raised platforms, pools and sunken conversation corners create interest, excitement and give the impression of closeness. Angles and corners break up solid walls and further distort the measurements of space and distance. Geometric patterns in the ceiling further break up spatial relationships and provide no focal point to distract from the visual attraction of the stores. Skylights with fins to angle the incoming light create patterned shadows to reinforce this intent." (Reprinted by permission from Chain Store Age, November, 1970, Copyright 1970, Lebhar-Friedman, Inc., 2 Park Ave., New York, New York 10016.)

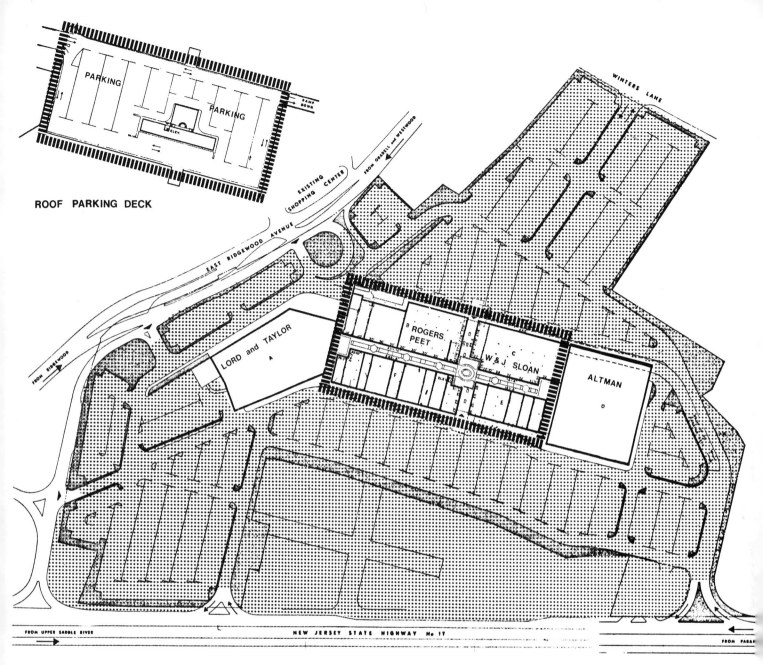

ROOF PARKING DECK

The Fashion Center, Paramus,
New Jersey. Site plan. (Architect:
Lathrop Douglass, FAIA.)

With new developments in carpeting for heavy traffic and for both indoor and outdoor use, carpeting is becoming another accepted material for floor covering. The higher initial cost of installation is offset by the lower cost of maintenance. Whether or not carpeting is used throughout the entire mall area, there are definitely certain areas where carpeting adds color and design interest, especially in the rest areas or in the larger sunken areas in the court, where steps leading down make a definite separation from the court floor.

In the mall, wall materials up to 8 or 10 feet high should be chosen for permanence and ease of maintenance. Often the use of the same material as on the exterior—such as brick, precast concrete, etc.—brings in a continuity of design and is a subdued element which allows the individual storefronts to be featured and accented. Above this 8- or 10-foot height of permanent material, any type of material which the design concept calls for can be used—plaster, dry wall, wood, metal, etc. Generally the center architect and the developer allow each tenant to have freedom of design between the dividing neutral piers for his own storefront design. In order to create some unity, the height and type of the general sign is limited to approximately 2 to 3 feet, and all placed under the established height level. However, in large centers with a number of malls and courts, these limitations may not apply. Imaginative and interesting super-graphic lettering and images without height and area limitations can be used to advantage to provide a change of mood and atmosphere.

As for ceiling materials, there is an infinite variety of choice, each expressing the architect's concept—exposed structural steel, concrete beams, shaped acoustical tiles, plaster, wood, etc. In general, the introduction of daylight through skylights and/or clerestory windows adds a cheerful and inviting element to the center (pages 74–78).

Mall Lighting

The illumination level for mall areas should be subdued and yet adequate to stimulate people and to create a restful and inviting atmosphere. In addition, the lighting source can be placed to create interesting ceiling patterns.

Lighting effects could also be achieved by using decorative pendants, chandeliers, architectural shapes, and specially designed wall and post lights.

Some mall areas will require special treatments related to their intended use. If an area is used for functions such as special displays or fashion shows, it will be necessary to provide spotlights and multilevel lighting control (theater-type lights and controls).

If the mall area gets a good deal of daylight, either through skylights or clerestory windows, multilevel lighting controls should be provided to save energy costs and related maintenance.

Mall areas accommodating heavy traffic should have not less than 20 foot-candles of light maintained, excluding the contribution of show-window lighting.

Most shopping centers employ a central environmental monitoring system. This system indicates the illumination level at one or more critical locations—and it is connected to the central control console which is generally located in the building engineer's office or the security office.

Show-window lighting is often affected by adjacent surroundings, and the illumination level required is determined by the items displayed. The displays in many show windows are related to the seasons and their characteristic colors. In general, show-window illumination should approximate 300 footcandles and should be designed for flexible multilevel illumination intensities.

The coming years will emphasize the trend toward dramatic displays encompassing theatrical lighting ideas. Many of the open-type stores in the enclosed centers will require new, ingenious approaches on the part of the designers to focus the shopper's attention on the store.

Another element which is an accepted standard for most shopping centers is background music and a paging system. These systems must be integrated with the lighting layout and with the architectural and acoustic design. The systems can be designed to distribute sound to all stores or only to the common areas. The music source is usually leased by the shopping center owner and may be a tape machine, record player, tuner, special radio station source, or special wired circuit via telephone or private underground distribution system. All systems are usually clock-controlled "On" and "Off." The smaller shopping center employs similar systems but often inserts a repeat timer in the circuit that interrupts the program and announces advertisement specials.

Berkshire Mall, Reading, Pennsylvania. Mall with fountain and rest area. (Architects: Evantash & Friedman Associates, Inc.)

Greenbriar Shopping Center, Atlanta, Georgia. Aerial view showing the extent of the continuous skylight. (Architects: John Portman & Associates.)

Harrisburg East Mall, Harrisburg, Pennsylvania. Mall and fountain, with wooden bridge crossover. (Architects: Evantash & Friedman Associates, Inc. Photographer: Lawrence S. Williams.)

Tyler Mall, Riverside, California. Interior court, showing domed ceilings (Architects: Burke Kober Nicolais Archuleta. Photographer: Jordan Lagman.)

Tyler Mall, Riverside, California. Mall, showing terrazzo floor patterns. (Architects: Burke Kober Nicolais Archuleta. Photographer: Jordan Lagman.)

West Towne Mall, Madison, Wisconsin. Court with sculpture, showing rest area and floor pattern of terrazzo and paving brick. (Architect: Louis Resnick, AIA. Sculptor: Joseph Anthony McDonnell. Photographer: Wollin Studios.)

York Mall, York, Pennsylvania. Mall with rest area. Plaster ceiling. (Architects: Evantash & Friedman Associates, Inc.)

Macomb Mall, Roseville, Michigan. Interior mall showing precast concrete T-ceiling and skylights. (Architects: Louis G. Redstone Associates, Inc. Photographer: Balthazar Korab.)

South Coast Plaza, Costa Mesa, California. Fountain. (Architects: Gruen Associates. Photographer: William Nelson.)

The general layout requires a consideration of acoustics—including reverberation time, sound absorption, sound reflection, sound-level distribution, spacing of speakers, type of speakers, etc. Spacing of speakers is determined by speaker mounting height, speaker output distribution, and established ceiling pattern design.

Interior tenant signs are also controlled with regard to brightness and size by lease restrictions, and some developers, at the suggestion of their designers, have called for uniform signs. Original planning should always provide for the illumination of signs, because nonilluminated signs are seldom used.

The type of lighting and the lighting layout is usually one of the most important elements the architectural designer must consider. The use of high-intensity discharge lamp fixtures in malls is increasing. This results from recent refinement in the high-intensity discharge (HID) lamps. High-intensity discharge lamps encompass mercury vapor lamps, metal halide lamps (metalarc lamps and multivapor lamps), and high-pressure sodium lamps (trade names Lucalox, Lumalox, and Ceramalux).

The main advantage of these lamps is high lumen per watt light output; and this efficiency, combined with improved color rendition, has made HID lamps highly acceptable for many commercial lighting installations. The efficiency and long lamp life of HID lamps parallel or exceed the efficiency and life of fluorescent lamps. In industrial installations, where color rendition is not a critical requirement, HID lamps have been used for many years. Supermarkets, discount stores, drugstores, and similar occupancies have rapidly accepted HID lighting systems.

Where HID lamps are used, it is necessary to take into consideration glare from the light source, noise from ballasts, color qualities of the lamps, and visual comfort.

For reasons of safety it is usually mandatory that incandescent and/or fluorescent lamps be combined with HID lamps to avoid the one- to six-minute blackout that results from instantaneous power interruption.

In addition to interior mall lighting, numerous exterior lighting functions must also be considered. Among these are building floodlighting, fascia lighting, sculptured features, and marquees. Lighting of this sort is often used in lieu of large signs to draw attention to the shopping center and to identify it. In such instances, the lighting must be more than adequate, otherwise it may convey undesirable impressions.

For large shopping centers, it is also necessary to provide flagpole lights that are in harmony with logos, insignias, and identifier pendants.

If planter lighting is to be provided, it should be considered in the early stages of landscape design.

Tenant signs are generally not allowed on the exterior of the closed-mall shopping center. If permitted, they are controlled by lease restrictions with regard to exact locations and size. Exterior sign lighting is controlled by photo cell and time switches or by astronomical-type time switches.

Good parking area illumination is very important. A minimum illumination level of 1 footcandle should be maintained at darkest location. It is desirable to have an even illumination level, but this is not essential. A high ratio of minimum to maximum illumination levels is seldom aesthetically objectionable unless you are viewing the parking area from a higher elevation (such as a plane) at night. The type of lighting standard used is often determined by cost comparisons between the various types that are being considered for the particular job and on the basis of relative aesthetic values. Among the things that must be considered are lamp life, lamp lumen maintenance, system maintenance, structural stability of lighting standards and components under the most severe storms, and periodic painting costs. (There are no painting costs in the case of aluminum and stainless steel standards, but these usually cost more initially.) If lighting standards are also intended to carry parking area graphics or signs, the wind loading must be considered in specification. Most parking lots employ high-intensity discharge lamps (mercury vapor, multivapor, and high-pressure sodium) with consideration to lamp color correction to avoid distorting the appearance of people and colors.

Driveway approaches that enter and leave main thoroughfares should have a higher level of illumination and, if practical, should have a distinctly different lighting standard or standard location so that the lights may serve as markers for entrances and exits. An illumination level of 10 footcandles at entrances is desirable.

Most shopping centers have walkways around building perimeters, and these walks must be illuminated by use of building-mounted lighting brackets or post-type walkway lights. The appearance of the lights is important and must complement the building design. Again, lamp life, lamp color, maintenance, weatherproofing, and durability must be considered.

Heating, Ventilating, and Air Conditioning (HVAC)

Another important aspect to be considered in the mall design is the comfort of the shopper as related to temperature control. The shopper should experience the pleasure of contrast and comfort whether coming in from summer heat or winter cold.

The generally accepted indoor conditions are 75 degrees Fahrenheit and 50 percent relative humidity in the summer and 70 degrees Fahrenheit in winter. Winter humidification would be desirable, but is impractical and costly because of the large proportion of outside air usually required for cooling. This outside air has a relatively low moisture content and would have to be supplemented with large quantities of water moisture in order to raise the relative humidity. In addition, the large winter cooling loads call for relatively low air temperatures in supply ducts. Such cool air has a low moisture-carrying capacity, and when humidity is added, condensation and dripping from ductwork may occur. Control of odors is very important and is best accomplished by maintaining a lower air pressure in odor-producing areas than in the remainder of the center. This is accomplished by exhausting air from the offending areas as required. If odor-producing areas are connected to a common supply-air system, exhaust quantities should exceed supply-air quantities.

Artwork

In order to add to the attraction of the center, it is also important to integrate works of art with the design of the various parts of the center.

One of the basic goals of a shopping center is to develop a festive and colorful environment, to create a marketplace set in attractive surroundings that makes shopping a gayer, more interesting experience. To carry out this concept, the architect has to be especially aware of the proportion, scale, and character of the malls. The use of related art—i.e., murals, sculpture, planting, fountains, paving design, special lighting, and graphics—adds a human touch and meaningful interest. The fact that many people visit shopping centers for browsing as well as for shopping, even on Sundays when many stores are closed, proves the validity of the concept.

The art form which emerged in the late 1960s and will no doubt have a more extensive use in the present decade is the supergraphic design. This is used in both exteriors and interiors of the centers in the form of large logo signing and symbols, parking identification, and entrance and exit signs. Large decorative art elements are being used in the form of murals applied to major exterior surfaces. In the mall interior, supergraphics are used in oversize scale and in many ingenious forms for storefront designs. They are also used effectively in the store interiors for department signing and wall murals. The colors, imaginative shapes, and special lighting effects which are part of the supergraphics are especially appealing to the young shoppers, who now comprise a very substantial part of the purchasing public.

There is no doubt that a well-programmed use of art could create a special regional atmosphere which would make the center a landmark. However, a word of caution is in order here. Indiscriminate or misdirected use of art could result in an unattractive image and would not contribute to the center's glamor. In any case, an art program, with the advice of the architect in charge and of a knowledgeable art consultant, is a prerequisite.

The enclosed-mall center, by its very nature, is intimate in character, and works of art have to be scaled to its interior spaces. This means that most of the art pieces have to be commissioned with certain limitations as to general size, height and width, solid or open space composition, and budget. The art program should be decided upon in the early stages of planning. Because of its community ties and the revival of interest in art, it would be good if works of art were commissioned from talented artists in the locality as well as from those who are nationally known (pages 82–87).

My experience in planning an overall art program for centers has been to include at least one play sculpture for children to climb and slide on. This design has to be low and smooth in shape and line so as to avoid any possible injury (page 88).

Whether a new or an experienced artist is being engaged, there must always be a businesslike approach in reaching a working arrangement. The following items need to be considered:

1. Preparation of detailed specifications for the artwork, similar to specifications for the building trades.
2. Guarantee by the artist of the permanency of materials used and of functional operation (as in the case of fountains).
3. Definite arrangements for the installation of the artwork on the premises.
4. Time limit for completion of the project.
5. Periodic visits by the architect to the artist's studio to check progress and solve unforeseen problems.

Detailed, written specifications are very important for a clear understanding of the proper materials to be used, the required finishes, and all component parts, whether mechanical, electrical, or other. Good specifications make it possible to avoid misunderstanding and friction between the parties.

Graphics and Signing

With the constant increase in the size and sophistication of regional shopping centers, the graphic arts have become an element of prime importance. The range for the design of graphic arts extends from the exterior main-center sign and logo (symbol), traffic directional signs in the parking areas, mall and arcade entrance signs, and special-events signs to the interior storefront signs, directories, and directional signs (telephones, lockers, rest rooms, public areas, and temporary storefront signs).

Many large developers (e.g., the Rouse Company), find it essential to issue a standard shopping center sign manual which specifies the requirements for all the above-named graphics. These requirements vary from project to project. This procedure is recommended for all major centers.

Prior to leasing, strict graphics and environmental design criteria should be established so that the shopper is easily and pleasantly oriented to all of the spaces. Store owners are rewarded with an oriented public that can search out

Belden Village, Canton, Ohio.
Mall fountain and sculpture.
(Architect: Louis Resnick, AIA.
Sculptor: C. E. Van Duzer.)

Belden Village, Canton, Ohio.
Mall sculpture. (Architect: Louis
Resnick, AIA. Sculptor: C. E. Van
Duzer.)

Smith Haven Mall, Smithtown, New York. View of mall. (Architects: Copeland, Novak & Israel International. Photographer: Constance Hope Associates.) Hanging sculpture, entitled Forty Feet of Fashion, is by Larry Rivers. This three-department-store, two-story shopping center (a development of the owner-builder, N. K. Winston Corporation) consists of four individual malls radiating from a central court. The 35'-high court is covered by a clear plastic dome and is planned for civic and promotional events. Outstanding in this center are works of art by internationally known artists. A mural by Sam Wiener is in the Abraham & Straus store.

Smith Haven Mall, Smithtown, New York. Fountain and mobile sculpture. (Architects: Copeland, Novak & Israel International. Sculptor: Alexander Calder. Photographer: Constance Hope Association.)

ABOVE: *Southridge Mall, Milwaukee, Wisconsin. Court and light sculpture. (Architects: Wah Yee Associates. Sculptor: Herbert Gesner.) This light sculpture features variations of light reflecting from prisms that are electronically controlled. The sculpture, 30' in height, has fourty-four lights in the tower operated by a program which produces 3,080 changes of light every twenty minutes.* ABOVE, RIGHT: *Genesee Valley Center, Flint, Michigan. Interior court with sculpture. (Architects: Gruen Associates. Associated architect: Louis G. Redstone Associates, Inc. Sculptor: Harry Bertoia. Photographer: Balthazar Korab.)* RIGHT: *Pompano Fashion Square, Pompano Beach, Florida. Entrance to Jordan Marsh. Stainless steel sculpture entitled Sailboat. [Architects: John Graham & Company. Sculptors: Saunders Schulz and William C. Severson (Scopia Inc.).]*

Westland Shopping Center, Westland, Michigan. East court showing 30'-high mobile sculpture and special clock with zodiac numerals. (Architects: Gruen Associates; Louis G. Redstone Associates, Inc. Mobile sculpture by George Rickey. Clock by Narendra Patel. Photographer: Balthazar Korab.)

Westland Shopping Center, Westland, Michigan. Play sculpture. (Architects: Gruen Associates, Louis G. Redstone Associates, Inc. Sculptor: Samuel Cashwan. Photographer: Balthazar Korab.)

Franklin Park Mall, Toledo, Ohio. J. L. Hudson Company court with sculpture. (Architects: for center—Daverman Associates, Inc., for J. L. Hudson Company—Raymond Loewy-William Snaith, Inc., Levine Alpern, and Louis G. Redstone Associates, Inc. Sculptor: Alexander Calder.)

East Towne Shopping Center, Madison, Wisconsin. Main entrance showing sculptured walls, each side 57' long × 30' high. (Architects: for center: Louis Resnick, AIA; for J. C. Penny—Daverman Associates; for Sears—Erickson Kristman, Stillwaugh; for Prange Company—W. C. Weeks, Inc.; for Gimbel's—Abbott Merkt & Company, Inc. Sculptress: Joan Robinson. Photographer: Wollin Studios.)

Ala Moana Shopping Center, Honolulu, Hawaii. (Architects: John Graham & Company. Fountain sculpture by George Tsutakawa.) The 15' silicone bronze statue cascades 1,000 gallons of water per minute.

Macomb Mall, Roseville, Michigan. Court with bronze fountain. (Architects: Louis G. Redstone Associates, Inc. Sculptor: Arthur Schneider.)

East Towne Shopping Center, Madison, Wisconsin. Fountain. (Architect for center: Louis Resnick, AIA. Sculptor of fountain: Joseph Anthony McDonnell. Photographer: Wollin Studios.)

their stores in an easy and orderly way. This is not meant to limit the variety that is inherent in a shopping center where the signs are all more or less individually designed by various interior designers or sign companies. But specifications that establish the framework of design and placement tend to organize all the message areas from the merchandising standpoint.

To produce effective graphics programs, the designer should be concerned not only with the problems of directing and identifying but also with the views of the architect and the owner. Together, they will set the desired taste and merchandising standards. The designer must be concerned with visually competitive or obstructive architectural forms, with space, kiosks, interior decoration or design, and also with lighting in making judgments regarding graphic concepts, design, and implementation. Exterior and interior graphics criteria for tenants must be established early in the development so that they can be written into tenant leasing agreements. A great deal of thinking must take place before design begins in order to ensure the maximum communication potential (page 89).

There are many effective ways to design the signing for storefronts. These signs may be in the form of individual letters of various materials—stainless steel, aluminum, plastic, porcelain enamel. The lighting may be built in as part of the letters, or the letters may be lighted from another source. One concept used satisfactorily in Galleria Post Oak, Houston, Texas, is described here in detail. This system, designed by Lindell Mabrey, using the Thomas lighting graphics channel installation, provides an infinite number of techniques with similar controls of size and constant plane. The variety of design, and the uniqueness of seeing letter forms identified only by back lighting, tend to provide a rich

(4)

(1)

(3)

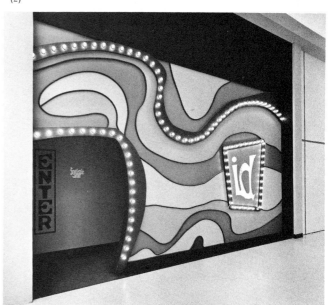

(2)

and high quality level. According to Mr. Mabrey, "Graphics should never shock the environment but should communicate easily and effectively in the environment. The typical shopper makes no thoughtful judgments concerning good or bad graphics, architecture or space design. He feels good or uncomfortable concerning buying or not buying, staying or leaving." This channel system provides lighting in the lower level and balcony area and provides a carrier for the individual store graphics. The channel is 2 feet high by 1 foot deep, the bottom of the channel being open with a louver to provide the down lighting for the balcony area. The front of the lighting channel is faced with a low-light-transmission glass and all signs are inserted directly behind it. The signs may be prepared in two or three dimensions, in any color, or in combination with design shapes. All graphics are provided by local sign companies of the store's choice. Complete specifications are supplied to ensure proper use and insertion of the graphics inserts. The images seen through the low-light-transmission glass are of a warm, deep, and rich color because the letter forms are identified by back lighting only. Very little of the ambient light in the mall areas is able to reach the face of the letter form because of the low-light-transmission glass. It gives an entirely new dimension to the viewing of graphics. In contrast, the light escaping from the bottom of the box is bright and relates visually to the light spill from store display spaces. It washes down in front of the stores as well as onto the walkway and provides a consistent, strong light level which directs attention toward the merchandising areas.

The above system would fit in best where the center comprises one major mall or court area. In the larger regional centers having four or five department stores, with a number of individual malls and courts contiguous to each department store, there is an advantage to varying the character and atmosphere through different types of signing and graphics. An example of this latter approach is shown in the Franklin Park Mall (see portfolio section).

This subject of lighting is complex and is in a continuous stage of development and research. Opinions vary widely as to the kind of lighting best suited for a relaxed shopping environment. The approaches range from a very dim, sophisticated atmosphere where even some of the store signings are left unlit to very bright lighting and oversize graphics covering much of the storefront. In many respects, lighting calls for scientific expertise; and much research is currently being done on this subject by consultant firms.

Security

The term *security* covers a large variety of elements relating to the center, starting from the exterior parking areas and going into the public areas of the center, i.e., malls and courts (including public washrooms) and the merchandising areas of the stores. It covers such topics as fire protection, pilfering and burglary protection, various methods of electronic surveillance, locking devices, cash control, emergency power, emergency communication, and handling of demonstrators.

Good lighting is of great importance in the parking areas as a deterrent to purse snatchers, car thieves, and burglars. Panhandlers and other undesirables normally will not frequent a shopping center that is well lighted. It is advisable to have the lights left on until about 2 A.M.

Fire protection in the form of a sprinkler system is a building code requirement for enclosed shopping centers, and the installation cost is more than offset by the low insurance rates. Fire protection is especially important in this decade with the frequent threats of fire bombs. For a more detailed description of the design of fire sprinkler systems, refer to the chapter entitled Mechanical Systems.

Security considerations in sprinkler systems start with alarms on the gate valves. Gate valves control the water flow from the riser to an individual system. An alarm is transmitted if the valve is turned off, thus depriving the sprinkler system of any additional water. In other words, if there were a fire, the only water available would be what was already in the small pipe coming off the riser.

In addition to the gate-valve alarm, there also should be a water-flow alarm. This is an alarm that sets into the pipe and immediately transmits a signal should water begin moving in the pipe. This way you know if the sprinkler head has been broken and there is a fire. It is important that an immediate alarm be given any time water flows out of the system, as extensive water damage may otherwise occur. Without an alarm system the water could flow for some period of time before it is seen or heard.

In addition to the automatic shutoff system, there are individual containers holding dry powder (a chemical similar to what is found in dry chemical fire extinguishers) that can be placed up against the ceiling. They are hemispherical in shape and approximately 8 inches in diameter. At the base of the unit is a single sprinkler head which, when the temperature rises to a predetermined point, will melt the fuse connection and release the dry powder with the necessary force to blanket a given radius. This is a very convenient way of giving fire protection to an isolated area where, because of the cost of construction or for some other reason, the use of the conventional system is not possible.

Since the potential damage caused by smoke can be great in a shopping center, smoke detectors and heat sensors should be installed. Both the smoke detectors and heat sensors can be tied into the alarm systems so that, prior to the time that the fire gets hot enough to cause the sprinkler system to open, notification will be received through the alarm system.

Smoke detectors, heat sensors, and fire dampers can also be tied into air-conditioning vents so that all the air flow—fans and motors, etc.—will be shut off early in the fire. This prevents smoke from becoming a hazard to the entire center, since it will not be picked up in the air-conditioning system and then dispersed throughout all the other areas, which may cause panic as well as damage to merchandise.

One of the considerations of a fire protection system is the location of the fire hoses and fire extinguishers in sufficient numbers to be of real value in case of a major problem. Proper location, as well as the design and labeling of the cabinet, can be essential to its immediate availability when needed. An unmarked hose cabinet hidden off in a corner somewhere is of little value if it cannot be found in case of emergency. One other consideration is the quality and type of hose that is to be used. It is suggested that the fire department be consulted on the grade of hose and the type and class of fire extinguishers selected.

Other considerations include the location of fire hydrants in the parking lots and areas surrounding the center and the use of interior standpipe connections.

Special attention should be paid to the construction and location of the central trash baling area. It should be of fireproof construction and easily reachable by the fire department.

Areas which have proved to be security risks in shopping centers include the dock areas. There are two approaches to receiving of merchandise in shopping centers. One is a central receiving operation for the entire center, where all merchandise received is checked in and then dispatched to the individual stores. The other approach, which is in general use, involves a separate receiving operation or dock for each store at the center. Regardless which of the two approaches is used, there are basic security precautions to be taken in the design of these areas. First, realizing that these areas are subject to attack by people interested in committing large-scale thefts, the security system designed must protect total shipments rather than just individual items.

It is recommended that the dock area be so constructed that it can be sealed off from the rest of the center in a way that provides fire protection as well as security for the area. One means of securing a dock area is to use reinforced concrete walls and steel fire doors.

The truck wells themselves should be designed so that the outer rolling overhead steel doors can be lowered electrically, or manually, should there be a power failure.

Somewhere adjacent to the dock area should be an area where valuable merchandise can be held while awaiting pickup or shipment out of the center. It is also recommended that the alarms for the dock area be put on separate zones. Each of the exterior rolling doors should be alarmed with some type of magnetic door contact. The use of the magnetic contacts on the exterior doors allows the dock platform area to remain in operation even when there is no movement of trucks.

A few construction details relating to security are worthy of mention. It is important that the outside walls be free of devices that a burglar could use for climbing on the roof of the building; also, roof entry areas have to be secured. Roof vents, where necessary, should have burglar bars and/or alarms whenever possible. When exterior display windows are used, it is advisable to specify shatterproof glass. Steel doors for service entrances should be used. Each door should have a magnetic contact alarming device that ties into the overall alarm system.

Entrance doors to the mall areas should be made of shatterproof glass with all hardware case-hardened. Hinge pins should face the interior if they are not hidden within the door. An added protection is the use of an electromagnetic door-locking system.

Burglar Protection Systems

"Burglar protection" means many things to many people. The shopping center has two approaches to the problem. It can install a central station—that is, take all of its burglar protection, fire protection, sprinkler-flow and valve systems, rate-of-rise temperature indicators, etc., and tie these systems into an alarm panel for the entire center. This panel is then monitored—along with the panels of its other customers—by an alarm company. An alternative is for the center to install its own alarm panel in the shopping center complex and have all the alarms throughout the entire center come to that panel. Smaller centers usually employ a simple coded or noncoded supervised system that sounds alarm signals in the area of signal origin.

With the proprietary system, the center provides a man to monitor the panel during its operation. Depending upon the types of alarms used in the center, this could be either during the hours the center is closed to the public or on a twenty-four hour basis. If such items as holdup alarms are tied into it, the panel would have to be monitored twenty-four hours a day.

Certain types of alarms used within a center should be put on what is termed *line supervision*. Professional burglars have the knowledge necessary to tap into the telephone lines or lines being used to transmit signals into the proprietary system. At the time they are entering a building, they "jump" the system and thereby prohibit the panel from receiving an alarm condition. Line supervision is a system whereby constant monitoring is done electronically of the resistance in the line. Any change in the resistance of the line used to transmit the signals will signify an alarm condition. The signal would mean that there was actually a line problem or that a penetration of the burglary systems had occurred.

For years, retailers depended upon two primary types of burglar devices: these were magnetic contacts on the doors leading into the building and window tape around the windows. However, with the increase in the crime rate and the development of space-age equipment, a need for better security became obvious. For one thing, burglars began to jump door contacts. Also, youngsters took pride in cutting across the window tape with just one slice of a razor blade. Once the tape was cut, the panel, whether central or proprietary, would not receive any message saying that the alarm had been activated. A search then had to be made tracing back all the lines, and sometimes it would take hours to discover that one tiny razor blade had cut into the window tape.

Photoelectric beams have been used, and initially a single beam would be put in. A photoelectric cell would transmit the invisible beam, which would run across an opening or down an aisle to a receiver at the other end. Any break in the beam, as might be caused by a person walking between the two points, would signal an alarm. However, burglars soon learned to climb over or go under this system. In order to prevent this tactic from succeeding, the beam was given a "lace" appearance.

One of the newer and most effective mechanisms is the motion-detection device that is now on the market. These devices, while somewhat more temperamental in some cases, are much harder to defeat than simple window tape, door contacts, or photoelectric systems. But a word of caution is due here: Any system, no matter how good it is at the point of actual use, can be inactivated more easily if line supervision is not included in it. The one thing that a motion detector must be able to do is discriminate between types of masses (e.g., a human body as opposed to a piece of paper that might fall off a desk).

There are basically two types of motion-detection devices that can be used. One is nondirectional; it floods an area with a field. The other is directional, which means that it can be directed down an aisle so that areas on either side can have people in them without disturbing the alarm system.

Some motion detectors will penetrate walls. However, since they are usually adjustable, they can be turned down to pull them back inside the wall. In some cases, where wall penetration is desired, the cost can be reduced by using a single unit to penetrate an interior wall, thereby providing complete protection of the premises.

Relatively new developments are the microphone systems. Again, the alarm from such a system can either go to a central station outside the center or be tied into the center if it has its own proprietary system. This system involves the placing of microphones approximately every 50 feet, depending on the type of coverage desired. These microphones have contacts in them which sound will break, immediately notifying the panel that an open circuit exists. The microphone will then allow the audible monitoring of the area.

Because this system involves many widely dispersed microphones, some method of detecting the origin of the sound is needed. The normal installation for a shopping center will consist of several speakers within the panel complex. When sounds occur in any protected location, a speaker at the panel will become active and will transmit conversations taking place. The monitors can then notify the proper authorities and request whatever assistance may be needed to handle the situation.

There are also alarms that sense vibrations. These alarms can be useful in supplementing a burglar alarm system. They are activated by vibrations that occur when someone attempts to break into a building through a window, wall, or roof with one of these sensory devices attached to it.

Another device, often called a capacitance field alarm, surrounds a specific area with an electronic field. Anyone entering the field upsets its balance and triggers the alarm.

The matter of a watchman tour-service system must also be considered. One system is nonelectrical and consists of key boxes, each containing a special key, placed throughout the center. The other system requires wiring to the alarm panel, and the guard carries a special key which he inserts into one of the several types of watch box stations, located throughout the center.

Each time the guard puts the key into a box, it registers at the panel, so the monitor at the panel knows where the guard is at all times. This system may also be equipped to transmit an emergency signal which indicates that help is needed.

All alarm systems capable of handling a shopping center will have available a device which permanently records all signals received at the panel on a printout system.

Door contacts may be placed on stairways that are marked "Emergency Exit Only." These contacts, tied back into the panel, will allow the alarm system to stay in operation during store hours. Should it be necessary for authorized personnel to use these areas, a bypass key system may be installed. Thus, when a key is inserted into the lock and turned, the alarm is bypassed.

Holdup Alarms

The success of the Federal Bank Act that requires all banks to have cameras able to take a photograph of someone committing a holdup of a bank suggests that retailers could make use of such a system.

To begin with, some type of automatic alarming device is needed. The button-, foot-, or hand-operated device that requires some overt action by the employee for its activation is dangerous. The person committing the holdup may be extremely nervous, and any added motion or movement by the employee could be fatal.

One automatic system now being widely used involves the placement of two money clips in the money drawer. One clip holds the last $20 bill and the other holds the bottom $10. Removal of these two bills automatically activates the alarm. Removal of just one or the other will not activate the alarm, so false alarms are reduced. When the alarm is activated, this can also turn on the cameras. Movie, 33mm, or TV cameras with a videotaping machine all will do an adequate job.

The next problem is deciding where the alarm will be received. The alarm can be received somewhere in the center office complex (as part of the proprietary system), at a central-station alarm company, or at the local police station. Regardless of where it is transmitted, it should be a silent system. No loud outside bell is needed to panic the holdup artist.

No matter where the signal is sent, decisions on actions to be taken will have to be made. If the central station answers, whom do they notify? The center, the police, or the individual store? If the proprietary system is used, is the center to respond, to call the police, or to call the store?

Electronic Inventory Control Systems

In the past few years there has been an increase in the use of inventory control systems which can be attached in one manner or another to merchandise to control shoplifting. A tag, wafer, or some other device may be attached to the merchandise, and when a person leaves the area with the device still attached, an alarm tells the security person that merchandise containing the antishoplifting device is leaving the area.

If the device is used on a large scale in the community, even the most casual pilferer will recognize it for what it is, namely, a theft-detection device. These systems can act as a theft preventive technique since the would-be thief knows what it is and realizes the likelihood of getting caught.

The other possible approach is to conceal the device in the merchandise. This system is not obvious to the would-be thief and is used primarily as a means of apprehending rather than deterring shoplifters. Good arguments can be presented for both approaches. However, the cost of apprehending a thief is much greater than that of deterring him. It is becoming known that preventive systems can force the shoplifters, which no center needs anyway, to concentrate on centers where the devices are not used.

With such systems, and there are several on the market, the device is either deactivated or removed at the point of sale, so the salespeople must be fully trained in the use of the system. As long as human error does not become excessive, false alarms are minimal with most systems.

If each store within the center put a system in and then manned each exit, the cost would be tremendous. However, the detectors may be set up at the center exits manned by center employees, and each store using the system may be charged a proportionate amount. With systems of this type, it is advantageous to have a small, private area where a suspect could be taken and questioned without excessive embarrassment in the event the person had, in fact, paid for the merchandise but the clerk had forgotten to remove the signaling device.

Most of these devices can trigger any kind of an alarm system that is desired—a bell, buzzer, light, etc. At each exit, the system could be left on twenty-four hours a day and an automatic counter could be sealed into the unit, allowing management to keep track of the number of times the alarm signal had been received at the exit point. If the system is tied into the center alarm system, an immediate alert would result in the possible apprehension of a thief. This system, when used to complement the regular burglar alarm system, tells not only that the door was opened but that stolen property was, in fact, removed from the center.

These devices are in their infancy and, as it appears now, they will within the relatively near future be refined to the point where, if properly used and installed and designed into the total center, shoplifting as we know it today could be virtually eliminated.

These systems can also be an aid in controlling employee dishonesty. If the system used involves a tag or wafer or something of that nature which acts as a triggering device, an effective audit can be performed by matching the number of tags removed against the number of items sold.

Another advantage of having the center personnel do the monitoring at the exits is that an employee who wishes to steal from his employer must be concerned with getting by someone who does not work with him and will not look the other way as he leaves the center.

Since each of the various inventory control systems has different requirements as to the size of the exit opening which works best with the system, this should be discussed with whatever company the center is planning on using.

Closed-Circuit Television

Closed-circuit television tied into a central monitoring panel can be an effective tool if properly used. Because of the tremendous cost of installing closed-circuit television (pulling of cables, wiring, etc.) early planning for maximum benefits is important to make it an effective tool and an economically feasible one.

A central closed-circuit television system allows full-time surveillance of receiving docks and of emergency exits and areas where traffic is normally light but potential danger is great (e.g., parking lots) both day and night. In short, the entire center can be monitored, thus eliminating the need for each store to either monitor its premises or to place security personnel on the docks or out on the parking lots. Cameras can also be used to either supplement or, in some cases, replace the motorized external control used by centers at night, which is expensive in terms of both manpower and equipment.

Television can provide excellent total-perimeter coverage of a shopping center. Of course, it can be tied to automatic videotape machines, and when parking lot problems arise, the security person monitoring has only to push a button to videotape the situation occurring in the parking lot, such as a purse theft or an altercation between a would-be auto thief and the auto owner.

If, for instance, cable is run to various central locations around the center where a camera can easily be plugged in, fewer cameras will be needed, because this provides the mobility to go where the problem exists. Live television cameras can become a very effective deterrent to the criminal—in the evening to the burglar and/or during the day to the shoplifter or employee-thief. It is possible for center planners, at the time they are discussing leases with potential store tenants, to work out the number of television camera outlets that tenants would like wired into their stores for future use. This does not obligate them to use their cameras on a 12-month basis. However, the center can lease cameras as the tenants request them.

This approach to closed-circuit television allows key selling areas to be monitored as individual stores change their interior layouts. While a retailer most certainly has to pay for this service, it can be an inducement for him to sign the lease when he realizes the potential value of the planning that is going into the center's closed-circuit television operation—a project that could very well reduce his losses and thus increase his profits.

An open display of some of the monitors in the mall area reenforces the impression that the television system is an operational system and not made up of dummy cameras as so many people are prone to believe.

Many people who sell television cameras may try to sell centers on drone of dummy cameras. The value of these is limited and temporary. Another step that can be taken to increase the public's awareness of the television system is to place in one store a monitor showing the interior of another store. The picture seen on the monitor does not show the would-be thief the entire area that the television cameras can cover, because he is never sure what location is being covered. It does, however, reinforce the idea that each store has television coverage and that he will risk getting caught if he attempts a theft.

Television can serve as a deterrent not only to the shoplifter but also to the employee, since neither employees nor customers can be sure of just how much of the center is protected by the television monitors. With the use of videotape, television can help in the preparation and presentation of court cases. Another aspect of this coverage is that a given suspect, once recognized, can be followed on television from store to store while each store's security personnel are being notified. Television can, of course, also be used in monitoring customer package pickup areas as well as the other nonselling and selling floors, and parking lots.

Locking

The center can be keyed on a master key system specifically designed for it by any of the major lock companies. Such a system usually consists of a grand master lock, submaster locks, and single-key locks below that, so that the center doors can be protected from unauthorized use. Another device that can be tied into this is what is called *the recording key lock*. Each key for this system is so designed that, when it is inserted into the lock and turned, it registers its number and the time on the tape inside. The tape container is removed on a daily, weekly, or monthly basis and checked to see who has used what key and at what time.

A single entrance for the center also means a single entrance for personnel working in the center. This single entrance would then be the only door with an exterior key receptacle or cylinder.

Cash Control

Most larger shopping center retailers will install their own cash offices—at least that has been the practice in the past. However, one technique that provides maximum security at reduced expense is to locate a bank within the shopping center and let it act as the cash office for the various stores. The bank could process each store's funds, take in each day's receipts, and even hold the money from the registers. The bank then would charge the stores a set rate per transaction. This also could provide a further deterrent to employee theft inasmuch as the employees will probably hold the generally accepted attitude that no one can steal from a bank and get away with it.

Again, in any of the stores, cash offices, or banks, the perimeter or holdup alarms used are of utmost importance and should be thoroughly checked to be sure that they are adequate.

Emergency Communication

In the event that evacuation of a center should become necessary, a means of alerting customers and employees within the center is needed. A speaker system throughout the shopping center can be useful in several ways. It can provide a means of paging parents of lost children and of supplying music throughout the center. It can also be the means of notifying personnel within the center that the center must be closed. The precise words to be used in the announcement must be carefully chosen.

Emergency announcements should be worded so as to avoid any possible panic. It is suggested that a recording be made in advance and placed on a standby recorder at a central point in the center. When evacuation becomes necessary, the tape giving the needed instructions can be played, thus avoiding the communication of a sense of panic to the shoppers. In addition, the speaker system can be used to tell key people within the center that their assistance is needed and that they should call the center office immediately. By using code numbers, it is possible to devise a system which can alert any particular group to respond at any time.

The location of the center security or police office is important since it must be so constructed and placed that it will be accessible to authorized personnel as well as to the county or state police in the event of a demonstration or other disruption.

Another point to remember is that, in many cases, shoplifters and other criminals may have to be held at the center station while waiting for the police to take them into custody. Since such people can be rather disorderly, it is preferable to place the security office away from selling areas.

Demonstrations

The management should establish certain definite policies regarding the holding and handling of group demonstrations. Understanding, tact, and diplomacy should guide the management in these decisions. If the demonstrators receive permission and are nonviolent, there should be no problems involved.

If, during the initial stages of the demonstrations, it appears that the group may become violent, then the center should take immediate steps to protect certain key areas. The central plant should be secured immediately and no one allowed to enter without proper identification. The communication and management offices for the center should also be secured and a guard posted.

In addition to securing the central plant area (i.e., heating, air conditioning, etc.), any major electrical panels or generators should be also secured. If the stores have individual receiving docks, then it should be possible—through advance planning—to secure these areas quickly.

The effectiveness of the actual handling of the problem is usually in direct relationship to the thoroughness and soundness of the planning effort. Responsibility for the protection of the property and the lives and safety of the people within the center cannot be passed on to the local authorities and disavowed by the center management.

The problem of handling public assemblies, demonstrations, or picketing is described in the form of an actual case study under the section entitled Center Operation.

Electrical Systems

The electrical systems for a shopping center vary from one basic power, lighting, and telephone system to many, depending on size and type of shopping center. Auxiliary systems often included are music and paging systems (described under Mall Lighting), a fire alarm system, a burglar alarm system (described under

Security), lighting and environmental monitoring systems, delivery signal system, and closed-circuit television system for specific tenant requirements.

The power distribution system requires numerous considerations. It is necessary to consider the power characteristics available from the utility company, the shopping center load requirements, the number of tenants, individual tenant loads, future load and shopping center growth, utility rules regarding resale of power to tenants by the shopping center owner, the cost of the owner's electrical distribution system (including requirement of electrical rooms, transformer pads, length of feeders, quantity of feeders, etc.) versus cost of distribution system as required if each tenant were served directly by the utility company. Other considerations are differential cost of electrical energy between primary and secondary rates versus amortization costs of transformers and primary distribution system, and, finally, space limitations. The reliability of service must also be considered, and the possibility of arranging for a second service from the utility company in the event of a blackout will often call for additional cost estimates. As a further precaution against blackout, auxiliary battery lighting systems or emergency generators are employed in the design. Outages and service interruptions as experienced by the serving utility company will help to determine if radial or loop distribution system should be used.

If the demand load for a shopping center does not exceed 1,000 kilovolt-amperes (sufficient for approximately 100,000 square feet of shopping space), primary service should generally not be considered unless all tenant power consumption is unmetered. To determine if secondary distribution voltage should be 265/460, 120/208, or 120/240, an evaluation should be made of costs for the power system and the fluorescent lighting system at respective voltages. Many times the costs for a step-down transformer (460 to 120/208 or 460 to 120/240) and related feeders will preclude the use of 277/480-volt distribution, but length of feeders and voltage drop considerations may sometimes require distribution at the higher voltage.

Regarding the site design, for esthetic reasons, the developer should install the electric wire underground, eliminating poles and overhead wires. It is a more expensive installation, but in many locations the underground system is a requirement.

A total energy system should also be considered; an engineering study should be made to determine the economics and priorities that may require a total energy system. Studies of power plant cost, including space, equipment, maintenance, etc., often show that investments in merchandising and real estate are preferable to total energy power plant investment. But if the local utility company has excessive power outages, if it is unable to handle the new load without large charges to the owner, or if a reliable and economical natural gas fuel source is readily available, then a total energy system installation should be considered.

In any event the owner should not proceed without a full knowledge of the system itself, the increased complexity of the mechanical systems required, and the overall increase in maintenance, space requirements, and personnel problems that will be involved.

The telephone system is the most essential auxiliary system to be provided, and, except for large department stores, the telephone service requirements are usually minimal. For department stores and other large stores, the telephone system requires detailed coordination with the layout of the store's merchandise fixtures and with its operational requirements. Branch conduit sizes, cable termination space, main service conduit, telephone relay rooms, switchboard space, telephone closets, etc., must conform to tenant's requirements. Unless severe restrictions are encountered, the telephone conduit layout should provide a flexible outlet layout that permits relocation and addition of telephones in conformance with revised merchandising layouts. For department stores with large volumes of telephone usage, the installation of under-floor ducts will provide maximum flexibility. If outlet boxes and conduits are used, spare cable capacity should be allowed at pull boxes and outlets for future growth and expansion of the system. (Example: provide junction boxes at columns for ready future conduit extension to new telephone outlets; provide conduit stubs into floor on a modular plan for ready extension.) For smaller stores, the telephone system usually consists of a few outlets at specific locations and of service entrance conduit. All telephone system layouts require coordination with the local telephone utility company.

As for power service, the main telephone service should also be underground, like the electrical service.

The fire and burglar alarm system is discussed in detail under Security.

The environmental monitoring system keeps track of such things as the status of fans, chillers, air conditioners, the temperature of various areas, and the temperature outdoors as well as main power service entrance breakers, power transformer temperature, and illumination level of various critical mall areas. The monitor console or panel is usually located in the building engineer's office or in the quarters of other qualified personnel.

The delivery signal system usually consists of pushbuttons, talk-back speakers, and door releases that permit entry for merchandise delivery to respective tenants after the delivery transport has been properly identified by that tenant. Thus unauthorized traffic in service areas is restricted.

Mechanical Systems

The following reviews several basic approaches in the selection of the mechanical system best suited for the individual center. The subject will be separated into the three broad categories of (1) heating, ventilating, and air conditioning, (2) plumbing, and (3) fire protection systems.

Heating, Ventilating, and Air Conditioning (HVAC)

The first step in selecting an HVAC system is for the mechanical engineer to analyze the schematic concepts of the architect and propose a number of schemes which would fit into the overall design. These schemes, accompanied by cost estimates, should be presented to the developer, with explanations of the pros and cons of each system.

Following are various types of systems to be considered. Where boilers are specified they are normally gas- or oil-fired. However, where climate and utility rates are a factor, the use of electric boilers or individual electric heating units should be investigated. No attempt has been made to rate systems as to their suitability for different types of construction (open- or closed-mall) or for different size centers. This decision is best made on an individual job basis.

Type A—Central chillers and boilers and related distribution mains are provided by the developer-landlord to serve heating and cooling equipment for the entire system. Equipment and distribution systems for common areas are furnished by the developer and equipment for tenant spaces is furnished by the tenant, depending on the lease arrangement.

Areas having odd-hour operations or perishable stock should be provided with supplemental or separate cooling capability in order to avoid running large central chillers at low loads and to provide necessary cooling during possible seasonal shutdown of the central system. Since there are interconnections between landlord and tenant systems, the tenant must meet certain criteria established as part of the lease. These criteria define equipment requirements and installation, conditions and times when chilled water and/or hot water will be available, and details on charges for utilities and related services.

Advantages of this system:
Reliable operation
Low maintenance
Little need for access to roof-mounted equipment

Disadvantages:
Possible tenant dissatisfaction with utility charge, initial high installation costs, and space requirement for this equipment
Greater initial cost than for completely separate systems for each space

Type B—Central chillers, boilers, air handlers, air-distribution ducts, and auxiliary heating piping to common areas and tenant areas are provided by the landlord. The extension of heating, piping, and ductwork is the responsibility of either the landlord or the tenant depending on lease arrangement.

Air is provided as required to cool the spaces under summer design conditions and heating coils in the duct system add heat as required under less than full load conditions. A refinement to this system can be accomplished by providing variable-volume terminal units for each zone. These units first reduce the volume of cool air before adding heat, thereby greatly reducing operating costs whenever cooling loads are reduced because of lower occupancy and lower transmission loads.

As indicated under Type A, areas with odd-hour operation or perishable stock should be provided with supplemental or separate cooling capacity.

Advantages:
Least amount of equipment required for overall operation
Reliable system
Low overall maintenance
Minimum maintenance for tenant
No equipment space required in tenant areas

Disadvantages:
Greater initial cost than for completely separate systems for each space
Main duct space may pose problems
Possible tenant dissatisfaction with utility and lease charges
Higher operating costs than other systems unless variable volume units are used

Type C—Rooftop multizone units containing refrigeration cycles, gas-fired heaters, and fans are provided by the landlord as required to serve all the heating and cooling requirements.

Because a unit may serve several tenant areas (each with its own zone control), the landlord should maintain control over and furnish the entire system including all controls and distribution systems. Ceilings would be laid out on a modular basis, with any required changes being negotiated with the tenant. If auxiliary heating is required, it should be provided by the tenant responsible for the space served.

Advantages:
Lower first cost than for type A or B
No equipment in tenant spaces
No maintenance required by tenant

Disadvantages:
Since rooftop multizone units are usually in the 30- to 40-ton range, a number of units are required
Rooftop multizone performance and quality (to date) is still to be perfected
Greater maintenance than for type A or B
All maintenance must be performed on roof
Possible leak problems through and at roof units
Possible tenant dissatisfaction with limitations of modular ceilings

Type D—Each space is provided with its own heating and cooling equipment. The landlord provides equipment for common areas, and each tenant provides equipment for his space.

Equipment can be of the packaged rooftop type or may consist of split systems. The latter are made up either of roof-mounted condensers with refrigeration compressors and air handlers located in the spaces served, or roof-mounted condensing units (condenser and compressor in one unit) are mounted on the roof and the air-handling unit is located in the space served. Condensing units offer the advantage of allowing the air-handling units to be suspended from the roof or mezzanine framing rather than taking up valuable floor space. Use of condensers on the roof with refrigeration compressors in the spaces served has the advantage of not requiring roof access for compressor maintenance.

Packaged rooftop units have the advantage of not requiring any space in the areas served.

In all cases heating units are furnished by the landlord for common areas and by tenants for their own spaces depending on leasing arrangements.

Advantages:
Lower first cost than for type A or B
Tenant assumption of all initial cost and operating costs may be advantageous to the landlord

Disadvantages:
Multiplicity of roof-mounted equipment requires special visual treatment and frequent access to roof for maintenance, with unavoidable damage to roof
Equipment not as reliable as for type A or B
Greater possibility of roof leaks because of roof-mounted equipment

Exhaust Systems

Exhaust systems for toilets, kitchens, etc., are furnished by the party responsible for finishing the space served. Kitchen exhaust systems are better served by up-blast roof fans, which offer superior cleaning and odor dispersal characteristics.

For toilet and similar exhaust systems, it would be preferable to mount fans inside of space in order to minimize the amount of rooftop equipment requiring maintenance.

Plumbing Systems

Plumbing systems are normally quite straightforward, with the landlord bringing water, sewer, and gas connections to leased spaces for extension by individual tenants (except in instances where the landlord supplies a turnkey job).

Water can be supplied directly from outside mains to each space, with municipal metering, or from landlord-furnished mains and meters if local authorities allow, and if the latter arrangement is advantageous to the landlord.

Where water pressure may exceed 80 pounds per square inch, pressure reducing stations should be considered. Also, water treatment may be necessary where excessive water hardeners and/or iron content warrants such action.

Sewers from food handling areas should be provided with grease traps and separate waste lines to large, easily maintained sewers.

Storm systems are provided by the landlord and are standard, as for any installation.

Fire Protection Systems

Code requirements and insurance rates are making it desirable, and in many cases mandatory, that shopping centers be provided with sprinkler systems throughout.

Before designing the sprinkler system, we must first look at the water source and its available pressure. A dual water source is normally desirable. This can be achieved by a service having two public water mains or one water main and a water tower or underground water storage tank. Water pressure is evaluated by its ability to adequately serve the highest sprinkler heads in the building.

Assuming that water is available, there are two main methods of serving the building complex. One method involves the use of a single on-site water main which acts both as the fire protection source and as the domestic water source. Another method involves separate on-site fire and domestic water loops.

The single-main method is most commonly used when cost is a major factor, but it presents problems of supervision, since each lead from the main to the building requires its own separate alarm. The alarm for each lead performs the function of locating the segment of active sprinklers within the building and allowing the fire department to attach its pumper between the fire hydrant and the active sprinkler connection, thereby increasing the pressure in the fire-affected area (page 104).

The disadvantages of this type of system are, first, that the fire department has to locate the area of the fire prior to starting its fire fighting effort. Second, since the fire and domestic systems are combined, the water in the circuit is in constant movement, making it possible for particle or mineral deposits to settle in the fire protection lines or heads, thus reducing the capacity of the lines or even plugging them entirely.

The second method of serving a building complex requires the provision of independent water loops, one for domestic use and the other for fire protection. This provides two separate sources of water. One advantage of this approach

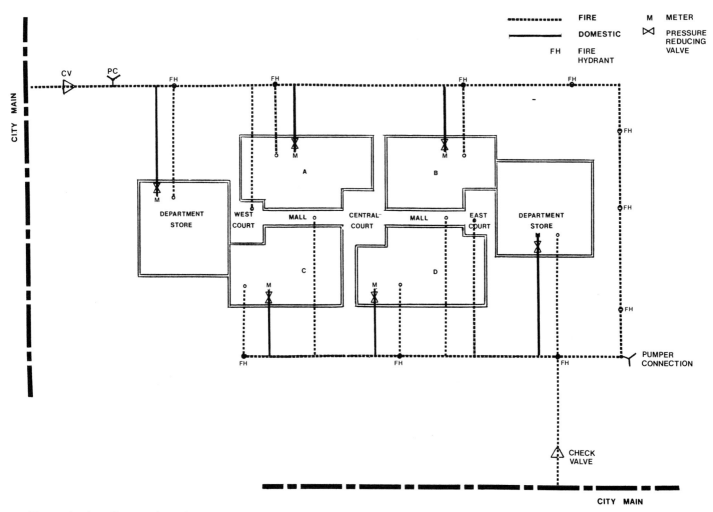

Diagram showing a fire protection system based on a single main water supply.

is that the fire department can pressurize the entire fire fighting system without first determining the exact location of the fire. Another lies in the fact that the independent fire protection loop is in a static situation, allowing impurities and particles in the water to settle out and thus eliminating any chance that they might hamper the operation of the system. It is generally advisable that two independent water sources be available to serve the general area of the center and to form a loop around this area. Also, separate fire protection and domestic loops should be provided within the center area. The initial outlay for such systems will result in substantial savings in insurance premiums, and the systems will pay for themselves over a period of only a few years (page 105).

The best-known and most widely used fire protection system is called the *wet system*. This is a network of water-filled pipes with sprinkler heads attached to them, the pipes being kept under a constant pressure. When a fire starts, it melts the fuse connection in the sprinkler head, allowing the water to flow out of the head and onto the fire.

Generally tied into the wet system is a dry system around the perimeter of the building. This is done so that there will be no danger of pipes freezing or bursting in cold weather. The normal type of dry system works in conjunction

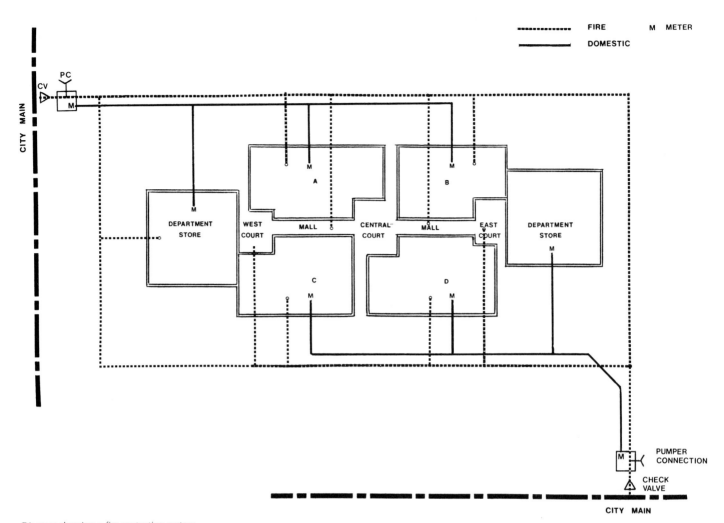

*Diagram showing a fire protection system
based on two separate water loops,
one for domestic and one for fire protection.*

with the total wet system, the pipes around the perimeter being under air
pressure. This is a constant pressure which holds back the water. At the time
the fuses melt from the heat of the fire, the air escapes, allowing the water to
flow in behind the escaping air.

A relatively recent development is an automatic shutoff for wet sprinkler
systems. Each individual sprinkler head has its own separate thermostat. When
the sprinkler is activated, the water flow will cover the fire. As the heat decreases,
the thermostat recloses the sprinkler head. Among the largest losses in many
retail store or shopping center fires are those due to water damage to merchandise. A system that can turn itself on and off automatically will greatly reduce
the amount of damage done by excessive water flow. This automatic shutoff
system can turn the sprinkler off and on as many as a dozen times if the fire,
each time that it is covered with water, is cooled but not extinguished.

In the design of the sprinkler system itself, one of the primary considerations
is the number of risers. The risers are the main feeder lines into the sprinkler
system—the lines that carry the water into the system itself. An insufficient
number of risers going into a building from the main source of water supply
can create a water shortage should there be problems in more than one area.

In case a system must be repaired or shut down, the availability of several risers makes it possible to shut a small area off from one riser rather than shutting down large portions of an entire center's water system.

Fire Protection in Existing Centers

There is no easy way to install sprinklers in an existing store or shopping center. It is costly and difficult to work in a confined attic space. Access through the existing ceiling must be gained in such a manner that installation work and repairs to existing finishes do not interfere with a store's normal operation.

Materials Handling

The sorting and storing of reserve merchandise, whether in the store facility or in a special warehouse (as in the case of chain stores), has always been a difficult and costly item. The chain stores are continuing to evolve new methods of mechanization and automation in their distribution centers. The primary objective of the automation is the efficient control of sold merchandise and its replenishment through the use of the computerized cash registers in each store. Data concerning every registered sale are transmitted instantly to the warehouse and replacement merchandise is ordered. Although the cost of an automated installation is relatively high, the labor- and time-saving advantages offset this.

The problem is more difficult to solve in the case of the individual retailer whose store rental is high. If he wants even minimal storage facilities for his operation, he must use valuable sales space for this purpose. It certainly would be worth exploring the idea of an automated warehouse to provide facilities for a number of individual storekeepers.

A few words regarding security precautions in warehouses may be worthwhile here. These precautions would include the use of windowless walls, the elimination of skylights, and the routing of truck traffic through a main control gate.

An example of an efficient automated warehouse is the distribution center for Strawbridge & Clothier in Philadelphia. Another, in a related situation where materials handling is of prime importance, is the Pan Am Cargo Terminal at the Kennedy Airport in New York City, which uses highly automated equipment successfully (pages 108–110).

Maintenance and Operation

Maintenance

Once the center is completed and most of the tenants have moved in, effective maintenance and operation become prime factors in the success of the center. It would be difficult in this limited space to describe all the elements that make for an efficient and economic operation. Some of the outstanding factors which require special attention include the common area maintenance procedures for indoors and outdoors and their approximate cost, the planning for promotional events, and the sociopolitical and public relations problems to be handled.

The term *common area maintenance* (CAM) is commonly used in most shopping center leases and refers to a charge that is added to the normal rent. This additional charge, or extra rental, covers the maintenance and protection of those areas commonly used by all tenants and, in some cases, by the buying public.

These common areas include malls, courts, sidewalks, truck areas, parking lots, and roadways.

Charges for common area maintenance vary from center to center and from area to area. Northland Center, an eighteen-year-old one-department-store, open-mall center consisting of 1,300,000 square feet of rentable area, is located in the population center of metropolitan Detroit. Its common area cost is 56 cents per square foot of rentable area, a cost which is charged to each tenant. Unlike many regional shopping centers, Northland Center has an open-ended lease clause regarding common area maintenance, and the cost for this service can be increased or decreased at the landlord's will. Many regional centers are tied down to a fixed charge of x number of cents per square foot, and the landlord pays the difference between this cost and the actual cost. An enclosed 1,000,000-square-foot center with a lot of terrazzo floor, natural tropical plantings, and other center amenities can run as high as 70 cents per square foot.

For examples of centers comparable to the two listed above, but in another area of the country, we may consider a 1,300,000-square-foot open center and a 1,000,000-square-foot enclosed center and put them into a warm climate, such as Texas. Here the common area cost could be as much as 50 percent less than at the previously mentioned centers, primarily due to the fact that there is no snow removal in the warm climates. Another item which affects the cost of common area maintenance is protection. In a metropolitan area such as Detroit, protection can run as high as 35 cents per square foot. Elsewhere in the midwest, as in Lincoln, Nebraska, protection cost may be as low as 5 cents per square foot. In analyzing the costs of operation of three regional midwest centers, the costs were broken down into three categories:

Indoor—average	25¢
Outdoor—average	16¢
Protection—average	24¢
Total average—	65¢

The following case study reflects the experience, in relation to maintenance operations, of Jerome L. Schostak, of Schostak Brothers & Company in Detroit, Michigan, a developer of a number of medium-sized regional centers. Except for guard service, he preferred to have his own staff rather than to use contracted services. The chief of such a staff must, however, be the sort of person who not only understands mechanical and electrical operations but who is also ready to participate in the physical work involved. He is the one who explains the entire philosophy of the operation and he often works right along with his men. The maintenance staff (besides the general maintenance superintendent) consists of a foreman and five men, none of whom had any special mechanical skills when they started. In addition, there is a middle-aged cleaning woman who uses an aluminum cart equipped with litter bag, cleaning rags, and a small, child-size broom to the handle of which a scraper is attached for the removal of gum spots from the floor. The superintendent and three of the men work on the day shift—normally from 7:30 A.M. to 4 P.M. Days off are taken by this crew on Tuesdays or Wednesdays, when the traffic is lighter, and the mall closes at 5:30 P.M. One man works from 11 P.M. to 8 A.M. His is the combined duty of night guard and cleaning man. He maintains a once-an-hour telephone

Located near the Philadelphia International Airport, this distribution center shows the necessity of this kind of auxiliary service in the merchandising field. It is designed for "better customer service through faster merchandising flow, avoidance of damage, closer coordination among all handling areas, more modern and attractive working conditions for employees, better records and controls, and adequate stock space for back-up merchandise," according to G. Stockton Strawbridge, Chairman of the Board, and Randall E. Copeland, President.

The ground floor consists of two major sections separated by a fire wall; these "high-stack" and "low-stack" areas refer to the height of storage racks that can be used. The high-stack area stores furniture, appliances, TV sets, bulk housewares, and other large bulk merchandise. A fire wall screens the receiving platform from the stock storage area. The low-stack area utilizes semibulk storage for items such as small housewares, smallwares, linens, toys, draperies, etc. It also accommodates electronic, furniture, and appliance workrooms; semibulk checking and marking; packing; transfer; distribution; shipping; battery charging; and the entrance lobby.

The mezzanine level is a key section for future store growth. It will be utilized for checking, marking, and sorting for new branch stores as well as storage for all hanging apparel, flatware, and nonbulk hard goods. Shipments will reach this level by overhead power conveyors from the receiving platform and will be processed on mechanized conveyor equipment including an overhead rail system to handle hanging apparel on trolleys and combinations of roller and belt conveyors for flatware. Present plans for the mezzanine include facilities for administrative offices. A freight elevator provides access to the mezzanine for food service, equipment, and merchandise that cannot conveniently be carried on the conveyor.

Miscellaneous area include the boiler room and transfer and delivery platforms. Receiving, transfer, and delivery truck wells occupy the balance of the ground floor.

Towveyors were engineered to automatically distribute merchandise anywhere within the ground floor. The system has a total footage of 5,370 feet and operates at a speed of 60 feet per minute. It is capable of accepting a cart every 20 feet on the tow line.

Conveyors are used to move shipments—consisting of small cartons from the receiving dock—horizontally through the checking and marking areas. Extension conveyors are included to allow for efficient truck unloading and merchandise transport from the receiving area.

Racking for the high-stack area includes cantilever racking plus specialized racking to accommodate bedding, mirrors, headboards, table leaves, and bookcases. The conventional racking for the low-stack area accommodates housewares, linens, and smallwares, with some specialized racking for rugs.

There are three fork-lift trucks in all. One standard fork-lift truck is used for the movement of merchandise on the receiving platform, and two lift trucks with basiloid and clamp attachments are used for the handling of major appliances, TV sets, and stereos.

Order pickers work in high-stack and low-stack areas. A fleet of eighteen tow carts takes operators into narrow aisles directly to merchandise. The guidance system attached to the floor makes steering unnecessary. Tow carts are used to put away merchandise as well as to fill customer's orders.

The helicopter landing pad measures 60 by 50 feet. The heliport allows for swift, comfortable air-passenger transport between the distribution center and the downtown Philadelphia Strawbridge & Clothier store. The landing pad is located just over the mezzanine area and provides direct access to the distribution center offices.

The building and equipment were designed to provide maximum safety for the employees. The tow lines and conveyors have stop and start buttons located conveniently throughout the building. A horn sounds before the tow-line system starts to move. The conveyor is shut off automatically in the event of jamming. All tow-line and conveyor systems are monitored by control panels. Lift trucks are equipped with emergency stop switches. Fume exhaust mechanisms have been provided in all truck docks. A complete security system and fire protection sprinkler system has also been provided.

STRAWBRIDGE & CLOTHIER DISTRIBUTION CENTER
Philadelphia, Pennsylvania
ARCHITECTS: Abbott Merkt & Company, Inc.

Incoming conveyors from order office station where paper work is matched up.

Transfer area. Conveyors feed run-out conveyors, each of which is directed to specific store area on truck dock.

Receiving mezzanine.

Package conveyor, receiving area to marking area.

PAN AM CARGO TERMINAL
JFK Airport, New York
ARCHITECTS: Abbott Merkt & Company, Inc.

*Cargo going from truck dock
into the system.*

Conveyor belts and controls.

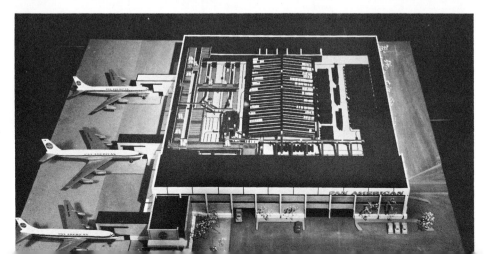

*Model showing
materials-handling equipment.*

contact with the local police, who have been instructed to come to the mall if the hourly call is missed.

Snow clearing in this midwestern climate is a chore which takes first priority after a snowfall. All the men are on twenty-four-hour alert. The night man calls the superintendent and foreman, who in turn contact as many of the remaining crew as conditions dictate. The snow is not removed, because this would be extremely costly. It is, instead, plowed into windrows along the center lines in the parking areas. This then serves as a "bumper block" against which cars will nose up even though a light snowfall has obliterated the striping. Without these windrows the parking pattern, after a light snowfall, would become chaotic.

It is advisable for management to prepare an operations manual and a maintenance manual. It should be detailed, showing recurring operations and maintenance procedures, which should be broken down into daily, weekly, monthly and semiannual operations. These manuals should be reviewed regularly with the maintenance superintendent, center manager, bookkeeping department, and other persons involved in these operations. A detailed maintenance checklist is available from the International Council of Shopping Centers in New York City.

The center manager should have brief staff meetings with the maintenance superintendent, the foreman, the promotion manager, and the mall office personnel. He should discuss and correct the shortcomings of the previous week. This creates a feeling among the personnel that they are "on the team" and that their ideas and opinions are valuable. In the case of preparing for special events, it is important that all the staff know the scheduling so as to be able to anticipate problems that may arise.

On the outside of the building, the landlord's responsibilities include parking lot cleaning, snow removal, lighting, striping, and repairs as well as policing (with patrol car) to enforce employee parking regulations and control "undesirable" elements in the parking lot. On the inside of the building the landlord is responsible for mall and court, community hall, public washrooms, all corridors, servicing lighting, heating and air conditioning; cleaning, maintaining planters, fountains, sculpture, aviaries, aquariums, etc.

Cleaning of fountains is a chore, but one which can be taken care of by a regular and not particularly skilled maintenance man under instructions from the superintendent.

Birdcages and fishponds are in a different category and require the attention of a man familiar with the problems of birds and fish. If the center has a tenant pet shop with a qualified operator, the maintenance arrangements could be readily made with him to care for these attractions.

As for the maintenance of planters, it is the opinion of this developer that it is less costly to maintain live plantings than artificial ones. The artificial plantings require cleaning, dusting, and polishing, which is no less costly than the normal watering, fertilizing, and trimming of the natural plants. Generally, it is advisable to use natural plants in areas where there is daylight from skylights and clerestory windows. The installation of sprinklers in the planting areas makes for less costly maintenance.

It is expected that the tenants will cooperate with the center regulations regarding parking rules for employees, and rules that carts not be taken into mall areas. Tenants are also expected to maintain the housekeeping in their own stores on a level at least equal to that of the mall itself, keeping uniform opening and closing hours and exercising control over signs in the show windows as well as those outside the leased premises.

Trash handling With the public's increasing awareness of air pollution factors, the problem of trash disposal has become increasingly important in the maintenance of the center. In the existing centers, incinerators generally are being replaced by baling or compactor systems. In many of the new centers, each tenant has his own trash collecting service whereby his trash, either baled or compacted, is picked up and trucked away two or three times a week. In planning a new center, it would be more efficient and economical for the landlord to provide an area to accommodate two giant-size compactors to take care of all the trash needs of the tenants. The landlord would also arrange for the pickup from the tenants and the common areas—mall, parking spaces, etc. Because the amount of trash accumulated by various tenants differs, the landlord has to negotiate the proportionate cost which each tenant has to pay. For example, chain stores very often deliver their goods unpacked directly from their central warehouses and accumulate comparatively little trash. Most of the independent stores, on the other hand, receive their packaged merchandise on the premises. The tenant will be able to utilize his expensive space more profitably through the central trash collection. In many instances, the pickup of the compact tanks is free of charge because this material can profitably be recycled.

In principle, the goals and procedures of maintaining a medium-sized center are similar to those for the very large center. Here, however, the administration has to be highly organized. In each of the four large regional centers owned by Shopping Centers, Inc., of Southfield, Michigan, a center management team consisting of a number of department supervisors had to be set up. This team consists of

1. A ground maintenance supervisor for both indoors and outdoors
2. Electrical and mechanical supervisors
3. A security lieutenant
4. An assistant manager, also responsible for promotional events

All these supervisors are responsible to the general manager, who, in turn, reports to the landlord.

Basic Function of the General Manager

Bruce Andrews, vice president of Shopping Centers, Inc., defines the duties of the general manager as follows:

Operation

Responsible for the operation and profitability of the center to achieve approved goals and objectives, establish a rapport between management, center tenants and local community, authorized to make decisions and act on all matters pertaining to the center's operation within approved policies and budgets.

Duties and Responsibilities	Standards
1. To maintain the profitability of the center by achieving monthly, yearly, and long-range goals.	1-a. Review budget monthly with the above department supervisors so that their monthly and annual goals are maintained at minimum cost. Monthly variances explained in writing.

1-b. Control and approve all purchase requisitions and all other expenditures within the center's budget.

1-c. Obtain from each supervisor a quarterly, written cost analysis demonstrating that the vendors they do business with give the best price and quality possible.

1-d. Obtain at least three sealed bids from the property manager on major repairs. Bids to be opened and reviewed at his office.

1-e. Obtain sufficient bids from all supervisors in their area and within their budget control, on any contracted new work so as to ascertain best price quality.

2. To assure the collection of all rents, utility charges, and service charges.

2-a. Past dues from tenants not to exceed 8 percent monthly.

2-b. The assistant manager should report in writing, that he has called the delinquent tenants within twenty-four hours after receiving tenant past due list.

2-c. Formulate a written plan of action within six weeks of the above date to hold past tenant dues to a low minimum. Report immediately, in writing, to landlord.

2-d. Correspond with each tenant at the end of tenants' six-months sales period to obtain certified gross sales on time, so that percentage rent is paid semiannually.

3. Preparation and evaluation of new and existing leases; meetings with prospective tenants in cooperation with the leasing department.

3-a. Screen and evaluate prospective tenants. Provide recommendations in writing to the landlord. This evaluation includes financial statement plans for the store, how store fits in with established tenant mix, etc.

3-b. Write a new or renewal lease within seventy-two hours after lease negotiations have been confirmed by the landlord and the lessee.

3-c. Tenants are informed in writing of lease renewals and required improvements three to twelve months in advance, depending on store size.

3-d. Upgrade lease renewals; rent, sales, and store appearance will be critically reviewed by lessor.

3-e. The Lease Analysis Book is maintained up-to-date.

3-f. A weekly lease report submitted in writing to the Landlord.

4. Maintenance of all buildings and common areas.

4-a. Daily inspection of entire center to ensure cleanliness, good appearance, and safety.

4-b. Coordinate with the property and security managers when technical advice is needed in their respective fields.

4-c. Encourage department supervisors, each month, by the method of "management by objectives," to maintain the center up-to-date.

Résumé of accomplishments to be submitted to the landlord each month.

4-d. Monthly progress report of center operations to be submitted to landlord.

5. Directing and coordinating the efforts of all center personnel.

5-a. Daily personal contact with department supervisors to assist them in maintaining and improving their job responsibilities.

5-b. Weekly staff meetings so that good communications, problem solving, and cooperation exist in all departments. Minutes of meetings to be recorded, copy sent to landlord.

5-c. Review semiannually the work performance of each supervisor. Evaluations to be submitted to landlord.

5-d. Review company's employee manual with new personnel.

5-e. Each month, evaluate promotion activities, their scheduling, and expenditures with the assistant manager.

6. Establish a line of communication with tenants of the center and with the community in which the center is located.

6-a. Issue bulletins and center memos to inform principals and store managers of lease stipulations and current owner's policies.

6-b. Written and verbal notices to store managers relating to irregularities; follow-up to ensure correction. Principals notified by letter of managers who continually ignore the lease agreement.

6-c. Promote a feeling of cooperation and good will with the tenants by personal visits within their premises.

6-d. Serve as active member of the Merchant's Association to clarify company policy when needed.

6-e. Monthly tenant sales comparison report is submitted to each tenant.

6-f. Initiate meetings, at least quarterly, with local officials to promote mutual understanding and cooperation, especially with regard to police and fire protection.

6-g. Personal community involvement through active membership in the local chamber of commerce and civic clubs.

7. Preparation of yearly budget, sales forecast, and other quarter- or year-end reports.

7-a. Review and scrutinize the tentative budget requests of each department to develop a realistic budget for the center. Prepare written back-up sheets to support every controllable account.

7-b. All financial reports requested will be submitted within the company's timetable.

7-c. Compile information on trends of the national economy, business categories, and local market area to forecast tenant sales accurately as possible. According to Mr. Bruce Andrews, local marketing sources can be contacted for securing pertinent marketing data as well as conducting surveys of the area. In Michigan, the University of Michigan students in marketing classes undertake surveys in cooperation with the centers. The marketing departments of the two daily city newspapers, the *Detroit News* and the *Detroit Free Press,* compile pertinent data in the marketing areas, as does the planning department of the Detroit Edison Company.

There is no doubt that there are other aspects to managing a center which have not been covered in this short space. However, every community in each geographic location will have specific requirements to which the capable manager will have to adapt himself.

Sociopolitical factors and public relations There is more to the methods of operating a center than establishing rules for fostering goodwill between management, tenant, and the public.

The social upheaval of the late sixties and early seventies, which expressed itself at the centers in youth protest meetings, picketing, and gatherings for various political and civic causes, caught center management off guard. In addition, there was a tremendous increase in crime on center property, shoplifting, assault, bomb threats, armed and unarmed robbery, purse snatching, car theft, narcotics, and larceny from cars. All this presents a very difficult and challenging problem which requires special understanding and handling.

Richard Frey, president of Shopping Centers, Inc., relates his painful experiences with these problems and explains the effort and the thinking that was put forth to improve and to restore the pleasant atmosphere that had prevailed at one center at its opening eighteen years ago.

It was a formidable task, and it may help to reflect on past occurrences in the hopes of not repeating our mistakes. One such reflection can be taken from the largest shopping center owned by Shopping Centers, Inc.—Northland. In 1969, during the Christmas Season, this Center unwillingly hosted four radical demonstrations that attracted hundreds of teens from all over the Midwest. The incidents took place on four consecutive Saturdays and dramatically affected the Holiday sales—for the worse. As our young people say today, "It was a bad scene." There was only one Saturday punctuated with real violence (fist-fights, some broken windows and a smoke bomb) and the presence of a large multi-city police force didn't seem to do much for the shoppers' sense of security during the other three Saturdays. It did restrain the disturbance, however.

Just a year later, Northland was calm and collected and its Christmas volume was the greatest in recent years. This complete turnabout didn't just happen—we worked at it.

There is a philosophic theory that simply stated says, "pain breeds awareness" and indeed we, as managers of Northland, became intimately aware of its every asset and flaw in a hurry. Initially, employee interviews were conducted to attempt to garner grass-root impressions of possibly volatile situations. Secondly, the entire community was invited to offer its opinion as to probable causes and solutions. The local city governments, religious and law enforcement leaders, and most importantly, the young people themselves were asked to serve on the "Northland Committee."

This Committee was organized and monitored by the Y.M.C.A. of Metropolitan Detroit—an action which is a great example of cooperation between two divergent segments of the same community. The "Y" acted as a very interested third party and were swift and thorough in their approach and suggestions. As a result, the "Y" has strengthened their position in the area around Northland and will continue to be a great help to the youthful patrons of the Center, and as a matter of fact, to the entire Metropolitan area.

The Committee unearthed some bitter truths:

Some of our Northland employees admitted hostility toward hippie-type youngsters and salutations like, "How goes it girlie?" "Why don't you stop by the Barber Shop for an estimate?" Or simply, "Get moving" were frequently used by the Center Security Force. (It may be well to note that the members of the security force at Northland are employees of the Center, but are accredited and licensed as Sheriff's Deputies in Oakland County, Michigan.)

The Northland Committee recognized the explosive atmosphere created by such actions and an immediate re-evaluation of security methods was undertaken. This resulted in not only the curtailment or end of such attitudes and actions, but also in the hiring of two people to be solely concerned with the young element in the Center. The Y.M.C.A. provided one young man (a "Y" outreach worker), a local schoolteacher, who had been specially trained by the "Y" to cope with and to counsel today's rebellious youth. He was to mingle freely on Saturdays and during the summer throughout the Center, and we (SCI) provided the other. We tested four of our security officers with the help of local and state police agencies and found one man suited to be a juvenile officer at Northland. He was then trained by those cooperating agencies and given a private office in the Center. This youth officer was directed to continue the work of the emergency Northland Committee and establish a working rapport with youth.

His dress and his demeanor are casual (not in uniform) and the overall result of his efforts are good. As I said, it has been more than a year now and all is quiet.

As is often the case, the duties for a specifically designated person have broadened and now our juvenile officer deals with all youthful offenders in the Center including, of course, shoplifters. When a youthful offender is apprehended, he or she is turned over to this officer for interview and disposition. So far, no youth ever released to the custody of his parents and subsequently interviewed at regular intervals by our youth officer has been caught repeating his crime, a record of which we are quite proud.

The juvenile officer has also learned some quite startling things in relation to youthful attitudes toward retailing. For one, young people are more than just mildly irritated by their inability to purchase items on credit. When they shop they must pay cash and this automatically limits their purchases at a time when people over 21 are paying later and later and later. Young shoppers also resent being put at the end of "imaginary" lines at cash registers and at restaurants. Long hair is still apparently unacceptable in many stores and other places of business.

Unfortunately, we cannot change things like this overnight. We can, however, use a little tact in relating our situation to theirs. More emphasis on lay-away plans, for instance, will help them make the large dollar purchase and a simple, "Be right with you" will make waiting a bit more palatable. Common sense, is, in our opinion, the basic ingredient.

There are more specific contributory things that shopping centers and/or merchants as an entity can do. I mentioned before that people are the root of the problem and shopping centers are the meeting place for people with buying on their minds. They bring both their money and their civil rights. They expect to be accepted with both and to be treated fairly and equally. They also naturally think of the center as a forum and *maybe* it should be, for constructive social and political activism. At our centers, we provide booths in several mall locations for some of these activities and make them available to anyone willing to comply with simple rules regarding their use. We ask, for example, that groups using the booths limit themselves to two persons per booth and that they refrain from "hawking" or directly soliciting customers, and use giveaways on a limited basis (offered to customers, *not* a forced handout).

Such groups as Zero Population Growth, Open City (a free village for young people in Detroit's Inner City), and the Boy Scouts are frequent visitors to the booths. Local community groups are encouraged to use our auditorium and meeting rooms, and are sometimes aided financially by our tenants' Merchants Association. Community involvement helps a great deal. It helps people relate to us as property owners and we believe helps to convey the fact that we are good civic and corporate citizens. We, at SCI, welcome this relation. We feel we have been and will continue to be an asset to every community in which we do business. Our personnel is active in all types of civic duties all the way from improving the cultural environment to acting as voluntary probation officers. For instance, at Northland in Southfield, Michigan, we provide the largest park type facility in the city. In short, we are proud of our relationship to the community and our corporate citizenship and if there were such a thing as shopping centerism, we would be its main proponent. We recommend this "People" approach to all.

It is no secret that several of our social ills stem from the battle (real or imagined) between property rights and human rights.

This disconcerting issue surrounding shopping centers was recently tested in the courts and the now famous Logan Valley decision resulted which says in short—shopping centers are "quasi-public property"—at least for labor relation oriented problems. The ramifications of this court action could fill many papers if properly expounded, but three basic truths are sufficient in regard to its effect. *First*—Picketing in labor relations matters will be permitted in shopping centers, even when it is conducted on assumed private property, so long as it is not excessive in numbers or conduct, quiet, and is limited to the immediate premises of the employer involved. *Second*—Given the 30-year history of the National Labor Relations Act, the doctrine of limiting picketing to the employer's premises, and not forcing it to the entrances of the entire center, is about the best practical result shopping center owners could have hoped for. It was presaged by a number of State Court decisions to the same effect, including the Wonderland Center case in Michigan in 1963. At this point, most of us are resigned to the realities of this decision and are prepared to live with it. *Third*—If shopping centers present the opportunity for shoppers to contend that we are trying to use our property rights to muzzle or censor their reasonable human rights—if we unwittingly present an unreasonable direct confrontation between human rights and property rights—I think we not only must expect to lose—we almost deserve to lose.

There is, however, a conflict that may result from this attitude. We, by acting leniently toward somewhat strenuous or unusual demonstrations for civil rights may find some of our customers claiming infractions of their human rights (Consumerism). The conflict is then between two sets of human/civil rights and property rights take a back seat. Thus, if you allow the DAR to offer American flags from your solicitation booths, do you then allow Open City the opportunity to distribute free abortion-reform literature? Distributions seldom hurt property—and it only costs a little to clean up the area. The age of absolute dominion is over.

The experiences related above could probably occur in any of the large regional centers, especially with the center becoming, eventually, the core of the new town. We can anticipate that people will increasingly expect to use the center for assemblies and meetings. It would be wise for center management to be attuned to these continuous changes in people's attitudes and needs. I would like to suggest to the center management that it engage professional, qualified personnel to handle unexpected, volatile situations with tact and understanding. Too often, sole reliance on the police force only aggravates the problem.

The study of center operations has naturally been geared to how best to increase the profits for both the landlord and the tenants. Until the 1967 social upheavals, the sociopolitical factors were never considered as an influence on the economic outlook. Today this is one of the most important elements in maintaining the center's inviting "image."

Merchants' association and promotional activity   It is generally agreed that all centers, small as well as large, must have a well-organized, well-directed, and smoothly functioning merchants' association. Such an association, which has the purpose of attracting more shoppers to the center by special promotions, should engage in strong public relations. It is advisable that the landlord share the expense of the association budget up to a third of the costs, thereby creating goodwill and confidence as well as team effort.

Circus performances Successful promotions that were used by Shopping Centers, Inc., for all their centers over a period of a year consisted of circus performances, which were scheduled for five centers in August. In the Northland Center, Southfield, Michigan, seventeen free performances were given which attracted 60,000 people. Equal success was experienced in all the other centers. The Center's merchants' association also realized a small profit from sales of candy and goodies on the circus site. Average cost per center is approximately $11,000, with the primary variable being advertising.

Magician's show (Genesee Valley) Genesee Valley Center hosted local amateur and professional masters of magic for a nine-day period in March. The shows featured both routine and unusual magic acts with the famed Water Cell Escape heading the bill. Over ten thousand people were estimated to have viewed the performances.

Mobil homes on display (Northland) As usual, this event brings several thousand shoppers to the center as the participants advertise very heavily. They bear this cost on their own and the center reaps the benefits. So far, by actual count, the homes have welcomed over four thousand people per day during a seven-day show.

Flea market and sidewalk fair (Northland) This event not only draws thousands of customers to the center to see the strange world of a flea market but it also gives the merchants a chance to participate directly in the fun and profit. The stores are invited to bring their merchandise outside the stores to the mall area. They usually offer sale merchandise and hope the shopper will be drawn into the store. The system works, and the five Mondays that the sale was conducted, participating merchants experienced great increases in sales.

Comments from some store managers may be helpful:

A ladies' apparel store: "When sidewalk sales are on successive Mondays, as in Northland, the first two are fine, then traffic tapers off. When they are three days in a row, like Thursday, Friday, Saturday as at another center, then word of mouth brings increasing traffic from day to day."

A men's shoe store: "Influx of traffic generated into our center by the sidewalk sale in conjunction with the flea market, on successive Mondays, is tremendous. Volume at our store accelerated by 20 percent for said period."

A men's clothing store: "Terrific idea! Great results! Fifteen percent increase in sales."

A men's haberdashery store: "Fantastic idea! Results were excellent! Every year has brought good results."

International festival (Southland and Genesee Valley) Over twenty countries are represented in this week-long promotion that attracts several thousand spectators who quickly become customers. Each country offers a bit of unique flavor to the impressive show of the promotion. They set up shop and sell merchandise and food befitting their origin.

Fashion show (Northland) Three of these shows were held during August and September of 1970, drawing many people to the center. Again, this is an opportunity for the merchants to highlight their wares in a tasteful pleasing manner.

The fashion shows themselves are punctuated by a five-piece orchestra, a vocalist, and two go-go dancers.

Black products expo (Northland) This promotion contributed in a big way to the strengthening of our relations with the community. Twenty firms owned and operated by blacks were invited to display their wares free of charge at Northland for three days. The Inner City Business Improvement Forum (ICBIF) was asked to participate and help coordinate the show. The public responded well and the companies that participated benefited greatly. Two of them, in fact, now have their products sold at Northland stores.

Vacation homes (Northland)   Two unique units for fun living were displayed on the Northland Terrace for three months at absolutely no expense to the center. The advertising and maintenance of these vacation homes were left up to their owners. The center (not the merchants' association), however, receives a percent of the sales of these homes as soon as they become final. This was an excellent way to utilize vacant nonpromotable space during the winter.

Other attractions include art shows, demonstrations of artists' techniques in various media, concerts geared for all age groups and other traditional attractions which all centers use, special holiday-season exhibits (i.e., Christmas, Easter), radio broadcasting booths in the center courts, etc.

The promotions described above are fairly typical of those that are currently used in most centers. However, this fast-changing life tempo and the ever-present desire for novelty in entertainment will require an imaginative new approach to develop new and exciting promotional activities.

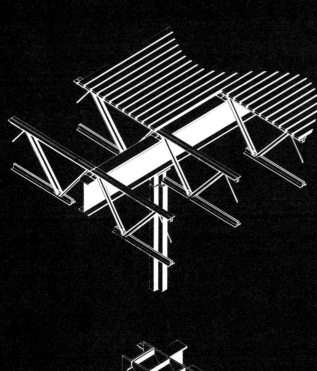

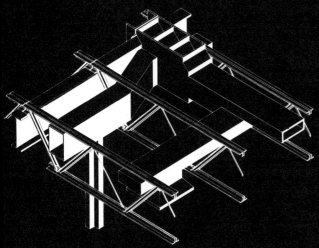

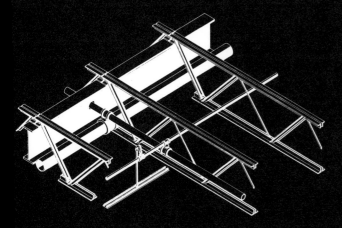

PART TWO

Implementation

When the results of the market area and base study have concluded that a market does indeed exist in the area; when the traffic analysis indicates that there are no major traffic problems and that the costs of perimeter site development are within reason; when the soils testing program indicates that suitable soil is available for constructing the type of center desired; when utility investigations have indicated the feasibility of the center concept in terms of zoning restrictions; and after financial sources have reviewed all factors and have determined that financing is, indeed, available; then implementation becomes the next step.

Schematic Design

This phase begins with some basic decisions on the number of major stores, the total leasable area, and the character of the center and its environment. Will it have one major department store, or do the studies justify consideration of two or more department stores? Will it be multistory, one level, or will the topography dictate $1\frac{1}{2}$ level center. These types of questions are typical of those that are asked when schematic designs are being developed.

After careful analysis of alternate solutions, final building orientation plans will be developed, parking layouts together with interior road and parking lot entrances will be made, and the portion of the site (it may be the entire site) that is to be used for the center will be firmly established. At this point, schematic design drawings are prepared to illustrate the scale and relationship of project elements, drawings that show basic decisions in terms of structure, materials, and services that will help to further define the center. The completion of schematic drawings and an outline specification is the signal for initiation of the preliminary cost estimate, which is prepared on the basis of these schematic drawings. At this point, the project has reached a convenient major evaluation point. Approvals are normally necessary at this stage, and a detailed review by the owner into the character of the center as it is being developed is appropriate. Cost data should be discussed with the financing agency and confirmation received that the project is financially within reason.

If the design is appropriate, if cost is within reason, if timing is proper and the continuing feasibility of the project is apparent, the next step is to prepare tentative leasing documents, consisting generally of floor plans of the center. These plans will show proposed store locations and tentative occupancy types as well as demising partitions and proposed tenant lease design criteria. These are basic tools for the developer and his associate, the leasing agent. Using these documents together with more detailed lease exhibit drawings for a particular space, he is able to show a prospective tenant the location and boundaries of his space, the types of utilities and other services available, and the general merchandising atmosphere that is planned.

Appropriate at this time are renderings, models, and other graphics which serve to illustrate the interior and exterior design concepts and familiarize the prospective tenant with finishes, proportions, and sizes of storefronts and similar areas. The leasing agent attempts to obtain as many tentative lease commitments as possible using these tools, and he works closely with the developer and his architect in adjusting minor variations to maximize the good points of the center.

Assuming that this early leasing proceeds satisfactorily and an assured interest is shown by a sufficient number of prospective tenants, the next step is taken.

Design Development

During this stage, the architect takes the schematic design drawings and develops them in considerably more detail. It is here that the structural bay sizes are finalized, selection of key materials is made, and color palettes are prepared to give a better view of the entire design approach. Decisions are made regarding the mechanical, electrical, and other services which establish the types of systems in more detail, and preliminary commitments are made with the utility companies.

Similar actions are taken with respect to the site design, including the establishment of final grades of building, parking, and site perimeters and development of site utility configurations. Furthermore, negotiations are initiated with required jurisdictions for zoning and parking, traffic approaches and utilities.

This phase is terminated by the completion of more detailed drawings than those defining the schematic phase and preparation of a more accurate cost estimate. If there is any question at all about the financial commitment, it should be ironed out at this time, since changes in project scope or size are now more difficult to make economically and many details of planning are already established.

From an internal standpoint, within the architect's office, the project manager is becoming more and more aware of the project's scope and complexity. He has participated in the preparation of design development drawings, and now his planning has advanced to the point where he has started to select personnel who will be involved in the final project. He has also made a number of logistical decisions basic to his operation. The project is now moving from the design department into production, where final working drawings and specifications are being prepared.

Similarly, the developer has advanced his efforts and his leasing agent has now acquired considerable knowledge of this project, with a positive grasp of the total leasing picture. At this point, the developer should be delegating certain liaison responsibilities to others in his office so that minor day-to-day decisions can be made and preparation of project documents can advance smoothly. He has, by this time, met the architect's consultants for the various engineering services and also any special consultants who might have been recommended in the areas of acoustical control, lighting, etc. He is familiar with the complete project team and is ready to make certain administrative decisions on how the project will ultimately be constructed.

He should become used to dealing with the same personnel in the architect and engineer's offices, and procedures should be standardized if at all possible. He should participate in regular reviews of the documents so that he will be aware of their status at all times and will be able to intelligently project the timing of the project in comparison with the proposed schedule.

The tenant coordinator should have a direct line of communication to the appropriate individual within the architect's office who can supply necessary leasing data, and he should be in a position to recapitulate (at any time) the exact status of the job. Once established, these procedures and duties tend to become automatic and make for a smoothly functioning process.

Administrative Considerations
Prior to Starting Construction Documents

Conventional versus Stage Construction

To allow for the efficient and tailored preparation of construction documents conforming to the actual method of construction that is to be used, it is necessary at this point to carefully review a number of aspects of the entire picture from a procedural standpoint. Early decisions in these areas will greatly facilitate the preparation of the documents; afford control of cost, time, and quality; and anticipate and resolve problems before they arise during the construction phase.

Probably the first consideration is whether this project will be constructed in the conventional manner or whether it will be constructed in stages. In the conventional manner, construction documents are prepared completely and then bids are received or negotiations are commenced with the ultimate aim of obtaining a lump-sum commitment on the cost of the structure—a commitment on the basis of which financing may be arranged and construction contracts written.

When the project is constructed in stages, only a portion of the construction documents are completed when initial bids are taken for some of the earliest site work. Then contracts are awarded for this work and it proceeds. As this work continues, additional bidding is accomplished on the next sequential step in the building process. This is awarded separately, and it too proceeds concurrently with the first step.

This form of multistage bidding results in scheduling described as "overlapping," "staggered," or "fast-track," and it achieves savings in time in many instances. It is not entirely a new technique, having been utilized in industrial construction for a number of years, but it is clear that the owner must have made certain basic decisions prior to its use. These include a positive commitment to the feasibility and desirability of the project and a rather general agreement on the projected cost of the completed project. This latter can be accomplished through accurate estimating at the design development stage, but in reality it requires not only good estimating but also disciplined adherence to the approved concepts, materials, and costs on the part of all concerned.

A detailed study of component costs is of particular importance so that, when individual subcontract bids are received, they can immediately be compared with budgeted amounts available for that work. Such a study also makes it possible to impose controls necessary to keep actual costs at the same level as budgeted costs.

Other key project decisions which must be made include the type of contractual relationship between the early bidders and the client, the type of management of construction that will be in effect on the project, and the ultimate contractual relationship between the construction management and the various bidders or between the bidders themselves.

The multistage method of construction offers the possibility of considerable economies in time if not economies in cost. Further, it places a considerable amount of detailed information on components and systems in the hands of owner and architect at an early project stage. This makes possible a simplified approach to the completion of construction documents by the architect, improved control of quality in the construction, and conceivably a reduction in extra costs experienced during the actual construction. The cost of the additional planning, coordination, and organizing required to achieve this method of construction can be somewhat higher than that of the conventional system of lump-sum bidding or negotiating. However, the potential saving in time and construction cost is also considerable and worthy of evaluation.

Methods of Contractor Selection

The next major consideration in the preparation of construction documents is the method of contractor selection, and basically there are two forms available: competitive bidding, and direct selection and negotiation. To become familiar with the details of the direct bidding process as conceived in its most usual application, the developer is referred to the AIA document called *Recommended Guide for Bidding Procedures and Contract Award,* which discusses the entire process in considerable detail. Basically however, it involves certain ground rules which should be understood by all parties to the process. Some of these are as follows:

> The Owner certainly has the right to expect that the Architect has exercised due diligence and skill in the preparation of the Contract Documents, and that these documents adequately describe the completed building to the Contractor, who can then provide such a building, certainly adequate for its intended purpose.
> The Contractor has a right to expect that information on the Contract Documents is sufficient to enable him to prepare complete estimates, and that the Architect is familiar with the local ordinances relating to the design and construction of buildings in that particular area. Unusual stipulations required by local authorities should be completely described in the construction documents.
> The Architect, on the other hand, has the right to expect full confidence from the Owner during the bidding procedure, particularly in connection with recommendation and selection of bidders, and the actual receipt of bids.
> Finally, all parties have a right to expect complete cooperation from the other parties to the process, as well as an ultimate contract award in line with accepted procedures and practices outlined in the documents, free from unwarranted negotiation or price cutting by Owner, Architect, or the low bidder's competitors. While such tactics may apparently work in the short run, it is apparent that their continued use affects the confidence of all participants in the process, and makes suspect future requests for bids. At this point, the laws of the market place take over, costs escalate, and trust diminishes.

When direct selection and negotiation is the method of contractor selection, there is reduced competitive incentive to the contractor in most instances, but this method offers the possible advantages of increased responsibility by the contractor, increased quality, and also decreased time of construction. This method of contract award is particularly useful in instances where a project will be started with incomplete drawings, as in multistage construction, but where the procedural aspects of that form of construction are undesirable because of either the size of the project or other factors. Further, if a specific contractor possesses capabilities especially well-suited to the requirements of the project, the emphasis on performance achieved through negotiation often outweighs the economies achieved by emphasis on price through bidding.

By and large, competitive bidding results in contract awards based on lump sum bids, while the negotiation method results in contracts awarded on either the cost of the work plus a lump sum or percentage fee, with the former more in evidence. When awarding a negotiated contract, the owner should consider the added cost of accounting and legal services required to adequately monitor a project of this nature, to determine his total outlay.

In either method of bidding, it is important to prequalify, or examine in advance the qualifications of the various bidders or selected contractors for negotiation, in sufficient detail to insure that uniformly high standards of ability, performance, and integrity are met. Since inefficient performance by the contractor can only be corrected through much time and effort, it is better to preselect responsible contractors who are capable of accomplishing the work on time, without unusual problems of cost or technical ability.

The developer should seek the assistance of his architect in obtaining the necessary experience and financial background of proposed bidders, so that they may be examined comparatively. Only those which meet the particular standards of the project should be prequalified for bidding or negotiation on that project.

Building Systems

Before the preparation of construction documents is begun, the developer should become familiar with a technique for design and construction known as *building systems.*

An informal definition of building systems considers the various components of a building as a sort of kit of parts, each part being compatible with the others and all parts being intended for application as a group. Many systems components have the advantages of factory prefabrication, with a consequent decrease in the amount of field labor required to complete that particular phase or subsystem of the building.

Common subsystems, or subgroups of building components, might include the building structure, its mechanical (heating, ventilating, and air-conditioning) components, an integrated lighting/ceiling grid, the exterior building wall, etc. One "system" in use for a number of years, with no fanfare whatever, is the building sprinkler system, which by and large is a modular arrangement of piping with sprinkler heads located at regular intervals and composed of piping precut and prethreaded at the factory and shipped to the jobsite for assembly with a minimum of on-site fabrication.

Proponents of building systems offer as advantages time savings in design, leasing, and construction; effective methods of cost control; the ability to offer interchangeable components on a modular basis, and all the other advantages of factory fabrication.

A recent application of building systems was in the construction of Franklin Park Mall, a regional shopping center in Toledo, Ohio, owned and managed by the Rouse Co. This center opened on July 22, 1971, two weeks ahead of schedule and an estimated $500,000 under the original budget.

On this project, the developer attempted to solve the complex management problem of shopping center development by applying a systematic approach to three aspects of development—design, leasing, and construction. The Rouse Co. collaborated with SYNCON, a building systems development firm, to develop a strategy in solving these three aspects, and the SYNCON set of industrial components provided the necessary order for control. These components were organized into six integrated subsystems, each having modular relationships, and they proved to be sufficiently flexible to accommodate the varying requirements of all types of tenants. The six subsystems used on Franklin Park Mall included structure; lighting/ceiling; heating, ventilating, and air conditioning; electrical distribution; sprinklers; and exterior wall panels (pages 128–129).

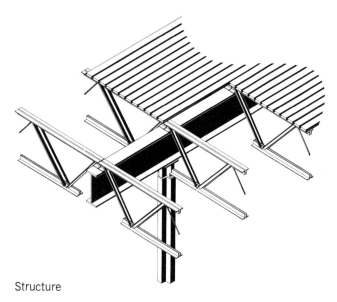

Structure

Structure subsystem. The subsystem is organized on a 5' module and consists of the four following elements:

The cruciform column is centrifugally cast concrete, reinforced for ceiling heights up to 16' and designed to meet a two-hour fire test.

The wide-flange primary beam is 24" deep, spans up to 35' and varies in weight for different loads.

The long-span trusses are 40" deep, spaced 5' on center and span up to 70'. They are designed to Steel Joist Institute standards.

The steel roof is standard 1½"-deep 22-gauge narrow-rib deck which will accommodate all forms of standard built-up roofing.

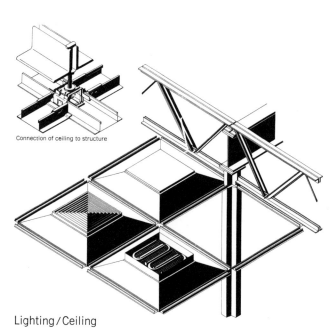

Connection of ceiling to structure

Lighting / Ceiling

Lighting subsystem. The subsystem, designed for applications requiring high levels of light and conditioned air discharge, consists of the following elements:

The spider connects the grid runners to the structure and provides leveling adjustment, lateral support, and thermal break.

The 4"-wide runners from the 5' grid supports the coffer and flat infill elements.

The coffer skirt is manufactured of light-gauge prepainted steel and is backed with acoustic damping.

The 30" square coffer infills can consist of fluorescent or incandescent light fixtures, air diffusers, and acoustic panels.

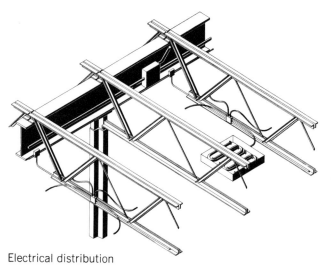

Electrical distribution

Electrical subsystem. The subsystem is designed to operate in the structural sandwich, providing power for roof-mounted HVAC units and lighting. The primary beam becomes the main avenue for distribution.

The large conduit for HVAC power runs only along the primary beams, since the roof-mounted units are always located above the beam. The junction box is positioned on the lower flange of the beam under the unit.

The conduit for lighting branches from the primary beam and runs down every other long-span truss. Junction boxes are located on 10' centers. This provides a power network on a 10' grid with each box servicing four lighting modules. All fittings and connections meet the requirements of the National Electrical Code.

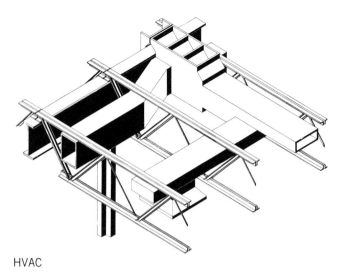

HVAC

HVAC subsystem. The subsystem is designed for structures requiring high-volume dusted-air discharge and plenum return.

The roof-mounted equipment services areas up to 8,000 square feet, either as a single zone or as a multizone with up to twelve separate controls. The units have an air-conditioning capacity up to 33 tons and air volume up to 11,400 cubic feet per minute. Both gas-fired and electric furnaces are available.

The duct network is divided by the primary beam, with half occurring on each side. All ductwork is designed to occupy the upper half of the plenum. Ducts up to 18″ square equaling 25 percent of the unit capacity can run perpendicular to the trusses.

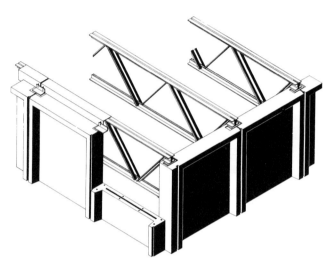

Wall panel

Wall-panel subsystem. The subsystem provides a building enclosure of precast concrete panels designed to complement the structural subsystem.

Adjacent 5′-wide load-bearing panels act as support for long-span trusses. The panels are of sandwich construction with a core of foamed plastic insulation providing a 0.20 U factor. The panels are prestressed, facilitating the handling of lengths up to 20′.

Weather sealing is provided by foamed plastic gaskets in the joints between panels, which are sealed on the outside with a polysulfide compound.

Non-load-bearing panels have the same configuration and attach to the structure with clip angles.

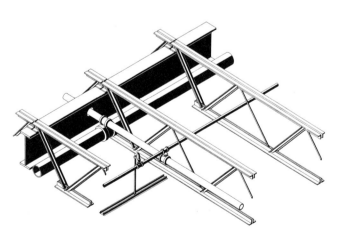

Sprinkler

Sprinkler subsystem. The subsystem functions within the structural sandwich and provides for a uniform coverage up to 125 square feet per head in basic modules up to 50,000 square feet.

The 8″-diameter bulk mains run alongside the primary beam and pitch $\frac{1}{8}$″ per 10′ for drainage.

Cross feeds occur at 75′ to 100′ centers along truss lines to either side of the bulk mains. The branch lines are spaced at 10′ centers above the secondary ceiling runners.

The sprinkler heads are located at either the midpoint of the secondary runners for 100-square-foot coverage or at the quarter point for 125-square-foot coverage.

All were based on a 5-foot horizontal module, and its use throughout the public mall and tenant spaces became a unifying visual element as well as an important planning tool.

The subsystems components directly affecting the tenant were those of the structure, HVAC system, 277-volt electrical distribution system, and ceiling grid and sprinkler system. Their use also allowed the Rouse Co. to provide the slab on grade and the dividing tenant partitions as well.

The tenant benefitted considerably by having certain modular components available for his immediate use, but in a number of instances tenants found this availability to be a limitation on their interior design and store planning, helpful only if they reoriented their planning in terms of the available systems. For instance, if a tenant wished to continue a previous policy of lighting with incandescent fixtures, he found it impossible to utilize the available 277-volt system which was suitable only for fluorescent lights. Or, if he normally utilized a textured plaster ceiling, the fact that a modular grid had been installed at a predetermined elevation in his space was more of a hindrance than a help, and he questioned the need to pay for something that he was not able to use.

By and large, however, this approach resulted in a superior shopping center with a number of innovative design results directly related to the use of systems components.

Further, in planning Franklin Park Mall, additional "software" (procedures) was developed through the use of the previously described "hardware." This included: (1) rules for leasing, (2) a comprehensive tenant manual explaining the logic of the systems approach with suggestions as to how the tenant could maximize its advantages, (3) a decision table plotting the relative importance of tenant decisions with reference to time and cost, (4) methods of selecting and compensating general contractors and subcontractors, (5) standard methods of installing the subsystem components, (6) a procedure for reporting construction activity progress on a daily basis, and (7) working drawings, scheduling, and planning procedures, prepared on a simplified basis, incorporating the advantages of the orderly use of systems components.

This "software" package became a most important management control which will undoubtedly be utilized by the developer on future projects and will be updated continually on the basis of the experience gained on each project.

Construction Management

Another concept intended to control costs, time, and quality involves the entry of the construction manager into the owner-architect-contractor relationship. The construction manager is a professional consultant engaged by the owner to assist him in the entire building process, to achieve more positive cost information from architects during design and positive scheduling and quality control commitments from contractors during construction. In theory, the construction manager provides the needed control over the entire building process, filling the void left by occasional poor coordination between architect and contractor. In point of fact, if the architect accomplishes his work properly, cost control is achieved; if the contractor accomplishes his end of the bargain, the schedule is kept or bettered and quality control is self-evident.

The construction manager's job is to provide the architect with feedback needed during the design and construction document phases, enabling him to select materials that have the requisite qualities of durability, finish, appearance, maintainability, etc. He is also to provide the architect with accurate cost data so that early estimates remain realistic. During the construction phase, the construction manager directly represents the owner and takes over the management and supervision of the job. In some cases he assumes full responsibility for confirming that the project is actually constructed in accordance with the documents, including the solicitation of bids and preparation of schedules, and can assume a number of the responsibilities and duties of the general contractor.

If given such broad responsibilities, the construction manager could divest the contractor of the assumption of risk that is a normal part of his responsibility, shifting it instead (since the construction manager himself is in no position to assume these risks) to the owner who, in many cases, is not equipped to handle such a responsibility.

In the instances where the construction manager does not assume these responsibilities of the general contractor but only acts as a coordinator for the owner during construction, he assists the architect in this area by providing expert services in terms of construction cost and management expertise, interpretation of schedules, and in normal procedures involving changes to the work, payment approvals, and quality control of the construction as it proceeds.

The basic assumption by those who advocate the use of the construction manager is that neither the architect nor the contractor are properly accomplishing their jobs and that an independent third party who supplies the necessary talent in the right place at the right time is better fitted to accomplish certain aspects of both of their operations. Probably the major reason for the advocacy of construction management is the increasing size and complexity of projects and increased complexity of contractual relationships between owner and contractor, and owner and architect.

Thus far, all parties to the contract, including the owner, the architect, and the contractor, have felt they can adequately provide construction management services and have indicated their availability to act as independent construction managers on projects. From these ranks have also risen the professional consultants who concentrate their efforts on construction management and who are refining the procedures involved in overlapping design/construction phasing, bid packaging, and the use of extremely specialized subcontractors on direct contracts to complete complex work.

As a technique, the use of a construction manager is not applicable to all kinds or sizes of projects, but there *is* a positive need for the construction manager in certain areas of construction.

The developer should select his project personnel with care. It may be preferable for him to select a construction manager with the requisite qualifications to directly provide the services that are desired, but he should be aware that when he does this, he (the developer) may also be assuming a portion of the risk inherent in the services of architect or contractor, and he should act accordingly.

Timing and Scheduling

The timing of construction of a shopping center project is a major administrative consideration in connection with the construction documents phase. Often, the developer has in mind a tentative date for the opening of the center, but a number of considerations relate to the final choice of an opening date.

One of the first of these considerations is the very practical one of the amount of time that construction should take combined with the amount of time required to complete the construction documents.

Another important area of consideration involves the developer's leasing program. Normally, the developer will have planned out the occupancies for the center and will be actively working toward total leasing during the preliminary stages. As construction is started, he normally comes under a certain pressure to complete the leasing arrangements so that tenants will be able to complete their store merchandising layouts and planning activities to meet the proposed end dates.

Often however, while the majority of the tenants will cooperate, a few, for reasons of their own, may be unable to come up with final layouts. These layouts may be delayed due to considerations of budget and expenditures in the parent company, possible changes in merchandising philosophy which cannot readily be resolved in time for inclusion in the planning for this center, and other equally important causes.

Thus a number of stores are unable to come up with the necessary layouts or to enter into the necessary construction agreements that would enable them to complete their premises in time for the center's grand opening. The effect of these delays can range from the mildly regrettable to the completely demoralizing, and the developer should have his tenant coordinator make every effort to spur the slower tenants into action, to encourage them to complete their layouts along with the rest of the tenants in time for the opening.

Total Project Scheduling—PERT and CPM

Consideration should also be given to other random factors which affect the completion of construction. These include projected trends in weather, the possibility of local strikes, delivery of materials, the availability of manpower, and other similar variables that will affect the setting of a realistic completion date.

Most of these factors can be categorized and included in the development of schedules which, until recently, have resulted in the preparation of a bar chart. This chart attempted to show the total duration of all activities in simplified form, but it generally did not provide sufficient detail to be useful except in a general way.

Recently, more sophisticated techniques of planning have become available, mainly involving the use of PERT or CPM scheduling.

PERT is defined as *program evaluation and review technique* and was established as a tool that would allow the manager to determine if, at a certain date, all activities scheduled for completion prior to that date had in fact been completed. CPM, defined as the *critical path method,* approaches the problem from the opposite standpoint, attempting to define all sequential activities progressing toward the completion of the various phases of a project. By assigning durations to each activity and combining phases, the manager is able to arrive at a final listing of activities which are critical to the completion of the total project. This sequence of activities is known as the critical path, since all activities on that path are without excess available time (float time) and must be commenced and completed on the critical dates.

In terms of construction activities, CPM has survived as the most useful tool available when expertly applied.

In practice, CPM becomes simply a method of preplanning which results in an accurate, two-dimensional graphic model depicting actual work to be done. In a sense, the manager, through a network plan, creates his project procedure on paper and simulates all major decision steps taken in the actual work.

In diagraming, the various network steps are tried in a short time period and those sequences of actions that turn out poorly can be analyzed, revised, and retried inexpensively before the work is actually performed. A major value of CPM is that it allows the manager to experiment with various courses of action and, based on job goals and his own experience and knowledge, to select the plan of action which promises the best results.

This method of planning effectively lengthens accurate prediction time for construction activities from three weeks to nearly a year, and if the progress of the work is monitored regularly and compared with the original CPM network, it is easily possible to achieve major savings in time as well as cost. CPM is not a cure-all, but when applied intelligently and with discretion, it can certainly increase the possibility of successful on-time project completion by a large factor.

It should be emphasized here that the preparation of a network plan is a cooperative responsibility, involving all those who are likely to be involved in the actual project. A network should not be prepared independently of the parties who will actually accomplish the work, since this method of operation automatically antagonizes the very people whose cooperation you desire and thus eliminates the benefit of their experience in the preparation of the network. Further, estimated durations should be as accurate as possible, derived from cost estimates, experience consensus, time-study evaluation of similar tasks, and available manpower analysis. The broader the range of experience of those who are involved in the preparation of the network, the better and more realistic is the result.

Finally, it is not enough merely to prepare the network accurately; it must also be followed up. One of the best methods of accomplishing this is to review progress on the jobsite periodically and to show graphically how actual job progress compares with the progress anticipated by the network. Work in process is continuously analyzed to improve upon the simulation provided by the network—so the network becomes an indication of the probable best method of accomplishing the result. This leaves the field manager sufficient latitude to accomplish those revisions in logic that he feels are necessary and it achieves a continual improvement in performance.

Without continual monitoring and reporting, interest in the network plan as a tool decreases to a point where it becomes just another piece of paper around the job office, not only ignored but in some cases used to prove the point that planning really does not pay.

Continual updating of the network, especially by computer, is not only expensive but largely unnecessary. Updating is clearly necessary when a major change in logic due to weather, a strike, or some other considerable cause requires a rethinking of the approach. It is also necessary when a number of small delays have become cumulative, throwing the logic pattern out of phase with reality. A common error is to confuse monitoring with updating. It is important that these differences are clearly understood.

Critical Path Method

Suppose we wish to review alternate series of steps involved in a given action, such as two separate methods of forming, reinforcing, and pouring a concrete wall.

The first step is to define each separate activity, in the sequence performed and to assign to it a duration.

To simplify the graphical representation involved, let us assume that the action is designated by a line, and at each end of the line let us draw a circle. These circles are called *nodes,* and the normal convention is to have an arrowhead at the right end of the line. This allows us to continue a sequence of activities from left to right. The estimated elapsed duration in working days is written underneath the line, and a description of the activity is written above the line. Let us say that this first activity is to partly form wall sections *A* and *B.* The duration listed would be, say, five days for four men. The next activity would be to set the reinforcing steel in wall sections *A* and *B,* so let us set up another arrow to the right of the first arrow, but not touching it, and again bound this arrow at either end by a node (see the diagram showing the critical path method). Further, let us connect the two nodes in the middle with a dotted arrow, the significance being that a dotted or dummy arrow represents only the existence of a relationship between tasks. The dotted arrow also allows us to insert an additional activity (if we have forgotten it in our original planning) without completely redrawing the diagram, and thus this becomes an important device in giving the diagram flexibility. Assume that the second activity will take two men three working days. Finally, let us draw another dummy arrow to another activity to the right, which should complete our sequence of events, and let us title the last activity "Complete Forming and Place Concrete in Wall Sections *A* and *B,*" with an estimated duration for four men of two working days.

Diagram showing the critical path method.

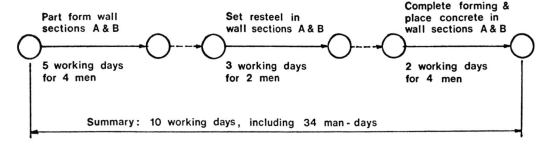

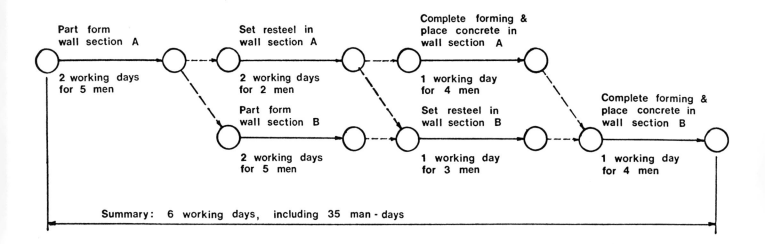

Summing the whole sequence up, it appears that we are dealing now with three separate tasks or activities. Each one has its own requirements in terms of the number of men required and the number of working days it will take that particular number of men to complete the activity. The summary would indicate that thirty-four man-days are required, making a total of ten working days to complete the sequence of activities comprising the total action.

Utilizing CPM, it is possible to further analyze these activities, as is shown in the graphical explanation of the diagram showing the critical path method. Here, wall sections A and B are separated, and activity is allowed to proceed in both simultaneously. The illustration clearly shows that a total of only six working days is now required to complete the total series of events at an increase of only one man-day, for a total of thirty-five man-days.

This illustrates the advantages to be gained by the positive and creative application of network planning. Briefly, these advantages are as follows:

1. The network shows the proper relationship among all tasks.
2. The method encourages all involved personnel to consider a project in great detail and motivates them to make early decisions on critical items.
3. It shows accurately how long a project will require to complete.
4. It allows the simulation of actions, permitting accurate evaluations and forecasts of the results to be gained from alternative plans of action.

Every effort should be made to set up the network plan in the best method possible, achieving the cooperation of all concerned on a realistic basis. It should be monitored, regularly and fairly, and the results reported to those in a position to make the necessary changes required in its further improvement and implementation.

Scheduling in Practice

In terms of the foregoing, when should scheduling start, and who is best equipped to provide this service?

Experience shows that a tentative schedule is an important part of the earliest stages of a project, if only to give some direction to the entire process. Meaningful scheduling is best accomplished after completion of design development drawings and documents, related cost estimates, and their approval by the owner. At this point, the design and its cost have been established, the preliminary decisions are made, and it is possible to achieve order by preparing a detailed schedule. Network planning is of considerable use during the preparation of contract documents, and any tightly scheduled project can be assisted in this manner.

Our best experience in on-time completion of projects has been through the efforts of an independent scheduling consultant reporting directly to the owner and cooperating with the contractor in the preparation of the schedule. Under these circumstances, the owner receives the benefit of the scheduling consultant's experience in his specialty and also of his continuing experience in parrallel projects under way at the same time, which are proceeding through some of the same job phases. The separate consultant provides the necessary distance between thought and action that is not provided when the contractor prepares the schedule directly. In the latter case it is difficult for the contractor to objectively evaluate his own performance.

The developer is cautioned that the process of network planning is a relatively simple one, but a number of "consultants" are on the scene who have derived their major experience in other disciplines. The best efforts appear to be those of a consultant whose background is construction and who is able to combine his scheduling expertise with that of at least one other specialty in the construction field.

Construction Documents Phase

Upon presentation and approval of the design development documents and after considerations involving the method of construction, contractor selection, scheduling, etc., have been resolved, the project enters the construction documents phase.

This phase consists of preparation of the final working drawings, details, designs, etc., required to set forth in detail all requirements for the construction of the project. These documents include the complete structural, mechanical, and electrical designs; complete construction specifications for all trades; and the necessary bidding documents requisite to the project.

During this phase, materials and products selected in earlier phases are utilized, together with all other materials which have not been selected until now, to provide a functioning whole.

Selection of materials is made on a number of bases, but generally standard products are used in the most critical places and special or unique products are used only in noncritical areas or for special uses. In many labor markets, the availability of skilled tradesmen is a major influence in the selection of materials, since often insufficient skilled labor is available to accomplish certain complex work. Maintenance requirements are legitimate criteria, but often they are unavailable at the time these documents are prepared and empirical decisions are made regarding these products or characteristics without sufficient knowledge. Accordingly, the developer and his staff often can assist in evaluating products from this standpoint before documents become finalized.

Mechanical and electrical systems are often selected on specific bases for given projects with cost as one major consideration, but too often the center will not have available technically trained personnel familiar with sophisticated operation. Mechanical and electrical systems intended to be "automatic" are generally more expensive in terms of first cost, often becoming more troublesome in terms of operation as their complexity increases. In most instances it is better to obtain the necessary personnel and stay with the simpler systems than it is to become too sophisticated and operate without trained personnel.

If the developer intends to sell utility services to his tenants, provision must be made early in the design process so the necessary systems can be established and metering provided. As is described elsewhere, this approach, where it is permitted by the various public utility commissions and/or municipalities which have jurisdiction, is often profitable for the developer.

Selection of Materials

A major criterion in the selection of all materials and systems is whether they have to be installed in strict sequence with other materials or whether they have the flexibility that would allow them to be installed on a nonsequential basis, simultaneously with other materials and equipment. The best solution, if a choice is possible, is to provide installation flexibility, since construction variables often dictate the sequence.

Other criteria established during the construction documents phase come from the developer's tenant organization and from tenants themselves. These relate to the selection of materials and structural systems involving provisions for special facilities (mezzanines, basements, stairs, roof openings, special roof loadings, special storefront line loadings, special floor depressions and others as required).

The lease should be specific in providing standardized basic facilities for the tenant. These facilities should be arranged in such a manner as to provide the maximum inherent flexibility.

For example, in order to avoid costly structural alterations resulting from tenant requirements developed during the leasing period, it is advisable to design the structural shell on the basis of the most efficient and economical grid layout. Future tenant requirements should not influence the basic steel structure. Rather, when the leasing is started, the tenant's space requirements should be adjusted to fit into the established grid system.

The developer and his architect should do their utmost to satisfy the tenants within the limits of the structure. If the tenant is still insistent, he may assume the cost of changes to fit his needs. However, in exceptional cases where the tenant is an important asset to the center, it may be to the developer's advantage to assume the cost of the changes involved.

Upon completion of construction documents, the architect presents final budget estimates together with the completed documents for the developer's review. Since this is the last chance for the developer to modify details and still obtain competitive bids, he should carefully analyze the proposed documents. If he finds that certain elements in the plans should be changed, now would be the best time to accomplish this, even though it may entail additional architectural fees. This procedure is preferable to going ahead with the bidding and making changes after the contract sum is determined.

Bidding, Negotiation, and Contract Award

Prior to entering this phase, a list of qualified bidders should be developed. Names may be suggested by the architect from his current experience in the marketplace, and the list may be modified as necessary by the developer. The total list of bidders should generally not exceed eight unless special considerations are present, and in most cases a list of six is preferable.

The roster of qualified bidders is best confirmed through early comparative analyses of ten to twelve contractors. This analysis should consider obvious criteria such as past work record, the number of projects presently in process and their status, possible interference with the developer's own project by other work already committed by the contractor, a review of financial statements to determine financial "health," a check of bank and trade references given, and, most particularly, a check of both owner and architect references for performance on other projects of the same type and size.

Similar prequalification measures should be taken in the case of a contractor who is being considered for a negotiated contract, with an additional check on his performance on similar negotiated contracts.

In line with the principle of keeping the bidding process as simple as possible, it is necessary that the bidders be given an adequate number of sets of bidding documents and that prompt clarification of questions raised in the bidding be made through addenda. A moratorium on issuance of addenda or other instructions to the bidders should be established during the last three days prior to the due date. Occasionally, a prebid conference is helpful, particularly where the project is complex or where a particular phase of the project is unusual in nature. An excessive number of alternates, complicated bid forms, a large number of required price breakdowns for accounting purposes (which could just as easily be obtained at a later date), and the use of "owner's option" clauses that give the owner free choice of any specified articles, makes, manufacturers, or styles of work (in lieu of allowing the bidder this same choice) are among the things that contractors object to and that tend to interfere with the bidding process. It should be emphasized and reemphasized that the best bid will be obtained when it is requested in the simplest manner possible, based on clear and explicit documents.

After bids are received and tabulated, their evaluation involves the clarification of any qualifications (and, where possible, the assignment of a cost to each qualification, so the actual bids can be evaluated on a side-by-side basis), the effect of alternates on the bidding, the possible cost of performance and payment bonds, proposed subcontractors for critical areas of the work, and recognition of the bidder's awareness of certain conditions which might be critical to the project. First among these critical items is the project completion date. While occasionally the bidder might be asked for his estimate of the total amount of construction time, in most instances the opening date of the center is already established and the contractor must give evidence of his ability to meet this date. It is most important that a clear understanding be reached on this point, since probably more misunderstandings and discussion, not to say litigation, involves construction timing than any other single matter.

A matter absolutely critical to the entire process is the identity of the project superintendent and his qualifications. Even if the bid sum is proper, the contractor is an excellent one, and all other considerations are quite satisfactory, the assignment of an unqualified superintendent is indicative of probable nonperformance on the part of the contractor. Most good contracting organizations will not give this kind of responsibility to such an individual knowingly, but occasionally it does happen, resulting in substantially increased costs and delays to the owner as well as the contractor.

Upon successful evaluation of bids, the contract award should be made as promptly as possible and every consideration and courtesy given to the contractor in the timely mobilization of his forces.

Now suppose the bids are not satisfactory, what are the conditions precedent to rejection of the bids, and rebidding the project?

If the proposal amount is excessive and cannot be reduced through appropriate alternatives and if the low bidder (or two or three low bidders if their proposals are very close) is unable to offer cost saving suggestions of any consequential amount, or if the construction time is clearly incorrect, or if no bid is acceptable for some other major reason, then it is appropriate to reject all bids and revise the construction documents to reflect a more realistic set of conditions which will allow the project to proceed.

This is an extreme circumstance, however, and it is rare that negotiations with the low bidder cannot achieve the desired result. If it is necessary to make this decision, it should be made promptly and your intent should be clear to all of the bidders.

Before the subject of negotiation and contract award is completely terminated, it should be mentioned that the ethics involved in this form of negotiation are rather clear. For instance, it is unethical to pit two or three low bidders against each other in a second unofficial round of bidding on substitutions or negotiated items. It is unethical to commence negotiation with an entirely new contractor after legitimate bids have already been received and a low bidder has been determined from a normal bidding process unless all bids are completely rejected. And it is unethical to approach the entire process from the standpoint that the contractor will be expected to finance the operations of the developer.

When bids are received for phased construction and bidding times are staggered, with various trades bid independently, or when bids are received for construction systems projects, the same general rules apply but the complexity of evaluation is considerably greater in either of these instances. The architect, or the construction manager if one is employed, is invaluable in helping to make a complete evaluation of bids and recommending a course of action involving contract award.

When contracts are negotiated and not bid directly, the contractor is expected to provide detailed general costs and other data relating to the proposed management organization, to define his overhead and explain how its costs will be determined, to develop a fee and describe how it will be applied, and to give specific information on personnel who will be associated with the project. Evaluation of proposals on negotiated contracts is often quite subjective, since charges for overhead and description of associated costs may be quite standard within the industry in a given locality, as is the fee. Particular attention should be paid to the method of bidding and awarding subcontracts to achieve the necessary controls required to restrain costs. The actual extent of the contractor's work should also be determined, and if possible, the contractor should be asked for a lump-sum bid covering work excluding management services accomplished directly by his own forces.

The Construction Phase—The Developer

The developer's primary concerns during this phase involve applying the necessary controls on cost and time to achieve his objectives as defined in the contract documents. He has every right to expect the contractor to construct the building properly, coordinating its various phases to achieve a well-built, attractive, functional project, free from major defects and experiencing only the normal amount of minor problems. He should expect his architect to exercise the necessary quality control measures during the construction phase and to cooperate with the contractor in achieving the final result. The owner can anticipate problems in the owner-architect-contractor relationship if the contractor's communications to the architect in the way of requests for approval, shop drawings and sample submittals, cost quotations, and other routine correspondence do not develop within a reasonably prompt period, or if the architect does not respond promptly to these communications. Perhaps the biggest complaint that the contractor has against the architect is that he tends to be casual in his use of time during the construction phase of the project, not realizing that this is the most important commodity available to the contractor. This criticism can also be shared by the developer, who is asked to make a number of decisions during the course of the project and must always respond promptly so the requisite action can be taken in the proper sequence, without unforeseen delay to other parts of the work.

It is imperative for the developer to ensure that tenant-supplied data necessary to the construction is obtained in sufficient time to allow its sequencing into the construction process. Delays in this area are particularly onerous to the contractor, and lead to a slowdown when decisions or information are unavailable when needed.

Often the developer will let separate site contracts, and this raises the question of coordination of site construction with building construction, particularly for curbs and sidewalks, underground utilities serving the tenant stores, parking lot lighting, and signing requirements. Specifically, the shopping center site is used by trades to a great extent during construction for deliveries, parking, storage of materials, and construction offices. These often interfere with the completion of the site work, and a high degree of cooperation, as well as specific definition in construction documents, will be required in order to complete the site work without interfering with the building and vice versa. (One device is to pave the parking area with base-course paving at an early date, leaving finish-course paving to the final construction period, one or two months prior to actual opening of the center, so parking areas will not deteriorate or be damaged. This procedure has the further effect of uncovering any soft spots in the subgrade and allowing repair prior to finish paving, which always results in a much better job.)

A further decision to be made by the developer early in the job, and in some instances prior to the actual bidding, is whether the contractor or his major subcontractors will be permitted to do tenant work. The purpose behind this is to maintain an adequate supply of labor and supervision for the construction of the center shell and to ensure that its on-time completion will not be affected by any tenant work which might fall behind. Owners have experienced difficulties in this area in the past, particularly during times when qualified mechanics in critical trades were in short supply.

To achieve necessary coordination, the developer, in addition to his tenant coordinator, should have a construction coordinator who is expected to maintain a good grasp of the day-to-day details of the project and to assist in processing the necessary authorizations involving cost and time, through the developer's office, so that delays will not occur. He should be joined approximately halfway through the project, when the center has been enclosed and the interior work is proceeding, by the individual who will be the developer's chief engineer. This will allow the latter to become familiar with all details of the project as it commences and thus be in a considerably better position to troubleshoot future difficulties than if he had been hired only after construction completion.

The Construction Phase—The Architect

The developer should expect that the architect will provide a supervisory field organization. Its job, backed up by the necessary office staff, is to oversee the construction as it progresses. The field observers are expected to help keep the project on schedule and details up-to-date. The developer should expect a principal of the architectural firm to be familiar with the progress of the work and to be available in case problems arise. This principal should also be the prime contact with the developer's organization. Ideally he is the same person who has provided coordination of this sort from the inception of the project.

The Construction Phase—The Contractor

The developer should expect the contractor to provide not only the necessary field superintendent and support personnel but also sufficient office personnel, including perhaps a project coordinator. His main function is to anticipate problems in advance of their occurrence and to resolve them, as well as to function as the chief contact between the owner and architect, and his firm. He should further expect that the contractor would also have a principal who would be familiar in detail with the progress of the work and be available for the prompt resolution of disputes or other difficulties involving relationships not only with the owner and architect but also with the construction trades and his subcontractors as well.

Finally, to achieve controls on construction time, a regular schedule of progress meetings, not over one month apart, should be established. Where appropriate, this may be done at intervals of two weeks, especially where job progress is rapid and coordination is critical. Through the use of network planning, close control can be kept on the construction, with the model provided by the network plan acting as a yardstick to measure actual construction performance early in the game, at a time when it can be corrected.

Cost Controls

The developer should recognize early that while conventional buildings of nearly every other type can be constructed from start to finish with a relatively small number of changes, this is not possible in the construction of shopping centers. Since such a multitude of individual entities ultimately become involved in their final operation, changes seem to occur constantly, and therefore some restraint on unnecessary changes becomes vital.

A small amount of time spent in the review of drawings and specifications is one of the developer's best possible investments, and at least one week should be devoted entirely to this effort after drawings have been completed. Unforeseen costs will always be with us, but they can be minimized through early recognition and the provision of allowances and contingencies in the developer's capital budget to cover the items in question.

Where possible, unit prices can be developed for the various tenant options and lease requirements affecting the shell construction, but in many cases it is impossible to completely define all possible combinations that can result. It is important to recognize that the building cannot be built on unit prices (since they are generally applicable only up to approximately 15 percent of the total cost of that type of work in the contract), and that restraint must be present in their selection so that those which are most important and most likely to be used often are precisely defined and obtained. Changes not susceptible to pricing on a unit price basis should be ignored and evaluated as they arise.

Because of the numerous changes in the work common to shopping center construction, the contractor's mark-up percentages become important criteria in bid evaluation. One possible control is to define the total amount of changes to be made in advance of bidding or contract negotiation and to establish one lump sum for overhead and profit to be obtained from the contractor for changes totalling that amount. This could then be adjusted upward or downward by relatively small percentages when the number of changes has been finally determined at the end of the project.

Tenant-induced revisions to the shell are the most numerous source of changes involving extra cost, and to a great extent these changes are involuntary but necessary on the part of the developer. The most usual types of tenant changes include

Revisions to the size and type of neutral piers

Addition of floor depressions or raised floor areas

The necessity of roof openings for the venting of HVAC equipment or toilet exhausts

Addition of conduit and piping within dividing walls or above ceilings in shell spaces

Additional electrical loadings added to the basic loads designed into the project

The addition of specially insulated spaces or spaces having special security requirements

Unusual heating, cooling, or ventilation requirements

The addition of storage or selling mezzanines

Extra heavy loadings at the storefront line to accommodate the storefront itself

Signing or other tenant facilities

Special roof loadings for roof-hung equipment

Special provision for receipt of tenant deliveries and/or removal of tenant wastes

The relocation of exit signs (which always seem to be required by the fire marshal in a location different from that shown on the drawings!)

"Interferences" between tenant and center piping, ductwork, structure, and so forth

Nearly all these changes are involuntary in nature and must be accommodated. At least the inconvenience and cost involved can be minimized if these changes are made as early as possible in the project so as to avoid the demolition, removal, and replacement of work that has already been completed.

Thus it would appear that the construction of shopping centers involves, by its nature, a multitude of changes. Orderly procedures for their timely presentation, quotation, review, and approval (including the issuance of field orders to allow them to proceed immediately where necessary), are a definite requirement to avoid misunderstanding and excess cost. Further, positive controls must be imposed by the developer on his tenants and upon the architect, contractor, and his own forces in order to minimize the number of unnecessary changes.

Construction of Tenant Spaces

We have already referred to the tenant coordinator and commented on his qualifications, authority, and responsibility. Perhaps his major responsibility during the construction phase is expediting tenant document completion in time for checking for conformance with lease requirements, coordination with shell construction, and for the timely bidding and award of tenant contracts. Particularly important in this area is the necessity for preordering and stockpiling of long-delivery and other critical items.

The tenant coordinator then follows up, during the actual construction itself, with a continuing review of the quality of the tenant work, and he lodges an immediate objection if it does not appear to be proceeding in accordance with the lease documents (although he has no responsibility whatever for its design or completion in accordance with the tenant's own construction documents). He also has the further responsibility of the coordination between the shell construction work and the tenant construction work. This most often involves the provision of utilities including heat, prorating of costs of interferences, cleanup, fire protection, debris removal, the installation of tenant-supplied utilities under the floor slab (if the slab is provided by the developer) or similar utilities above ceilings if the ceiling is provided by the developer, coordination of roof cutting, patching, and traffic.

He may also find himself directing cars so that tenant construction parking is restricted to given areas on the site and arranging for tenant deliveries which might arrive prior to the time the tenant's construction forces are on the site. In short, he is "all things to all men" insofar as the tenant is concerned, and during this period he is indispensable. When the center is complete and tenant work is nearly done, he has the further responsibility of seeing that tenant and center security is maintained during the period of final completion of the center, while store fixtures and final decor are installed in the tenant spaces. Finally, he arranges for and coordinates the tenant opening with the center grand opening, preferably on a simultaneous basis.

Completion and Occupancy

Already mentioned was the necessity for the operating personnel of the developer and tenants to become acquainted with the construction as it proceeds. Then, instead of attempting to achieve this familiarity all at once, at the end of construction, when all the operating instructions are being conveyed by the various subcontractors at one time, it can be developed in an orderly sequence.

The developer can then set up the maintenance programs for his equipment and also for finish surfaces as the work progresses, being attuned to operating instructions given by the construction personnel who actually did the assembly.

As the project approaches completion, final details become numerous and involve staffing as well as the administrative functions related to the center opening. Operating and engineering personnel, together with the tenant coordinator and his assistants, often continue to assist the developer by forming the nucleus of the center management staff.

At completion, the developer must reach a final point of understanding and initiate the guarantee period with the contractor on the completed construction, complete his final financing arrangements, resolve all tenant allowances against the actual cost of tenant spaces, and generally achieve a transition from the construction stage to the operating stage.

The architect and contractor can assist the developer in this transition by preparing the necessary documents in an orderly fashion and presenting them in the best sequence for their ultimate use. Documents should include the final as-built drawings and operating instructions, guarantees, and final waivers of lien. Furthermore, all outstanding claims or problems that might still be present should be promptly resolved.

The developer, on the other hand, can assist by accepting the construction in a timely manner and considering all the miscellaneous minor items that crop up after this date as items to be settled under the guarantee. In nearly all instances the contractor will be happy to honor requests presented in this context, it being unreasonable for the developer to withhold large sums of money until all of these minor problems have been resolved. This procedure is rarely necessary to ensure compliance with the precise working of the contract. To withhold payments at this stage, presuming a normal relationship of cooperation and confidence has been present throughout the course of construction, would unreasonably restrain the orderly progression from construction to operation.

Observation of normal business practices, including trust in the continued performance by both architect and contractor, is further evidence that this, perhaps the most difficult of all construction types because of the coordination problems involved, can be successfully completed to the satisfaction of all.

PART THREE

A Survey of Significant Centers

View of shopping center with Ala Moana Hotel at left background. Office building at left foreground with revolving La Ronde restaurant on top. Fourth level—top-level parking area. To right is mall-level parking area. To far right, street-level parking area. (Photographer: Camera Hawaii—photograph by Ted Needham.)

Monumental Tiki, an example of Polynesian religious art, fronting one of the stores. (Photographer: David Cornwell Productions.)

RIGHT: Ground level. Parking area extends under the Liberty House department store. Above this level are the street and mall levels. (Photographer: Camera Hawaii.)

Built on reclaimed land from the sea and strategically located in the center of metropolitan Honolulu, Ala Moana is owned and was developed by the Dillingham Corporation. The center was built in two stages. In addition to 12 acres of double-deck parking, a four-level parking deck was added. In planning the center, careful attention was paid to the concealment of mechanical housing, air conditioning, and other equipment.

A truck concourse inside the building accommodates all delivery, garbage, and similar "back-door" functions completely concealed from the public eye. Also established were strict sign regulations. Moving neon signs were not permitted.

Art forms at Ala Moana reflect the rich cultural origins of Hawaii's cosmopolitan population and represent some of the finest art talent in Honolulu.

According to Lowell S. Dillingham, President, "Bringing art to the marketplace has helped make the center successful, and the merchants and the developers believe that art and architecture are important elements of a successful business and that a business should make a cultural, sociological, as well as an economic, contribution to the community and its citizens."

ALA MOANA SHOPPING CENTER
Honolulu, Hawaii

ARCHITECTS: John Graham & Company

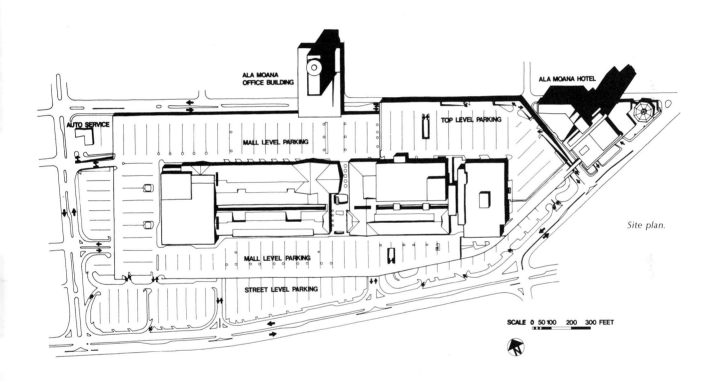

Site plan.

SCALE 0 50 100 200 300 FEET

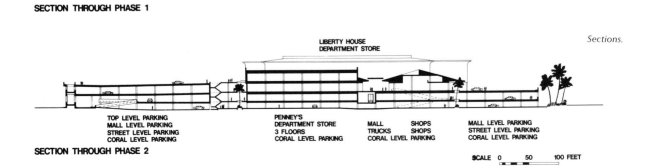

Sections.

SECTION THROUGH PHASE 1

MALL LEVEL PARKING
STREET LEVEL PARKING — SHOPS SHOPS — MALL TRUCKS — SHOPS SHOPS — MALL LEVEL PARKING SHOPS — MALL LEVEL PARKING STREET LEVEL PARKING

LIBERTY HOUSE
DEPARTMENT STORE

SECTION THROUGH PHASE 2

TOP LEVEL PARKING
MALL LEVEL PARKING
STREET LEVEL PARKING
CORAL LEVEL PARKING — PENNEY'S DEPARTMENT STORE 3 FLOORS CORAL LEVEL PARKING — MALL TRUCKS CORAL LEVEL PARKING — SHOPS SHOPS CORAL LEVEL PARKING — MALL LEVEL PARKING STREET LEVEL PARKING CORAL LEVEL PARKING

SCALE 0 50 100 FEET

Parking and pickup. (Photographer: Ern McQuillan's—Photographic Illustrators.)

Customers viewing heating plant. (Photographer: Ern McQuillan's—Photographic Illustrators.)

"The Square," on a 21-acre site, consists of a three-level department store (David Jones), a two-level junior department store (Big W), supermarket, over a hundred speciality shops, and many services including a child care center. A feature of the center is the self-service World Fare Restaurant seating up to 650 people. The international theme is carried out by the use of flags of many nations. The food retailing concessions prepare many international dishes and are appropriately named (e.g., Old Heidelberg serves German specialities; Drovers Barbecue provides typically Australian dishes; Giovanni's specializes in Italian food; Olé provides excellent Mexican and Spanish cuisine; The Texas Burger Bar has a wide range of hamburgers; Neptune's Haul serves a wide variety of seafoods; The Willow Pattern Plate specializes in Chinese food; The Last Course and the Forty-Second Street Donut Bar have desserts, pancakes and cakes; while sandwiches, pies, etc., may be purchased from Ye Olde Sandwich Bar.) Additional atmosphere is created by four separate alcoves, each decorated in the styles of certain countries. They are named Le Petit Paris, Taj Mahal, El Cantina, and The Ginza.

BANKSTOWN SQUARE
Sidney, Australia
ARCHITECTS: Hely, Bell & Horne

Exterior. (Photographer: Ern McQuillan's—
Photographic Illustrators.)

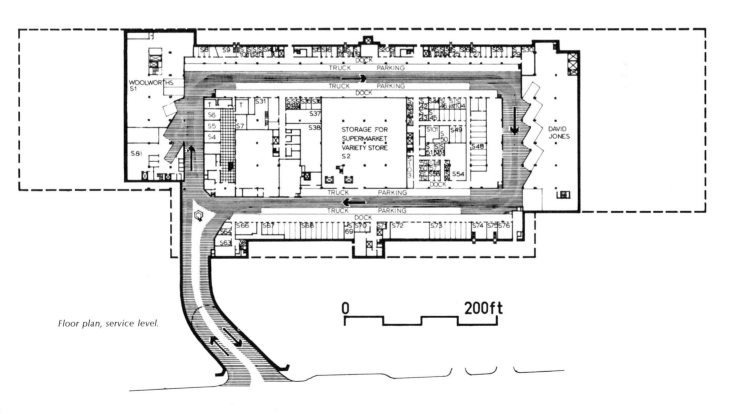

Floor plan, service level.

0   200ft

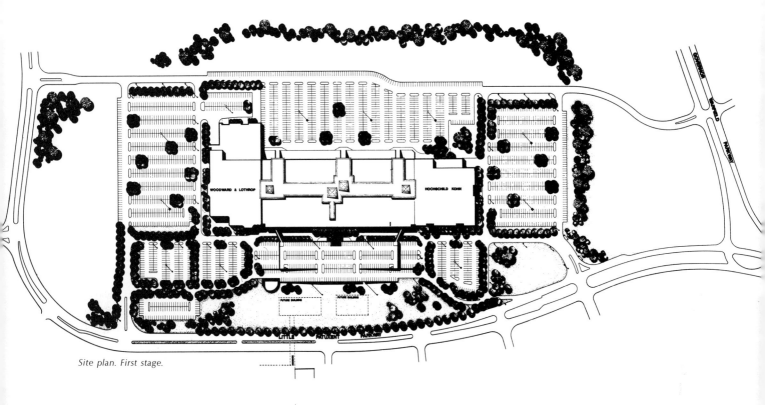

Site plan. First stage.

COLUMBIA MALL
Columbia, Maryland
ARCHITECTS: Cope, Linder, Walmsley

This center, developed by the Rouse Company, is situated on a 70-acre site and designed as the first phase of a town center, with stages two and three ultimately to contain five major department stores and approximately 2 million square feet of selling space. Future plans call for the center to be linked with the existing town center plaza by minibus routes.

According to Gerald Cope of the architectural firm of Cope, Linder, Walmsley, the concept was based on the following premises:

a. A compact center in a cartwheel formation is preferable to a linear one, giving relatively short walking distances between department stores placed at the extremities. The arms of the cartwheel may also extend in linear fashion (for example, eastward across the Little Patuxent Parkway to the waterfront and north, south, and west to the office areas). The department stores at the corners would have the opportunity of merchandising from two major pedestrian malls, while a central department store would receive traffic from all four sides.

b. A good balance between public and retail space may best be obtained with a two-level mall having a narrow ground-floor width (30 feet from storefront to storefront) and a wider upper-floor width (52 feet from storefront to storefront across an open gallery); i.e., T-shaped in close section. The lower level takes on the character of a narrow shopping street, the upper, that of a *galleria*. The mall, common to both shopping levels and adjacent to the center department store entrances, connects the major public spaces.

c. Least earth moving and maximum tree preservation could be obtained by adopting a split-level section through the center in an east-west direction and placing it across the valley so that access to parking decks could follow the rising ground on the north and south sides. Each parking level is in turn related to the shopping level within the center it serves.

d. Clarification of traffic circulation and entrance may be obtained by boulevard approaches centered on the major shopping entrances and flanked by associated office and commercial buildings.

Materials and Construction

a. Steel-frame construction with bar joists and concrete on metal decks for stores with textured-block infill panels are used for economy, flexibility, and speed of construction.

Interior, showing two levels.
(Photographer: George Pohl.)

Court and fountain.
(Photographer: George Pohl.)

b. The public spaces are roofed over with a 5-foot module space frame as an effective way of creating a consistent ceiling which can be double-decked for larger spaces, at the same time producing opportunities for varieties of light, seasonal displays, and special effects. At major courts, the space frame turns upward, forming pyramids over 70 feet high which dramatically light and emphasize these important spaces.

c. By lifting the structure 20 feet above the upper floor level, fireproofing of the individual members is not required.

d. The lower-level pedestrian streets are paved with brick or tile for appearance and maintenance and the upper walkways and bridges are concrete on metal deck, carpeted.

e. Interior and exterior surfaces are metal, consistent with the character of the building's steel-framed construction.

f. The mechanical system—package units for upper floors and a split system on the lower—is designed for initial economy and flexibility due to the various phases of the project development. A central mechanical plant is located in the east parking area and services both the retail and office facilities nearby.

Mall area and fountain.
(Photographer: Morley Baer.)

DEL MONTE CENTER
Monterey, California

ARCHITECTS: John Carl Warnecke & Associates
LANDSCAPE ARCHITECTS: Lawrence Halprin &
  Associates

In order to maintain the character of an unusually beautiful site and to preserve the magnificent oak trees, this center is conceived, both in plan organization and in visual terms, as a hillside village. It was also a question of satisfying the local residents, who would reject any project that would change the character of their area. The clusters of buildings, which are of varied heights and sizes, are so arranged as to minimize the presence of the large department store.

The project consists of a complete regional center with a wide range of shopping facilities that include quality women's apparel, a major department store, several retail chain stores, a market, and a large number of specialty shops. These are located within ten buildings, with a total gross leasable area of 408,000 square feet. The specialty shops are used in small groups to create an intimate scale. The individual buildings, located on a 44-acre site, vary in size, giving a variety of height and silhouette to the overall composition. Hipped roofs of terra-cotta tile on all buildings unify the complex. The site has been developed so that cars are parked on many terraces, each relatively small in size and landscaped so as to reduce the obtrusiveness of the automobile. A total of 2,400 cars can be accommodated. Construction materials were selected to harmonize with the traditional masonry and wood style of the area. Storefront material consists of adobe brick and slump stone, with stained redwood paneling. The structure is of precast exterior columns, with a system of glue-laminated members for the interior spaces.

152

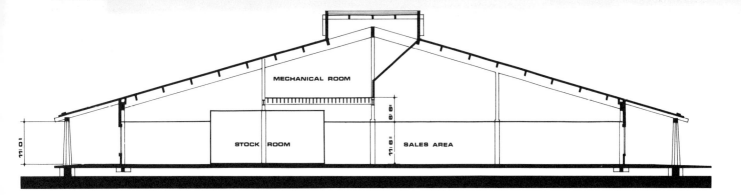

MECHANICAL ROOM

STOCK ROOM

SALES AREA

11' 0"

8' 8"

11' 8"

Section through Building No. 3.

0   10   50

*Exterior of Macy's, showing
special landscape. (Architect:
John S. Bolles. FAIA.
Photographer: Robert A. Isaacs.)*

*Mall area. (Photographer: Morley
Baer.)*

Main entrance and drive. (Landscape: Warren Edwards. Photographer: C. H. Guernsey & Co.)

THE DISCOVERIES, INC.
Oklahoma City, Oklahoma

ARCHITECTS: Guernsey & Watkins, Architects
   & Engineers
PROJECT ARCHITECT: Robert Hope, AIA

This center is located in northwest Oklahoma City, approximately fifteen minutes from downtown, in a middle upper-class residential district.

According to the architects, the owner desired a collection of small specialty shops combined under one roof, where the shopper might come and have lunch or dinner. The building also offers child care services to encourage longer stays by the mother. A prime concern was to create a casual, noncommercial atmosphere. No advertising by any of the tenants is allowed, either within the building or on the exterior. All shops use identical lettering next to or above their doorways. For the handicapped and elderly, all areas of the building are accessible by ramps at the front entrance and by an elevator between floors.

The Tea Room on the first floor and the private dining room on the lower level are available for use during evening hours, for wedding receptions, private dinners, etc., without the necessity of any shops being open. A small card room is available downstairs for bridge parties and luncheons.

All corridors and public areas are used to display paintings and art works. These are handled by an art dealer and instructor who has her studio within the building. The dress shop provides modeling during the noon lunch period within the Tea Room.

Fluorescent lay-in light fixtures were used in some shops which required a high level of illumination. However, approximately 90 percent of the building, including all corridors and public areas, is lighted with incandescent down lights and spots. All lighting was laid out to achieve the best possible illumination of the merchandise and no attempt was made to have a consistent overall footcandle level.

The developer-owners are Mr. and Mrs. Robert S. Kerr and C. E. Duffner.

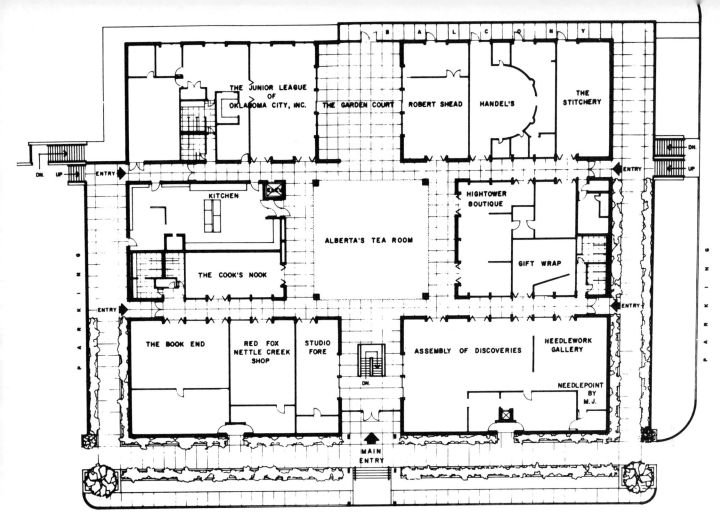

Floor plan, garden terrace level.

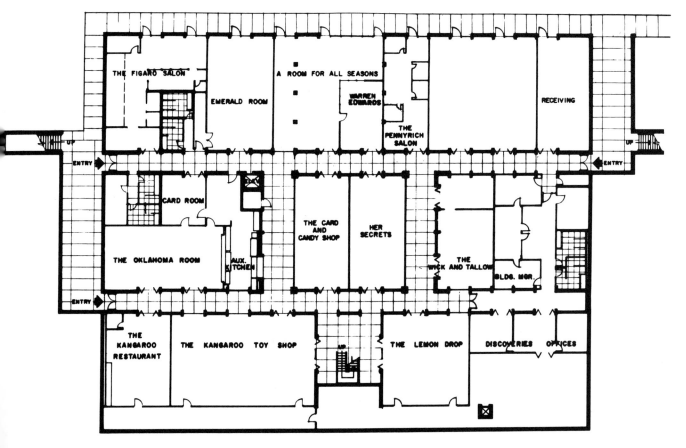

Floor plan, promenade level.

DONAU EINKAUFSZENTRUM
Regensburg, Germany

ARCHITECTS: Manfred Rappel,
Josepf Neumeier

This two-level center follows the same principles and concepts as those of the American regional shopping centers. The significant feature here is the addition of a multistory bank and office building. This feature is also becoming an integral part of the centers in the United States.

Artwork, fountain sculpture, plantings, and floor patterns add to the center's attraction.

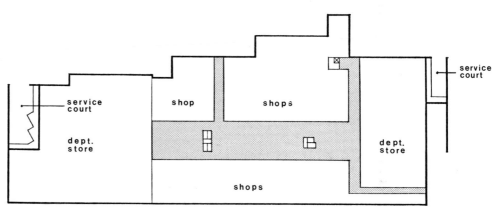

First-floor plan.

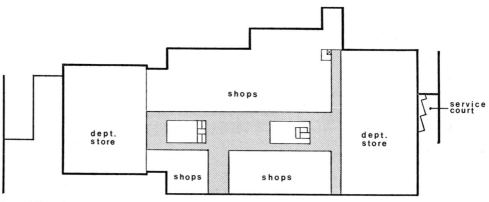

Second-floor plan.

156

Interior court and bronze fountain sculpture. (Sculptor: Peter Mayer. Photographer: Wilkin Spitta.)

Exterior view. (Photographer: Wilkin Spitta.)

Interior court and stone fountain sculpture. (Sculptor: Richard Triebe. (Photographer: Wilkin Spitta.)

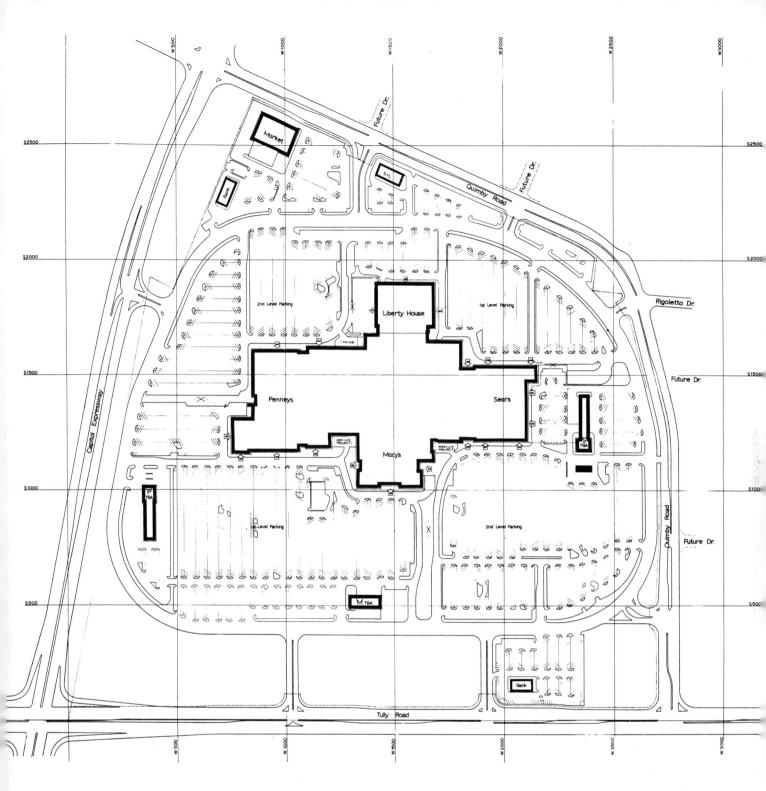

EASTRIDGE SHOPPING CENTER

San Jose, California

ARCHITECT (for center and Liberty House):
   Avner Naggar, AIA

This center, owned by Bayshore Properties and Homart Development Co., occupies a 100-acre area for retail development and has approximately 40 additional acres for adjacent peripheral uses.

Architect's Comments

The program called for an enclosed, climate-controlled regional retail development mall, with 1,400,000 square feet of gross leasable area, consisting of four major department stores as anchors and residual tenant space of 500,000 square feet of gross leasable area, and balanced parking—of equal accessibility to all tenants—providing spaces for 8,000 automobiles. In addition, the program outlined a peripheral convenience center, as well as ancillary uses such as banks, savings and loan associations, and office buildings.

The main objectives called for the following:

LEFT: *Location plan.*

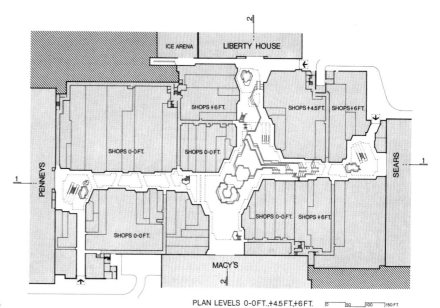

RIGHT: *Plan levels.*
BELOW: *Longitudinal section 2-2.*

PLAN LEVELS 0-0 FT., +4.5 FT., +6 FT.

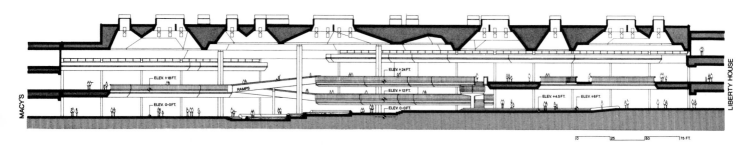

1. Compactness

Establishment of the shortest walking distances between anchors, with a maximum mall lineal front footage.

2. Shopper impulse motivation through visual comprehension of mall shops.

3. Ease of shopper orientation within malls and galleries.

4. Parking accessibility to all levels.

In order to eliminate the corridor-like feeling within the malls themselves, undulating lease line fronts were introduced. Basically, the two-level malls have been placed at varying elevations: ±0' and +18' on one end and +6' and +24' on the other end. An overlap of the +24' level over the ±0' level in the Grand Hall—the busiest commercial area—afforded the opportunity to include an additional level at +12'.

In order to make the transition from ±0' to +6' in the Grand Hall, an intermediate drop to +4.5' was introduced. The Grand Hall is open to three fully exposed levels of tenant stores, with the intermediate levels separated from other levels in this instance by only 6'. On the main levels, the transitions were made using wide steps and ramps (always not more than 3 risers, to satisfy code requirements and eliminate intermediate hand rails).

What appears in the plan to be a multiple-angular storefront arrangement is, in fact, achieved through the use of a single angle, arrived at by using the diagonal of two bays. (The basic bays are 24' × 28'. With the skip in the mall, the rectangular bay space becomes 24' × 56'. The diagonal of this rectangle is a 3° to 7° angle.) This angle was carried through in the mall paving and was closely adhered to in all storefront lease lines. It contributed to the interest of all storefront designs.

The multilevel arrangement also affords good visual proximity; it helps in the reduction of the distance between the department stores along the long axis of the center to less than 800 feet.

A popular attraction to the center is the 23,000-square-foot enclosed ice skating rink.

In order to conform to the even distribution and equal accessibility parking requirement, the site has been sectioned into quadrants with the ring road at a constant elevation. Each quadrant ramps up or down to meet the respective four basic floor levels (±0', +6', +18', +24'). There are six basic mall shop entrances from the various levels. The department stores are accessible in all cases from both upper and lower quadrants. Traffic is fed from the public arterials to the ring road through magazine roads, providing separation between shopper and through-traffic. Most of the existing mature trees on the site were saved through use of retaining walls or tree wells.

The structure is concrete frame with cantilevered galleries and steel frame for roof and high mall section. Metal and gypsum roof deck diaphragms were used for earthquake loading.

Interior mall materials include precast terrazzo tile units for the floors, with carpeting used for the depressed seating areas. Ceilings are of sculptured gypsum boards. As for lighting, mercury vapors were used in the high malls and incandescent at gallery soffits.

Among the highlights of the interior decor are three major art pieces:

Grand Court: Stainless steel sculpture by Stephanie Scuris.
Penney Great Hall: Light tower sculpture by Boyd Mefferd.
Liberty House Great Hall: Aluminum sculpture by Roger Bolomey.

Exterior of J.C. Penney store.
(Photographer: Joshua Freiwald.)

Exterior of Liberty House.
(Photographer: Joshua Freiwald.)

160

Court with pool and sculpture.

Court with sculpture.

Interior of Liberty House. (Interior designers: Wells, Squier Associates. Photographer: Joshua Freiwald.)

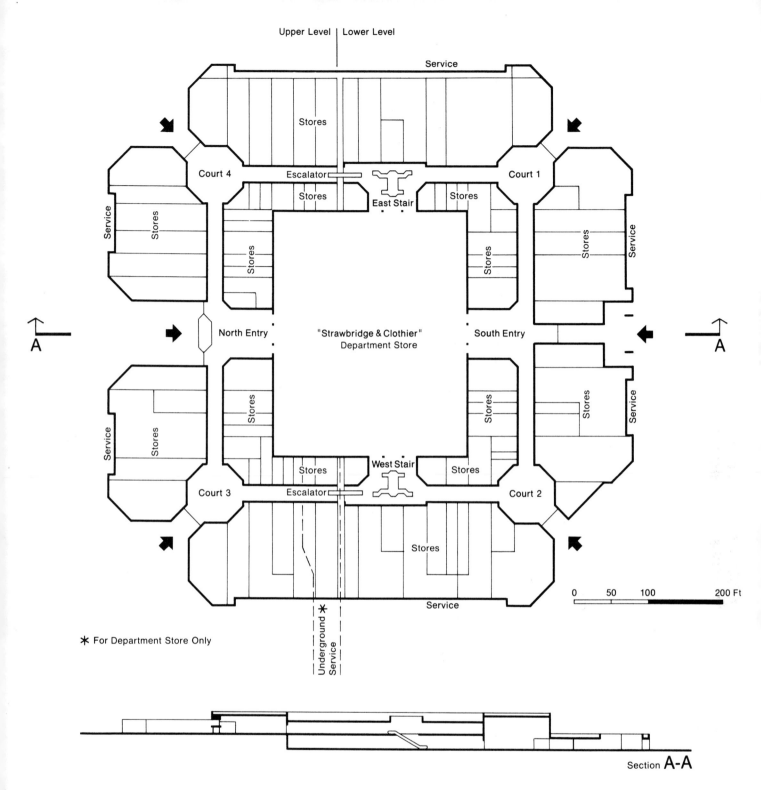

Upper Level | Lower Level

Service

Stores

Court 4   Escalator   Court 1
                                East Stair
                 Stores   Stores

Service Stores   Stores Service

       Stores   Stores

A→   →   North Entry   "Strawbridge & Clothier"   South Entry   ←   ←A
                              Department Store

Service Stores   Stores Service

       Stores   Stores

                 Stores   West Stair   Stores
Court 3   Escalator   Court 2

Stores

Service

✳ For Department Store Only

Underground ✳ Service

0   50   100   200 Ft

Section **A-A**

Floor plan and section.

EXTON SQUARE
Exton, Pennsylvania

ARCHITECTS: Katzman Associates, Inc.

Exton Square is located 35 miles from Philadelphia. The unusual feature of this plan is that Strawbridge & Clothier, the only department store, is placed directly in the center. The smaller stores are continuous to the periphery of the main store except where this is broken by the four main entrances, one in the center of each side. Corner entries to the center lead to four major courts, which are interconnected by a continuous arcade.

The project is split-level, with the back portion raised above the front area. The owner-developer is The Rouse Company.

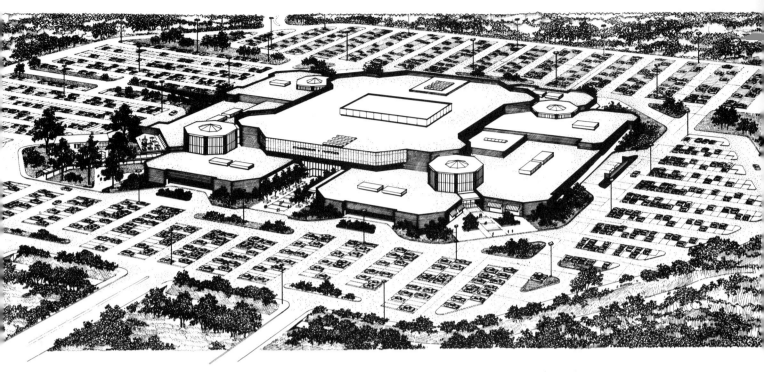

Bird's eye view of center.

Court No. 2.

LEFT: *Aerial view of site.* BELOW,
LEFT: *Parking area. (Photographer:
Panda/Croydon Associates.)*
BELOW: *Mall area. (Photographer:
Panda/Croydon Associates.)*

FAIRVIEW MALL SHOPPING CENTER
North York, Ontario, Canada

ARCHITECTS: Bregman & Hamann
DESIGN CONSULTANTS: Gruen Associates

This two-level regional center is situated on a 46-acre site some 10 miles from downtown Toronto. The complex includes two major department stores, 100 retail shops, a major food market, a 750-seat movie theater, a community hall, and related facilities.

A third level is planned to contain office space for professionals, insurance agencies, and other offices. It also contains heating, cooling, and other mechanical equipment.

An important feature of this mall is the inclined moving ramp between the shopping levels. The incline is gentle enough to accommodate baby carriages and wheelchairs as well as pedestrians. The moving ramp has worked out quite well in handling a large number of people.

A survey of the users was conducted and a significant finding was that:
1. Users aged twenty-five and under liked the moving ramp more than escalators.
2. Those aged twenty-five to thirty-five had no preference
3. Those aged thirty-five and over preferred escalators.

One problem that does exist from a merchandising point of view is that the length of the moving ramp inhibited the physical movement of shoppers from one side of the mall to the other, so that comparison shopping became more difficult. Shopkeepers facing the ramp also complained about restricted visual contact with the shoppers on the opposite side of the mall.

The structure is concrete frame at the first level and steel frame at the upper levels, with exterior walls of brick and exposed-aggregate precast panels.

The site is generously landscaped and provided with pedestrian access paths from the surrounding residential development of 25,000.

FASHION ISLAND
Irvine Ranch, Newport Beach, California

ARCHITECTS: Welton Becket & Associates
LANDSCAPE CONSULTANTS: Sasaki-Walker
  Associates, Inc.

The 75-acre center developed by Irvine Company includes four major department stores—Robinson's, The Broadway, Buffum's and the J. C. Penney chain—and fifty-two individual special shops and restaurants.

Special attention was paid to the landscaping of the three major and four secondary plazas to give each its own identity, character, and function. The mall complex has become a major tourist attraction as well as a park and focal point of activities for the residents of the new town of Irvine.

The site of the center overlooks Newport Beach, Corona Del Mar, and the Pacific Ocean.

The commercial part is the first phase of the center. The second phase will include office buildings, financial institutions, high-rise apartments, medical facilities, and entertainment centers.

"Our staggered plan for Fashion Island's mall encourages shoppers to go through shops rather than past them, and results in a mall some 200 feet shorter than possible under the more conventional in-line design," architect Welton Becket, FAIA, explained. "The offset mall also yields a higher percentage of corner locations—an important factor for customer identity and traffic."

The plazas, designed by Sasaki-Walker Associates, Inc., are individual in appearance and purpose yet so related that they flow into one another.

The largest plaza, which is designed as a park, also contains a stage for concerts and plays and a sculpture garden by Bella Feldman where children can play with sculptures mounted on a series of 24-inch wooden cubes.

The secondary plazas are paved space, sheltered by a formal pattern of tall shade trees, containing glassed-in merchandise display cases and large square redwood benches.

Another major plaza—175 feet square—is depressed three steps and paved with blue and white tile set in a triangular pattern. This is Fashion Island's principal outdoor display area for special exhibitions and includes a sizable stage. A highlight is a sculpture of three court jesters, held aloft by concrete columns, which gives the plaza scale and dimension.

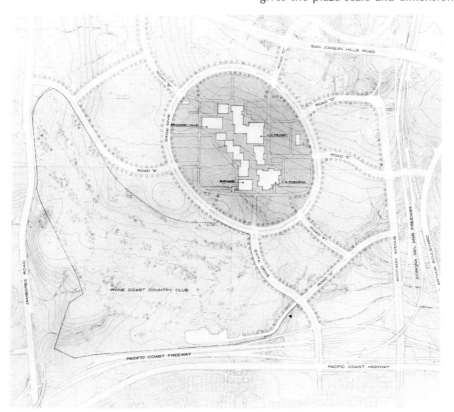

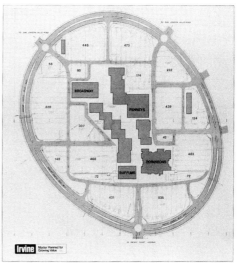

ABOVE: *Site plan.*
LEFT: *Final-phase road system.*

Attractive to youngsters is the children's play area in another plaza equipped with safe, modern playground apparatus created by sculptor, Jacques Overhoff. Surrounded by long hedges with benches for adults around the interior periphery, the slightly depressed play area is semisecluded. A wooden bridge above a fish pond bisects the area.

The third of the three major plazas provides a community facility—the Island House—designed as an arbor and including a kitchen, pantry, and lounge. This facility is available without charge to community clubs and groups for meetings and other social functions.

Another smaller paved area, overlooking the Pacific Ocean, features water jets from a round, stepped-up fountain and is used for fashion shows. To avoid blocking the shops, landscaping of all plazas was designed to allow a clear view—except for tree trunks—from a distance 3 to 10 feet above the ground.

The exterior of dark split-block curtain walls and terra-cotta-colored tile on the sloped roofs of the buildings contrasts with white, precast-concrete sculptured posts and beams which support 12-foot roof overhangs. This provides a continuous protective veranda along both sides of the staggered mall.

Welton Becket and Associates prepared the master plan and designed the Buffum's department store. William L. Pereira Associates designed the J. W. Robinson's department store and Charles Luckman Associates were the architects for J. C. Penney's and The Broadway Store.

LEFT: *Plaza.* (*Photographer: Marvin Rand.* BELOW: *Plaza with sculpture.* (*Sculptor: Jacques Overhoff. Photographer: Marvin Rand.*)

Plaza in front of Buffum's department store. (Photographer: Marvin Rand.)

Plaza with pool. (Photographer: Marvin Rand.)

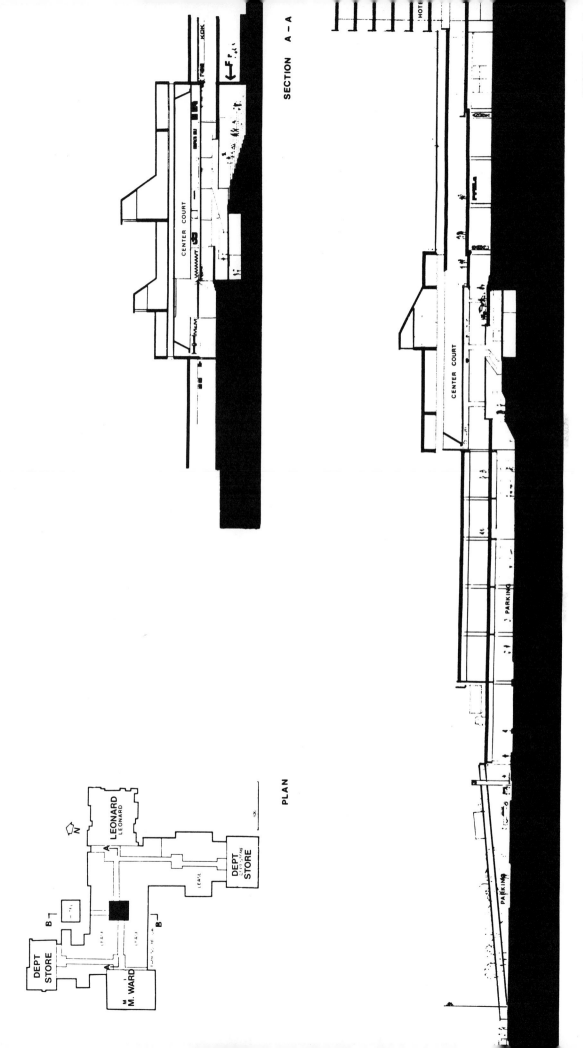

SECTION A – A

SECTION B – B

PLAN

CENTER COURT

CENTER COURT

PARKING

PARKING

LEONARD

DEPT STORE

DEPT STORE

M. WARD

168

OPPOSITE PAGE: *Sections.*

RIGHT: *Exterior view showing entry to Leonard's department store.*

Exterior view showing one of main entries.

The two-level center, located midway between Dallas and Fort Worth, is anchored by two major department stores, Leonard's and Montgomery Ward's, with planned phased expansion capabilities for a third and fourth department store. Also planned is a high-rise hotel connecting directly with the center.

The architects took advantage of the natural slope of the site and provided the shopper with more than 3 acres of covered parking, a feature not often planned in today's cost-conscious shopping centers.

In the interior, the architects created a large central Forum Court which features a 320-seat amphitheater to be used for various activities.

The amphitheater is integrated with both the retail areas and lower-level covered parking; the seating arrangement is, in fact, part of the vertical circulation system connecting the two. Upper-level shopping tiers serve as viewing balconies for performances or are simply for the pastime known as "people watching."

Another subsidiary mall area, below, is an activity court specially planned for children. Here graphics are integral to the architects' design concept. Besides the children's space, where they abound, graphic panels in walls and floors serve as traffic controls, area definers, or call shoppers' attention to displays and shop windows.*

Natural light enters the Forum Court through two tall light wells. This interplay of light, space, and form create a setting which, along with the people-noise, bright colors, activity, recreation, and entertainment of the center, adds to the shopper's enjoyment.

*Reprinted from *Architectural Record,* March, 1970.

FORUM 303
Arlington, Texas

ARCHITECTS: Omniplan Architects
  Harrell & Hamilton

169

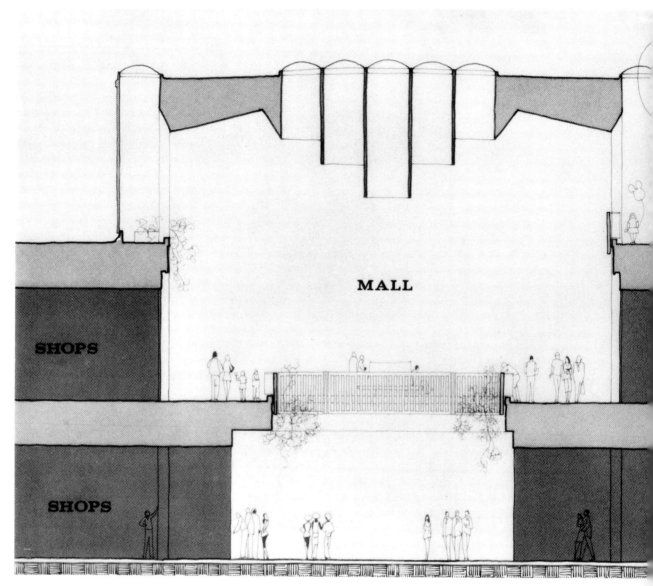

MALL

SHOPS

SHOPS

Section.

Exterior perspective.

This center is planned in the initial phase as a two-story, three-department-store complex. One of the features of this design is the provision for future expansion of a third floor. In the case of the department stores, the third-floor exterior walls are built initially as parapets. As for the other store buildings, the exterior third-floor walls were not built in the first stage.

The mall is tiered like two ziggurats side by side, and the lower mall storefronts undulate in and out in relation to the face of the balcony above. The former feature tends to reduce mall volume while greatly increasing tenant exposure between levels, while the latter eliminates the potential tunnel effect at the lower level.

Special attention is paid to night lighting, color-corrected mercury vapor. Approximately one fixture per 30-foot bay is used in central skylight boxes and at second-level crossovers.

For accent illumination at night, store design criteria required projection of an additional 35 footcandles at storefront lease line. Ceiling light-level modulation from a basic 15 footcandles to as much as 60 footcandles along the center mall is achieved by the addition of quartz lamp fixtures within skylight boxes to produce accents of downward shafts of light.

The arrangements for parking take into consideration the third-floor expansion. South and west parking are at the second-mall level, while north and east are at lower-mall level. The five-level parking-deck structure to be built at the time of third-floor expansion is planned to tie directly with a pedestrian bridge to upper-level parking grade at northwest and southeast corners of the center.

As for outside signing, only the department stores have building-mounted signs. Other tenants have ground-mounted signs located in the landscaped area separating the porte-cochere from the inner circulation lane. The long-range planning of the peripheral site calls for a unified design concept by using the same brick exterior material as the major material elsewhere.

The site is planned for a high-rise office building, hotel, and convention center. Already completed are the Bell Laboratories building and town houses and garden apartments.

FOUR SEASONS MALL
Greensboro, North Carolina
ARCHITECTS: Valand, Benzing & Associates

RIGHT: *Space frame canopy.*
BELOW: *J. C. Penney Company entrance.*
(*Designers: The Law Company.*)

This three-department-store shopping center, developed by The Rouse Company, comprises 940,000 square feet and is located in the suburban northwest section of Toledo on a former airport site.

One of the main objectives in the design of the mall was to make the traditional logo and major architectural features synonymous and directly identifiable with the center.

The mall, which features many natural materials, incorporates a great deal of white—the Unistrut ceilings, and bulkheads. The stores use natural wood cedar and bronze, and the two kinds of quarry tile used throughout the mall are of natural colors. The mall ceiling height is 12 feet and the width is 35 feet. However, the mall leading to the Lamson Court has a somewhat different design criterion. The ceilings, which are 16 feet high, are painted dark, and the mall is 50 feet wide. A completely different storefront concept was applied in this area, where large, bold graphics were used. The storefronts are 8 feet high with 8-foot decorative panels above them. Storefronts and bulkheads are lighted externally from the mall ceiling rather than internally from the store. The design objective was to achieve a carnival atmosphere.

All three courts of the department stores can be characterized similarly as having depressed areas with a water feature, planting, and seating. They are relatively quiet rest areas with light filtering down through the trees.

The Exhibition Court is 70 by 110 feet. The fountain is 35 feet high. Cedar wood has been used in the area to contrast with the white of the 40-foot Unistrut cube, which rises to a height of 85 feet.

Between the promotion courts and the department store courts where the mall jogs, there are landscaped "knuckle" areas where seating and telephones are provided. These areas are lit by special light boxes that hang down from the ceilings.

The dim lighting in the mall is planned so that the storefronts and merchandise will be lit at a maximum, thereby focusing shoppers' attention to them.

The design of the structure is of exposed Unistrut system painted white. It is used in the raised court areas as well as being featured in the high cube structure of the main exhibition court.

The modular Syn-Con construction system is used throughout. The utilization of this system provides flexibility for the installation of heating and air conditioning units, sprinkler system, ceiling and electrical distribution. This is discussed in more detail in Part Two.

According to Ken Ball, the architect and project manager for Daverman Associates, special attention was paid to the design of the promotional court. There, a freestanding stairway leads to a mezzanine gallery which contains the 250- to 300-seat community hall with kitchen facilities, a board room, and administrative offices. The finished material used throughout is cedar wood. The gallery provides an overall view of the grand court.

Architects for the center are Daverman Associates, Inc.; for Lamson's, Samborn-Steketree-Otis & Evans; for Hudson's, Raymond Loewy–William Snaith, Louis G. Redstone Associates, Inc.: consultants for mall interior and storefronts: Cranfield Stephens & Associates; interiors for Hudson's, Raymond Loewy–William Snaith and Robert B. Alpern Associates; designers for Penney's, The Law Company.

FRANKLIN PARK MALL
Toledo, Ohio
ARCHITECTS: Daverman Associates, Inc.

Mall interior showing the use of similar tile on floor and walls.

Court area.

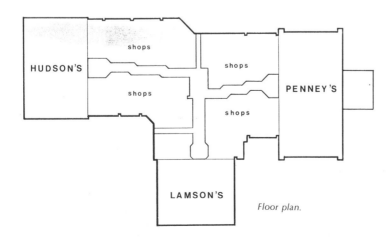

Floor plan.

HUDSON'S

shops

shops

shops

shops

shops

PENNEY'S

LAMSON'S

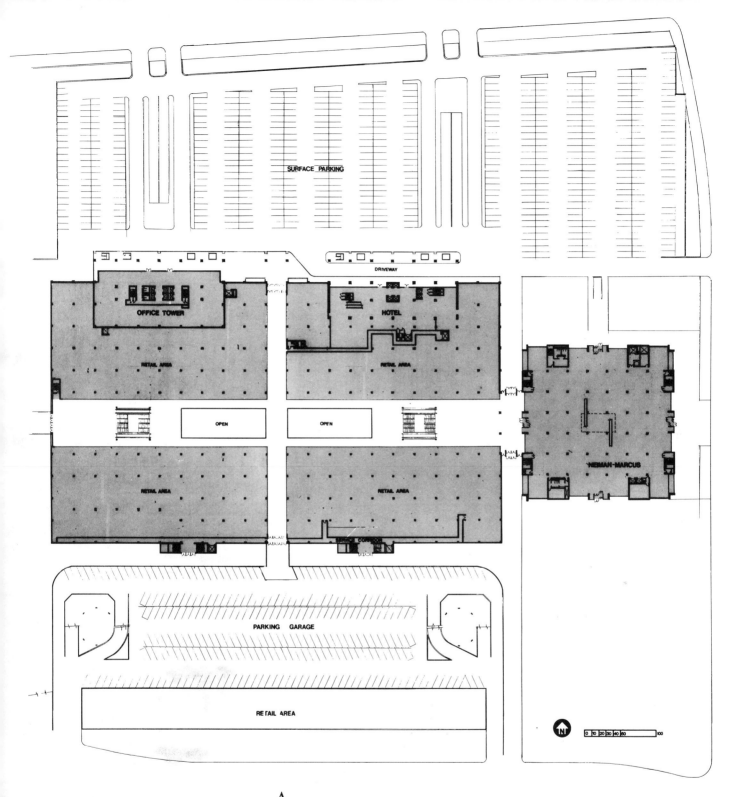

SURFACE PARKING

DRIVEWAY

OFFICE TOWER

HOTEL

RETAIL AREA

RETAIL AREA

NEIMAN-MARCUS

OPEN

OPEN

RETAIL AREA

RETAIL AREA

PARKING GARAGE

RETAIL AREA

0 10 20 30 40 60   100

GALLERIA POST OAK
Houston, Texas

ARCHITECTS: Hellmuth, Obata
  & Kassabaum, Inc.
ASSOCIATE ARCHITECTS: Neuhaus & Taylor

An interesting example of a multilevel shopping center which includes an office tower and hotel in its total planning concept is illustrated in this center, developed by Gerald D. Hines Interests.

The mall is covered by a continuous circular skylight reminiscent of the Galleria in Milan, Italy.

An attraction to the center is the adjoining five-level Neiman-Marcus store connected by a passageway. The multilevel galleries around the open center of the mall, reached by escalators at both ends, create excitement and visual interest. The traffic generated by the office tower, the hotel, and the additional recreational facilities, such as the skating rink, adds to the success of the center. Parking is provided both on the surface and in a parking garage.

The exterior of the Neiman-Marcus store is a departure from the windowless-type facade. Its inviting character stems from the use of show windows, sculptural shaping of the building masses, and careful planning of the landscaping around it.

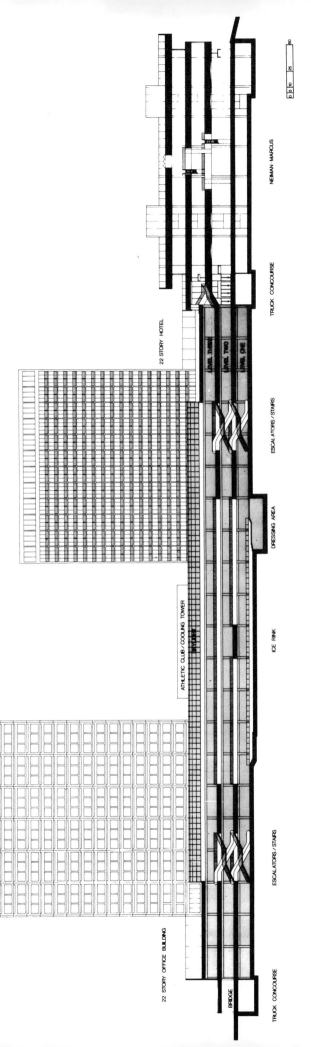

OPPOSITE PAGE: *Floor plan.*
LEFT: *Section.*

22 STORY OFFICE BUILDING

BRIDGE

TRUCK CONCOURSE

ESCALATORS / STAIRS

ICE RINK

ATHLETIC CLUB / COOLING TOWER

DRESSING AREA

ESCALATORS / STAIRS

22 STORY HOTEL

TRUCK CONCOURSE

NEIMAN-MARCUS

Skating rink. Lower level.

Exterior, Neiman-Marcus store.
[Photographer: Ezra Stoller (ESTO).]

Banque de Montréal—minibank.
(Photographer: Roger Jowett.)

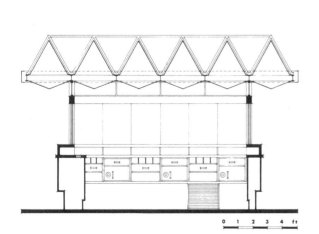

Section, minibank.

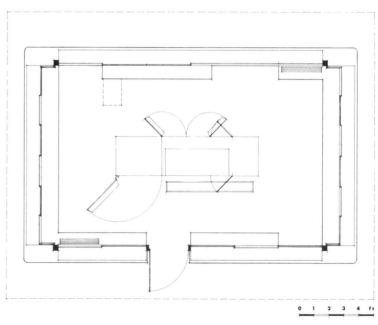

Floor plan.

According to John Kryton of the architectural firm of Greenspoon, Freedlander, Plachta & Kryton, an important consideration in designing this center is the Quebec law relating to earthquake design. It holds the architect responsible if the building is destroyed in whole or in part, and he can be charged in court with criminal negligence. Neither can an owner ignore these laws. He may also be charged with criminal negligence if such recommendations have been made known to him and he has refused to apply them to the structure.

The earthquake design of this center gave consideration to the store layouts. The earthquake design is based on the bracing of the various elements of the structure against a horizontal force applied laterally to the building. The result of such a force is expressed in practice either by bracing with diagonal elements the opening between two columns or by securing a special connection between columns and roof beams.

In large-span areas like the supermarkets, circular columns were used, these being equal in strength on all facets. (I-beams can withstand stronger forces only at the ends and not on the web.)

An interesting feature in the mall is the placement of a minibank. The minibank is a light and airy kiosk placed for customer convenience in one of the spacious aisles, where it provides attraction and service. Its main structure consists of four hollow steel columns surmounted by a space-frame roof with built-in pyramidal lighting fixtures. There are six tellers' windows. Counter writing space for the use of customers is provided at the corners. Working counters are blue, sides are black, and the area beneath the counter is decorated with carved copper panels. The bank stays open as long as the stores, with service all day on Saturdays.

Behind the sliding glass facade, the latest streamlined banking techniques have been artfully condensed into a 300-square-foot space. There are built-in tables, filing cabinets, and other accessories, as well as an air-conditioning system independent of the main building. The bank already has plans for minis in other centers.

In contrast to the experience of United States developers that supermarkets do not contribute to the success of a regional center, two of the most important chain supermarkets are connected, side by side, to this very successful center.

The center is owned and developed by Simpson's Ltd. and Cemp Investments Ltd.

GALERIES D'ANJOU SHOPPING CENTER
Montreal, Canada

ARCHITECTS: Greenspoon, Freedlander, Plachta & Kryton

ABOVE: *Eaton court with fountain.* BELOW: *Simpson's court. (Consulting architects: Gruen Associates. Photographer: Hayward Studios, Inc.)*

This center, a colorful showcase for the artistry of Mexico's finest artisans, was developed by Los Arcos Investments.

The focal point of the main court is the Mexican colonial fountain, 8 feet in height, hand-sculptured from cantera stone by skilled artisans in Tlaquepaque, Mexico, near Guadalajara.

A large stained-glass sunburst set in the octagonal glass dome of the center court is the work of Felipe Derflingher and his associates of Articulos Feder's Glass Studio in Mexico City. Another attraction of the enclosed mall is a colorful gazebo roofed in Tiffany-style glass. This is a Feder design, as are a number of glass lanterns.

Of unusual interest are the murals by the Mexican artist Jose Servin of Guadalajara, who is also the chairman of the Fine Arts Committee of the state of Jalisco, Mexico. His murals depict the varying cultures and crafts of the Mexican Indian and the American Indian. Colorful Mexican tiles are used extensively throughout the mall. These hand-painted, glazed tiles depict favorite Mexican designs of flowers, sun, animals, witch doctors, etc.

A variety of restaurants includes the Heidelberg Inn and Delicatessen, specializing in Bavarian dishes; Hobo Joe's; Rob Roy, an old English pub restaurant; The Robbers' Cave, a wine-cellar lounge with cheeses and gourmet foods; and El Jardin (The Garden), with an ornately carved fountain.

While Sears and The Broadway each had its own architect, architectural plans for the buildings were modified to harmonize with the general architectural concept of the mall. Uniform arches were used and Spanish motifs repeated.

LOS ARCOS
Scottsdale, Arizona

ARCHITECTS: For center and Sears:
  Burke Kober Nicolais Archuleta
For The Broadway Store:
  Charles Luckman

Site plan.

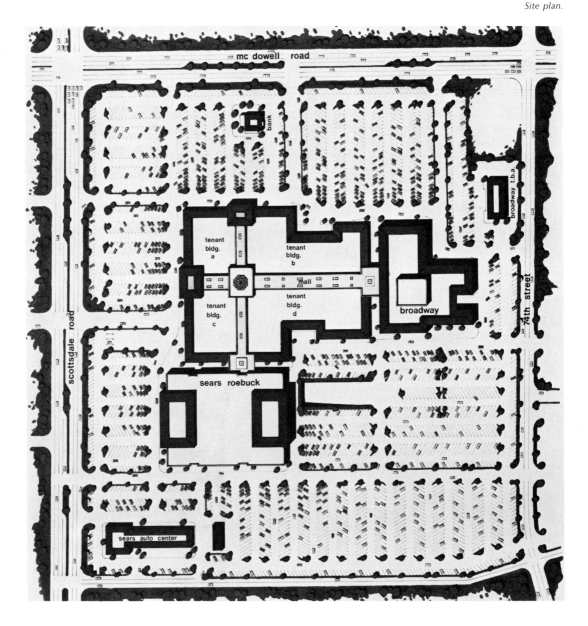

Entrance, showing lighting and arches. (Photographer: Koppes Fine.)

Entrance to court. (Photographer: Koppes Fine.)

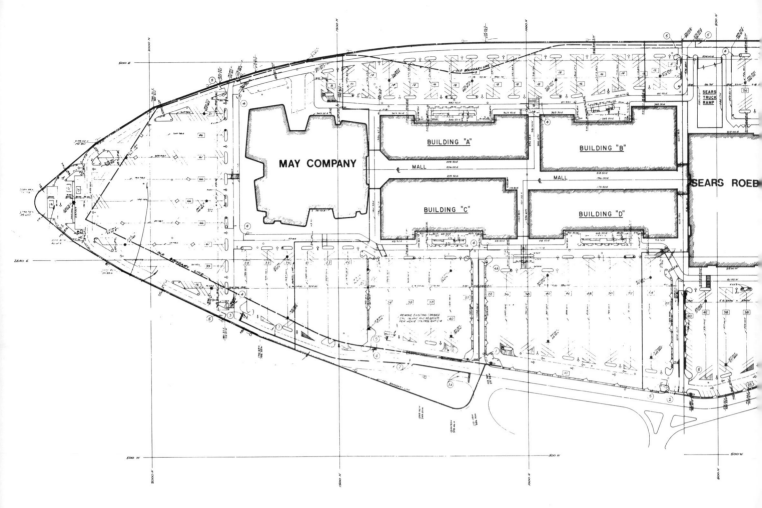

MAY COMPANY

BUILDING "A"

BUILDING "B"

MALL

MALL

BUILDING "C"

BUILDING "D"

SEARS ROEB

SEARS TRUCK RAMP

May Company site plan.

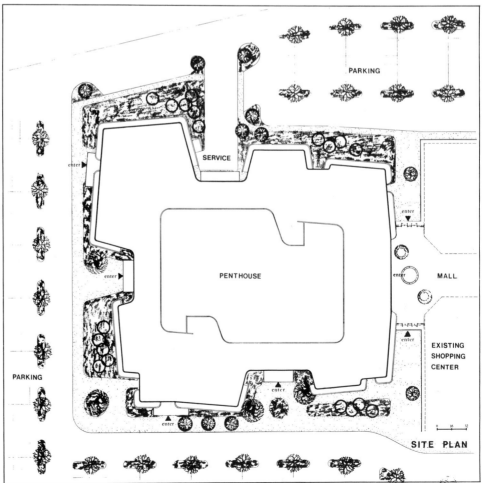

PARKING

SERVICE

PENTHOUSE

enter

enter

enter

enter

enter

enter

enter

MALL

EXISTING
SHOPPING
CENTER

PARKING

SITE PLAN

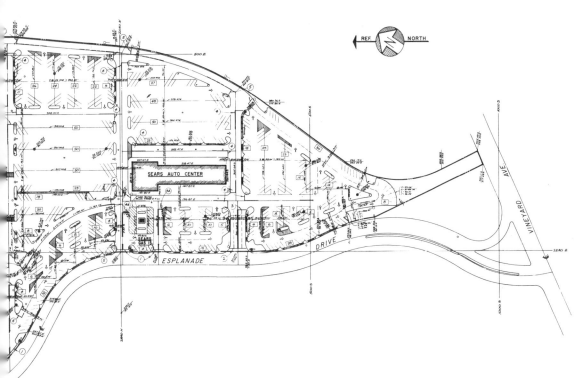

Esplanade site plan.

SEARS AUTO CENTER

SEARS GAS

ESPLANADE DRIVE

VINEYARD AVE.

The May Company store, one of the anchors of the center, has strong sculptural forms. The exterior material is of white split-face concrete block and concrete block covered with Celadon glazed tile.

According to the architects, the early California style of the Sears store was decided upon because of Centura County's heritage of early development under Spain and Mexico. This style was carried through the interior by use of arches plus brick, tile, and stucco in warm colors, as well as grillwork and decorative fountains and lighting fixtures. (See also following page.)

THE ESPLANADE
Oxnard, California

ARCHITECTS For center:
  Burke Kober Nicolais Archuleta
For May Company: Ladd & Kelsey

Exterior of May Company.

Exterior of Esplanade, showing entrance to center and Sears (building at right). (Photographer: Jordan Lagman.)

Interior mall and court of Esplanade. (Photographer: Jordan Lagman.)

NORTHLAND SHOPPING CENTER
Melbourne, Australia

ARCHITECTS: Tompkins Shaw & Evans

This center, developed by The Myer Emporium Ltd., is a three-department-store center. It is single-level except for the four-level main department store.

Special features include a circular market building housing thirty-five open stalls, each approximately 100 feet square, with access for goods via elevator from the storage area and truck dock below. This circular building is freestanding but connected with the center by covered walkways.

Another feature is the covered transit stop for passenger buses, accommodating 400 bus trips per day. This bus station is also connected to the center by covered walkways.

Professional and medical offices as well as the community auditorium are included in the center.

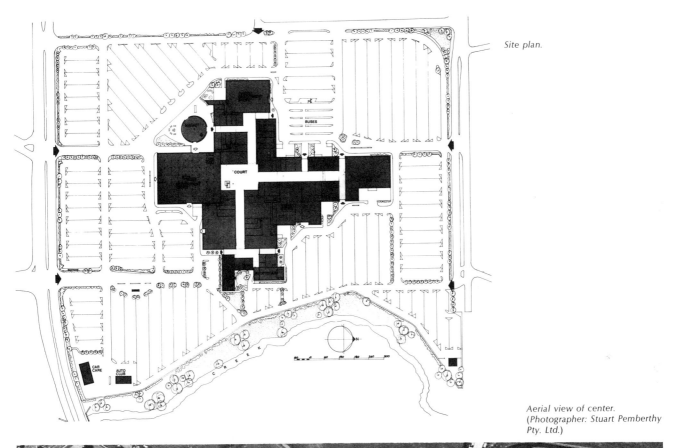

Site plan.

Aerial view of center.
(Photographer: Stuart Pemberthy
Pty. Ltd.)

The center occupies a 9-acre site and is located approximately 5 miles from the city center. The district of Coolock is a low-cost housing area, with no urban center as such, and is served by public bus transport.

The three-stage plan is laid out in the form of a central area at the "crossroads" of several two-story pedestrian shopping malls connecting directly with the pedestrian routes to the west and north and to the east to a pedestrian way running directly through the technical school complex. These malls are carefully designed

NORTHSIDE SHOPPING CENTER
County Coolock
Dublin, Ireland

ARCHITECTS: Stephenson Gilbrey & Associates

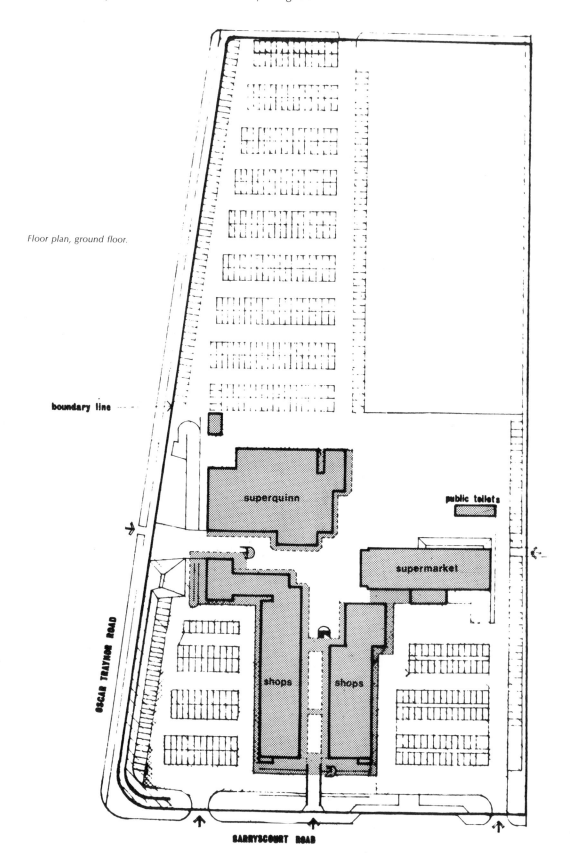

Floor plan, ground floor.

boundary line

superquinn

public toilets

supermarket

shops

shops

OSCAR TRAYNOR ROAD

BARRYSCOURT ROAD

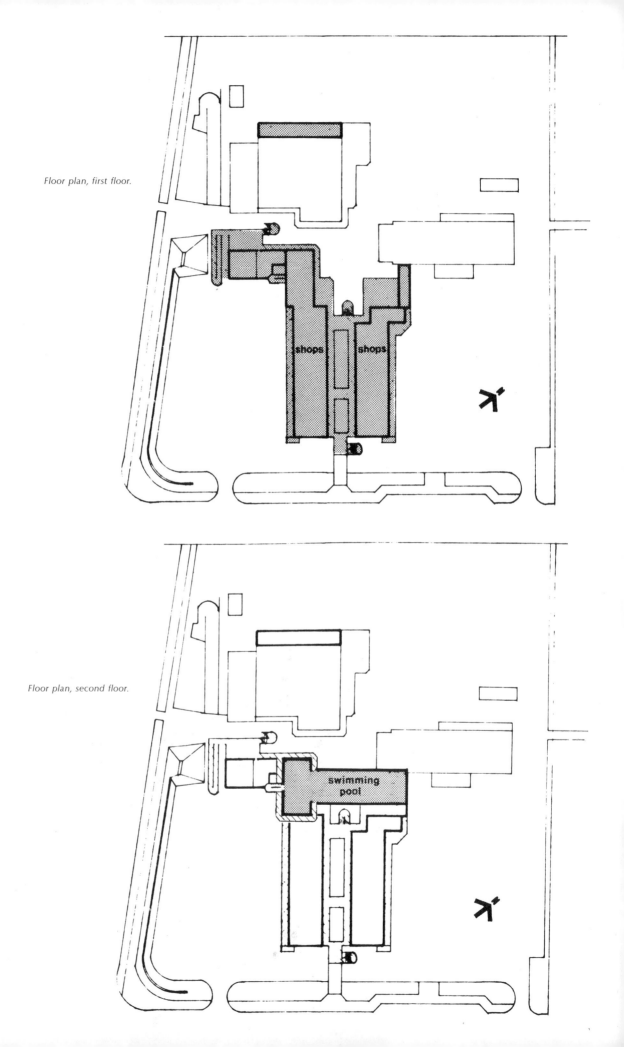

Floor plan, first floor.

shops shops

Floor plan, second floor.

swimming pool

185

to create pleasant, convenient areas for shoppers, and the use of space, shelter canopies, bridges, seating, and planting combine to achieve this. Incorporated also is a first-floor pedestrian walkway system approached by ramps and staircases and giving access to all upper-level accommodation.

Forty-six retail shops, two supermarkets, a swimming pool, cafe, public toilet facilities, and post office, included in the first two stages, are located in the complex. Stage three envisages a further twenty retail shops, a department store, and a community house.

Car parking spaces number 550, all at ground level, with a planned expansion to 1,000 which may require deck parking.

The pool, a special feature of the center, is covered and heated for year-round use and is reached from the first-floor public balcony of the center. This balcony is served by a pedestrian ramp and three staircases from ground level. The structure is of reinforced concrete, cast in place, with all external surfaces board-marked. Shutters are made of sawn Oregon pine.

Certain selected surfaces on the soffits of balcony overhangs are painted in continuous stripes of primary colors—red, blue, and yellow. The object of the colors is that they should act as a foil to the flat concrete surfaces which, in the prevailing dampness of the Irish climate, tend to mellow to a dull finish.

The center had to be visually recognizable as the focal point of the district, and as it was to serve an area the major part of which had already been developed, it was necessary to follow the extension of the already established pedestrian circulation patterns of the neighborhood. At the same time, provision had to be made in the initial stages of the project to allow for the needs of future expansion.

A major consideration was that the malls within the center should be used as streets and that residents should be encouraged by the layout of the malls to use the center as a main thoroughfare rather than walking around the perimeter or using the center only when actually shopping. In order to encourage this traffic flow, densely planted areas are planned to form a visual barrier to the perimeter, thus directing pedestrians over the link routes from the surrounding housing areas and into the center itself.

General interior view of center mall showing the texture of the concrete structure. (Photographer: Norman McGrath.)

Exterior view of center showing ramp arrangement leading to the upper floor and the supergraphic color stripings. Exterior combines cast-in-place concrete and concrete-block curtain wall. (Photographer: Norman McGrath.)

View showing the interesting effect of the concrete design. (Photographer: Norman McGrath.)

Aerial view of center and surroundings.

NORTHWEST PLAZA

St. Louis, Missouri

ARCHITECTS: Architectural Design Associates
LANDSCAPE ARCHITECTS: Lawrence Halprin & Associates

This center, located on a 117-acre site, is one of the few five-department-store centers designed around an open mall. The attraction of this center is due in part to the well-designed open areas between buildings, which was part of the initial concept of the architects, Architectural Design Associates. The successful integration of the buildings and the landscaped areas, as well as the "distinctive shingled and copper mansard roof which blends with exterior facades of lava stone, brick and glass present a unified, overall character."* There are eight fountains, some of which are designed by Lawrence Halprin, landscape architect. The malls also contain sculpture, shaded walkways, and colorful garden arrangements. One of the important water sculptures is created by Aristides Demetrios of San Francisco.

Another feature of this center is the twelve-story office building with a restaurant at mall level.

Although the accepted trend for the present and the immediate future is the closed-mall, climate-controlled center, the success of this center demonstrates that given the right location, design, tenant mix, and an attractive program for community events, there is still room for the well-planned open mall.

The owner-developers are Louis and Milton Zorensky.

*Reprinted by permission from *Chain Store Age,* Executive Edition. Copyright by Lebhar-Friedman, Inc., 2 Park Avenue, New York, N.Y. 10016

188

Court and fountain in front of
Famous-Barr department store.
(Store's designers: Raymond
Loewy and William Snaith.
Photographer: Jeremiah O.
Bragstad.)

Exterior court and fountain.
(Photographer: Jeremiah O.
Bragstad.)

This center was built by Lincoln Property Co. as part of a country-club apartment community. Clusters of shops were planned to open onto landscaped malls. Although the styles of the stores vary from rustic to contemporary, the unifying elements are the shapes and materials used in the canopies and the shingled roofs. The use of wood, red brick, walkways, and landscaped areas using fountains contributes to an enjoyable environment. Inside the shops the variation in ceiling heights from 13 to 24 feet allows flexibility in interior design, i.e., balconies, mezzanines, etc.

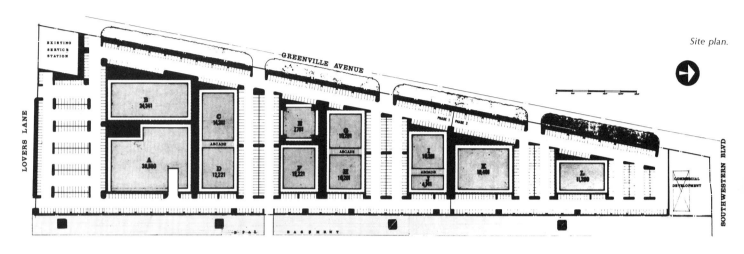

Site plan.

LEFT: *Mall.*
BELOW: *Sign and parking area.*

190

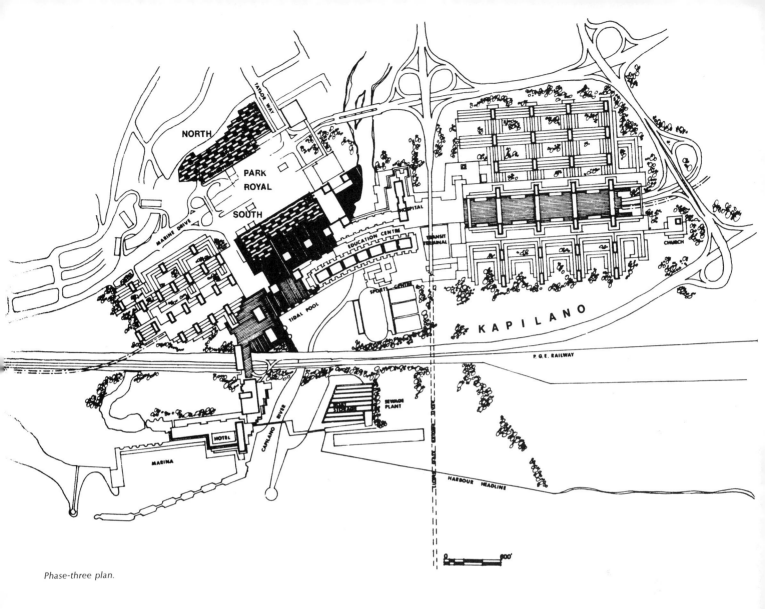

Phase-three plan.

This center began in 1950 as a one-department-store open-mall plan with a few small shops. Since then, the successful growth of the market compelled the owners to expand periodically, still retaining the open mall until 1968. At that time additional expansion, which included enclosure of the mall, increased parking facilities, and improved access and vehicular circulation, was started. This short-range type of planning proved costly not only moneywise but also in terms of inconvenience to shoppers and merchants.

According to Peter Blewett,* of the architectural firm of Wade Stockdill Armour & Blewett,

PARK ROYAL NORTH

Vancouver, B.C.

ARCHITECTS: Wade Stockdill Armour & Blewett
CONSULTING ARCHITECTS: John Graham Ltd.

> the Park Royal project is highly unusual and yet the problem is probably developing all over North America—i.e., how to pace the development of a shopping center to the rapid growth of its market area. I have seen throughout the United States and Canada the appalling land waste that occurs when a Center in a good location is neglected to the point where a new center can establish in close proximity and 'steal' the market area. It is my belief that all center owners should establish long-range development plans and implement staged growth ahead of the actual demand, thus preventing the market for a new center from building up. Naturally the traditional concept of low-density development surrounded by a vast surface parking area cannot be justified once the suburban land values climb to reflect the urban function of the large center. Greater use has to be made of original land mass, and the multilevel urban center will evolve. I found that at Park Royal the cost of intensified development could only be justified by the prohibitive cost of additional land acquisition. If the original center had been planned to allow for staged

*Excerpts from a paper given at the International Council of Shopping Centers Convention. May, 1970.

191

growth, then the normal economics of building would have applied. As it happened, we had to clear-span over parts of the existing center with our parking decks. This raised the unit car costs considerably and the entire planning resulted from a balance between car parking cost and anticipated income from increased space. This mathematical relationship involved constant juggling with costs and areas and was complicated by the need to elevate and separate the shopping center circulation from the municipal traffic.

The major factor influencing the planning was the site limitation. Major municipal arteries border the east and south sides of the site, while a steep hill rises to the north and apartment towers exist on the western boundary. The original Center required additional parking spaces without any retail expansion. Feasibility studies quickly proved that the cheapest provision, grade parking, was hampered by site restrictions. Next, deck parking was considered, but the cost of construction, with no return from parking spaces, was prohibitive to existing tenants. Consequently the only means of providing additional parking was a major retail expansion, with parking-deck costs being spread over a much greater number of shops. This concept initiated the economic, feasibility, traffic, and planning studies necessary for a major expansion. As a result of the studies, multilevel parking decks were built over the tenant shop and mall spaces with escalator and elevator connections directly from the decks down into the main shopping area. This not only provides customers with the minimum time/distance to shops but also creates under-cover parking areas. In addition, overflow parking is housed in a 485-car parkade structure located on a site to the east of the center.

The north mall is a high-volume space with completely artificial lighting techniques. In principle, individual shops provide a flood of light and activity and hence attraction, while the mall, particularly the ceiling, forms a darkened background against which revolving displays can be shown. These may take the form of seasonal concepts or individual displays such as fashions, fabrics, or automobiles. Another mall, to form a contrast, has a lower vaulted ceiling resulting in a much more intimate atmosphere for the smaller individual "domestic" shops. For visual warmth and ease of maintenance, brick tile forms the major floor finish, which in places continues up the walls in panels to provide continuity. This is punctuated by individual display windows or complete shop fronts. In the interior of the malls a high standard of visual continuity is achieved by establishing a design control line which penetrates the individual tenant space. By this means, all shops are limited to a base building material upon which their motif, symbol, or medallion is displayed. Encouragement has been given to the design of medallions for each store forming a back-lit panel in the canopy. No flashing or moving elements are permitted within the design control area. The result is an effective coordinated total design policy for the entire center.

Park Royal North site plan.

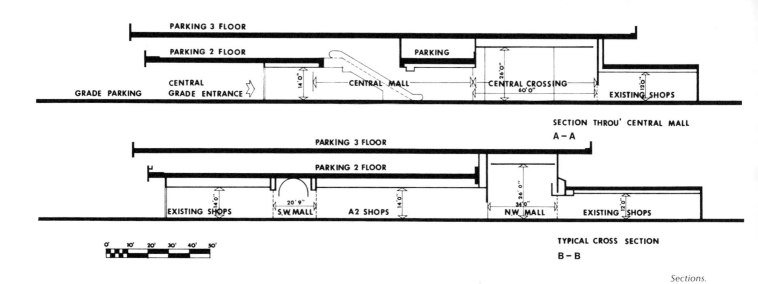

PARKING 3 FLOOR

PARKING 2 FLOOR

PARKING

GRADE PARKING CENTRAL
GRADE ENTRANCE 14'0" CENTRAL MALL 26'0" CENTRAL CROSSING
60'0" EXISTING SHOPS 12'0"

SECTION THROU' CENTRAL MALL
A – A

PARKING 3 FLOOR

PARKING 2 FLOOR

EXISTING SHOPS 14'0" S.W. MALL
20'9" A2 SHOPS 14'0" 26'0" N.W. MALL
34'0" EXISTING SHOPS 12'0"

0' 10' 20' 30' 40' 50'

TYPICAL CROSS SECTION
B – B

Sections.

LEFT: *Parking area, showing bridge connection over highway.* BELOW, LEFT: *Mall, showing furniture items, seating cubes, trash receptacles, light stands. (Interior designers: Cranfield Stephens & Associates.)* BELOW: *Southwest arcade mall, showing oxidized steel slats in ceiling. (Interior designers: Cranfield Stephens & Associates.)*

PARLY 2

Paris, France

ARCHITECTS: Lathrop Douglass, FAIA,
and Aaron Chelouche, AIA
ARCHITECT OF RECORD: Claude Balick

Near Versailles, this two-level, two-department-store regional center with approximately 100 satellite stores is one of the first large fashion centers in France.

A departure from the American-planned centers is the addition of two levels of office space over the satellite stores. Faced with parking and traffic problems similar to those in the United States, the architects depended on governmental support to obtain additional highway access. (Concessions were impossible to obtain.) The problem of providing space for 3,000 cars was solved through a partial double decking with a large auto service station located underground.

The center is near a 6,000-unit apartment development. Because of the high income level of the region, each store vied for a glamorous and spectacular image. The climatized center has marble floors, columns encased in natural wood, and a unique ceiling of plaster blocks with a color scheme of Prussian blue and white. In the two department-store courts are coffee bars on the lower mall level. Mall amenities include fountains, landscaping, and art. Special attention was paid to the design of light fixtures. Although the Frenchwoman had to learn new ways of shopping, the center has been extremely successful, with some 40 percent more sales than anticipated. Graphics have been designed with a center motif carried out in the ceiling block pattern, the cross-mall bridges, the benches, the planters, and even the door handles.

As is the trend in the United States, Canada, and in many places in Europe, this commercial center is the nucleus for a completely new town.

The owner of this center is LaSociete Anonyme Immobiliere de Construction; the developers, Messrs. Robert de Balkany and Jean-Louis Solal.

This is a "village scaled" center for shopping and dining with sufficient second-floor office space for professional people.

To meet the needs of small shop owners, especially to promote impulse buying, shops are planned along corridors, arcades, and several open landscaped courts. The architects have reinforced the village planning concept with natural materials—wood doors, wood trim, stucco, wood screens and grilles, brick walkways and courts, handcrafted terra-cotta lights—and with controlled graphics and signs. The planning assures easy movement of shoppers through the center in a leisurely and pleasant atmosphere.

Outdoor courts and a 400-seat auditorium provide ample space for community functions and merchant promotions. The center has played host to such varied activities as a children's art exhibit, a wine-tasting event, a ladies' bazaar, and various private parties.*

*Reprinted by permission from *The Texas Architect,* August, 1970.

QUADRANGLE
Dallas, Texas

ARCHITECTS: Pratt, Box, Henderson & Partners

Site plan.

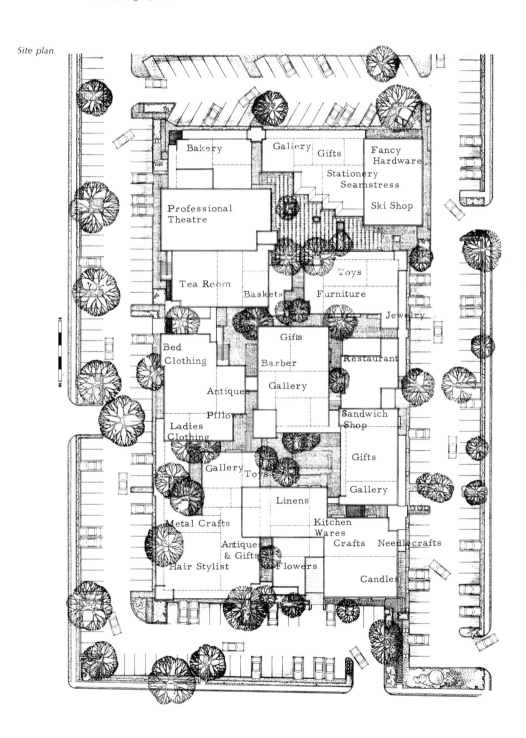

196

Coffee bar in main court.

Fountain sculpture.
(Sculptor: Lartigue)

195

View of mall and fountain.
(Photographer: P. Colacicco.)

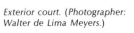

Exterior court. (Photographer:
Walter de Lima Meyers.)

FAR LEFT: *Exterior court.*
LEFT: *Interior court,
terra-cotta lighting on wall.*

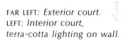

Exterior views.

QUAIL CORNERS SHOPPING CENTER
Raleigh, North Carolina

ARCHITECTS: Valand, Benzing
   & Associates
LANDSCAPE ARCHITECT:
   Geoffrey McLean

Quail Corners community, although 7 miles from downtown, is now within the corporate limits of the city of Raleigh, North Carolina. The developers are Austin Development Co. and Cameron-Brown Co. of Raleigh.

This mini-mall center stresses the integration of buildings and parking areas with well-designed landscaping. In addition, the exterior uses materials which harmonize with the contiguous neighborhood.

The exterior of natural cedar reverse board-and-batten siding is augmented in its residential feeling by many full-grown trees moved onto the site (originally a meadow). The concrete walls of the entrance garden and fountain were formed in place with board-and-batten cedar, the texture and the fibers of the wood remaining in the concrete after stripping. While the extensive landscaping was furnished and installed by Quail Corners, Inc., it is now fully maintained by a community garden club.

Both bank and service station (on the site) adhere strictly to the center in design, each identified with two relatively small black back-lighted signs. The gas-station owner contributed to the general landscaping cost.

Exterior lighting consists of 150 watt incandescent bulbs boxed with cedar boards at the tops of columns, casting a dramatic pattern of light up and down.

The special feature of locating professional offices on the second floor over the mall area has generated additional traffic into the mall. The mall is extensively used for civic events.

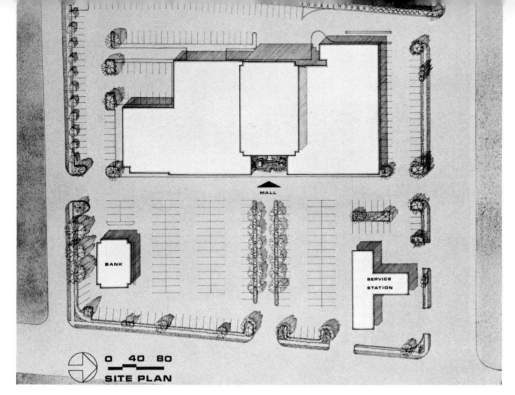

Site plan.

SITE PLAN

0 40 80

MALL

BANK

SERVICE STATION

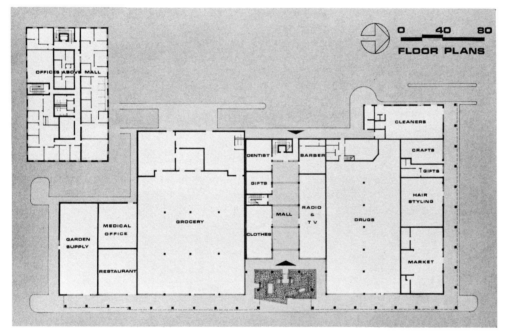

Floor plan.

FLOOR PLANS

0 40 80

OFFICES ABOVE MALL

CLEANERS

CRAFTS

GIFTS

DENTIST   BARBER

GIFTS

HAIR STYLING

GARDEN SUPPLY

MEDICAL OFFICE

GROCERY

MALL

RADIO & T V

DRUGS

CLOTHES

RESTAURANT

MARKET

Mall and plantings.

THE FINE LINE GIFTS

199

View showing three levels of shopping area (perspective). (Photographer: Gordon Sommers Photography.)

SANTA ANITA FASHION PARK
Arcadia, California

ARCHITECTS: Gruen Associates

This four-department-store center, including a professional and general tenant office complex, was developed by Santa Anita Consolidated, Inc.

The boutiques and specialty shops open into the mall on two and in some areas on three levels, connected by escalators and stairs. The mall features an angular roof, with a full-length section of transparent glass.

Patios, restaurants, and a theater provide facilities for relaxing, recreation, and social events.

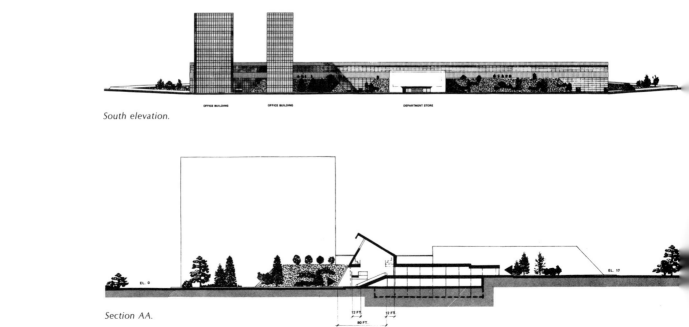

South elevation.

Section AA.

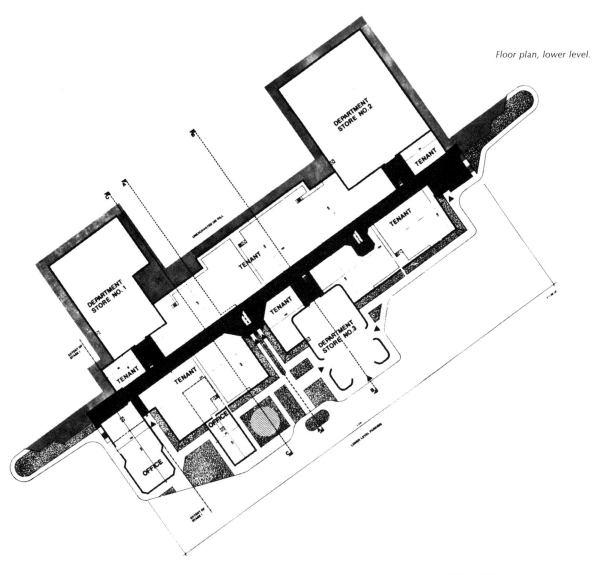

Floor plan, lower level.

Bird's-eye view of center (model). (Photographer: Gordon Sommers Photography.)

This pinwheel-shaped center uses new materials and advanced construction techniques.

Four malls converge at a central plaza. Clerestory windows furnish natural lighting. Skylights of special design are located along the walls, creating a feeling of contact with the outdoors. Some 800,000 square feet of commercial space opens onto the malls, which are offset at the plaza to preclude any feeling of great distance separating the two major department stores at either end of the center. The center is designed to add a third department store in the future. The design was intended to minimize storefronts exposed to the outside while giving maximum encouragement to traffic into the mall.

Both pavement and carpeting are used in the malls to create a landscaped street scene that includes shopping kiosks, rest areas, and children's play areas.

As to the interiors, a double cantilever roof with a massive 40-foot-high plexiglas skylight composed of multifaceted "gems" covers the central plaza. This skylight is also the source of a dramatic waterfall which falls freely into a sculptured concrete pool with colorful inward-spraying fountains.

Structural aspects of the center highlight precast concrete tilt-up exterior walls with the exterior ceramic facing bonded in a shingle fashion to the wall. The method of fastening the pieces and preventing the leakage of the cement around the joints in the shingle overlaps was developed in a test program before construction with the cooperation of the owner, contractor, architect, and structural engineer.

The method involved laying out the finish material face down on a casting bed in the tilt-up panel forms, hand-spreading about $\frac{3}{4}$-inch-thick mortar over the back of the units, placing a prefabricated reinforcing mat with tilt-up inserts attached, and placing the concrete before the mortar had set so that a complete bond was developed between the facing and the concrete wall.

Panels were lifted from the form on a three-day cycle and stockpiled in a vertical position for later attachment to the steel frame with a bolted connection at the top. They were dowelled and poured in at the foundation.

The enclosed interior malls have a raised roof which is supported on flexibly hinged columns above the storefront framing of the eight individual buildings on opposite sides of the malls. The structural system takes into consideration the earthquake code requirements. The buildings are seismically separated by this flexible construction. Seismic bracing consists of a unique system of rigid steel bents at the storefronts and X-braced frames at exterior walls and certain interior walls between stores. The final locations of these interior braced frames were established during the leasing of the store spaces.

The two major materials used throughout for the exterior walls—the ceramic shingles and precast concrete—give a unified effect to the entire center.

The center was developed by the Suburban Realty Co. of San Francisco.

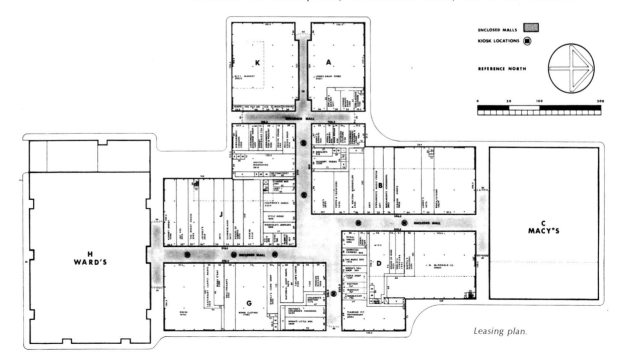

Leasing plan.

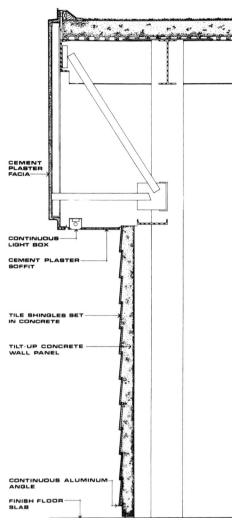

CEMENT
PLASTER
FACIA

CONTINUOUS
LIGHT BOX

CEMENT PLASTER
SOFFIT

TILE SHINGLES SET
IN CONCRETE

TILT-UP CONCRETE
WALL PANEL

CONTINUOUS ALUMINUM
ANGLE

FINISH FLOOR
SLAB

ABOVE: *Exterior wall section.*
ABOVE, LEFT: *Exterior view.*
(*Photographer: Wayne Thom.*)
LEFT: *Central plaza, Plexiglas sky-
light.* (*Photographer: Wayne
Thom.*)

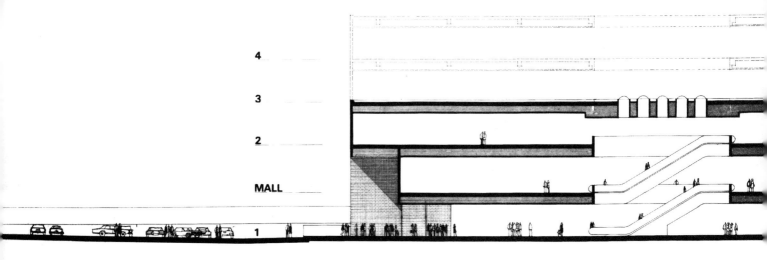

SHERWAY GARDENS
Toronto, Canada

ARCHITECTS:
For center and Eaton's department store:
   James A. Murray and Henry Fliess
For Simpson's department store and court:
   Searle Wilbee Rowland

This center, owned and developed by Sherway Center Ltd. (The Rouse Company), is situated on an 80-acre site at an interchange of two main highways in the western area of metropolitan Toronto. It is surrounded by a heavily populated urban area containing industrial plants and also commercial and residential areas that reflect nearly all income brackets.

The two-department-store center embodies a rather unique approach to questions of future growth, public spaces, and circulation as well as new thinking relating to human scale in the center environment.

The center was designed to be built in two stages. Stage one, includes two three-story department stores, two major food stores, and 125 retail stores, plus community facilities and executive offices, with a total gross leasable area of 750,000 square feet.

In Stage two the department stores will expand by two floors vertically to 350,000 square feet each and the retail store space will expand horizontally to a total of 450,000 square feet, giving a total gross leasable area of approximately 1,200,000 square feet.

The center was designed and executed on a team basis, involving representatives of the developer, the leasing principals, the architects and consultants, the interior designers, and the preselected general contractor.

The design concept for the base building was arrived at after an extensive period of exploration by the architects. A general contractor was then appointed. The work proceeded on a budget estimate toward subsequent confirmation of certain subtrades and a final translation to a fixed-sum contract. When the design concept was in an advanced stage of development, all the above-mentioned principals involved presented the basic concept to a large meeting of leading store designers and potential tenants so that they might make proposals in response to the design proposals.

In order to have a unified exterior design, the color and major materials were selected for walls and major department stores. The exterior walls between the department stores are of off-white matte-faced brick. The same material is used for the Eaton's department store. The matching off-white color in 2-by-4-inch glazed ceramic tiles (cast into large precast-concrete panels in the shop) is used in the exterior wall construction of Simpson's department store. Tenant work for individual stores was generally done by separate store designers and contractors. This was checked by the interior design consultants and coordinated for technical and mechanical implications by the architects and their consultants.

Colin Stephens, of Cranfield Stephens & Associates, prepared a tenant design brochure specifying materials and colors of storefronts along the S-shaped mall. Mall furniture was also designed by the same firm. With the exception of lighting standards, the furniture is custom-made beige or white molded Fiberglas, mostly tubular in shape. Chair seating is individual rather than bench type. These chairs have seat, back, and circular base molded in one piece. Tables, 20 inches high with 2½-foot-diameter round tops, are mushroom-shaped with lighted undersides. Waste bins are cylindrical on illuminated pedestal bases; ashtrays are miniatures of them. Store directory and fire-hose cabinets are 4-foot cylinders with the tops cut off at a 45-degree angle to provide a flat surface for lettering and for fire-hose housings. Triangular telephone stands, with concealed lighting in the base, each have three stainless steel pushbutton phones with privacy wings coming out from the center. The lamp standards, suggested by the architects and lighting consultants, are placed 20 feet apart in each mall section. They are 8-inch white metal tubes, 7 feet high. The lighting unit is concealed in the top and light is reflected off the ceiling. Each column has outlets for auxiliary flood- or spot-lighting fixtures.   (*continued*)

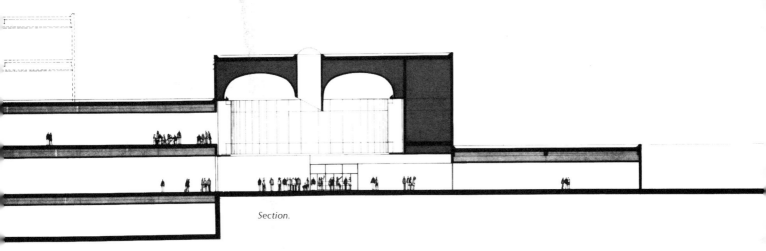

Section.

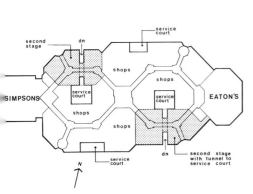

Floor plan showing future expansion.

ABOVE, RIGHT: *View of parking area and entrance from northwest. (Photographer: Panda/ Croydon Associates.)* RIGHT: *Aerial view. (Photographer: McCullagh Studio.)*

Court. (Design consultant: Gruen Associates. Photographer: Panda/ Croydon Associates.)

Cactus garden. (Landscape architect: George Tanaka. Photographer: Roger Jowett.)

Gourmet Fair, specialty shops. (Retail planners: Sherwood & Partners. Photographer: D'Arcy Glionna.)

Special attention in the design of the Simpson store has been given to the varying vantage points from which the building is seen. From the highways, the short time interval for viewing and the long distances dictated the need for a strong, distinctively recognizable form. From the parking areas, the mass of the building—with its indentations of entrances and mechanical areas—provides interest; while at close range, in contrast to the massive building, the bright-colored walls and lighted supergraphics of the entrances relate the building to the scale of the pedestrian and welcome the shopper. The form of the store acknowledges the merchandising requirement of windowless space in a vigorous manner. The store has entrances from both the lower and upper parking levels surrounding the building. It connects with the enclosed mall of the center by means of the Simpson's Court. There are a total of six entrances into the store. The soffits and walls of each exterior entrance are finished in glass mosaic tile, either green, gold, blue, or red. Forty-three super-graphic disks, 4 feet 6 inches in diameter, enclosed in 5-foot square boxes, are located at three entrances. Landscaping, flags and banner poles provide detail of interest on pedestrian circulation routes.

The Simpson's Court, between the store and the mall, is a domed area with a central light well. The court is finished with a black-and-white bull's-eye pattern on the floor, mirrored walls, and a domed ceiling with a skylight and rings of fluorescent paint. Neon tubing in red, yellow, and purple has been designed, and there are flashing black and fluorescent spotlights, psychedelic color effects are reflected to the floor. The Arcadian Court Restaurant on the second floor overlooks the domed court. The store's departments are fashioned as individual boutiques, each with its own distinctive decorative character.

One of the main features of Eaton's Sherway is the 6,000-square-foot court, which faces the store's mall-level west entrance and is one of the largest of the many garden courts. Dominating the Eaton Court is a circular fountain flanked by two crescent-shaped planters filled with tropical trees and plants. Sculptured masonry murals enhance the walls of the court.*

Gourmet Fair. Among the interesting innovations in the center is a farmers'-market-type area of 35,000 square feet. The Gourmet Fair, housing twenty-five independent merchants, includes prepared-food shops, florist shop, produce market, winemaking shop, tobacco shop, basket shop, and party favors shop. An interesting arrangement has been achieved by creating an irregular layout that gives the impression of being casual. This is helped by the ample public area which contains furniture for either stand-up or sit-down meals.

The floor is of quarry tile. Some columns are of plain, deep-colored wood and some of rustic copper metal. The furniture also uses the same basic materials—tables of copper metal and quarry tile surrounded by hassock-type stools of the same rustic copper metal capped with green cushions. The ceiling and walls, where exposed, are neutral in a dark brown, thus serving as a background for the many multicolored cloth banners hung from the ceiling. In addition to their color, they carry the various graphic designs of Gourmet Fair. These designs are also employed on some items of group-purchase packaging, such as book matches, shoppers' bags, etc. The object of these designs is to reinforce the merchants' efforts under the total Gourmet Fair "umbrella." The central public areas are lighted with a modest level of light, allowing the light from the tenants' areas to spill out onto the central area. Again, the aim of this approach is to focus the eye primarily on the tenants' merchandise.

*Reprinted with permission from *Building Management,* Canada, September, 1971.

Eaton's Court, one of three major courts in Sherway Gardens, where textures interplay. Here the hexagonal motifs of the sculptured wall are seen against clean gray tile; deep square wells of the grid ceiling stand out against a wall designed for film and slide projection; and fountains are set against deep green foliage. (Landscape architect for interior gardens: George Tanaka. Fountain design and wall mural: Count Alex Von Svaboda of Conn Art Studio. Associate architect: E. L. Hankinson. Photographer: Roger Jowett.)

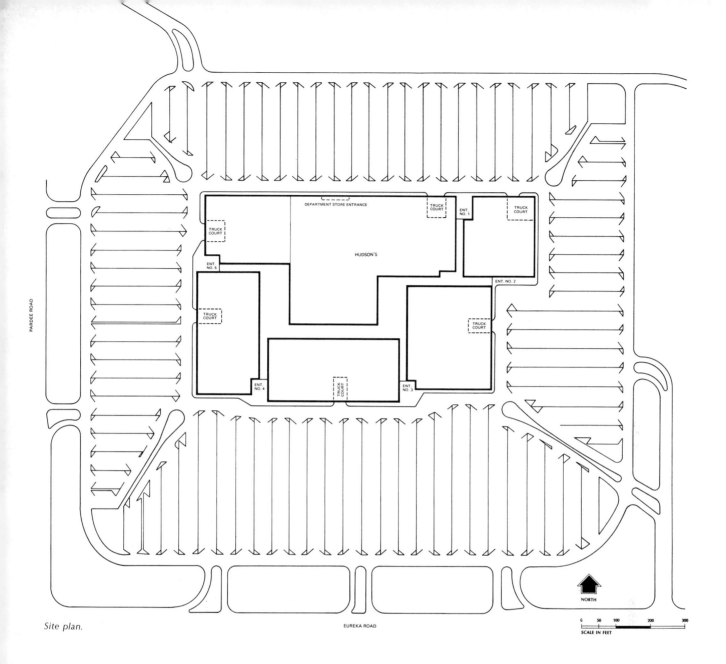

Site plan.

PARDEE ROAD

EUREKA ROAD

NORTH

0   50   100   200   300
SCALE IN FEET

Another example which emphasizes the importance of the main courts is this one-anchor department store center developed by Shopping Centers, Inc.

The concept of use of water as part of sculptural form is introduced in one of the courts as the main feature. In the other court, a large mural dominates one main wall. Both courts have freestanding sculptures by internationally known artists, extensive plantings, and intimate seating arrangements all designed to make the shopper's experience a delight.

Special attention is paid to the secondary entry arcades where plantings and artwork are also introduced.

SOUTHLAND CENTER
Taylor, Michigan

ARCHITECTS: Gruen Associates
ASSOCIATE ARCHITECTS: Louis G. Redstone Associates, Inc.

Cross section (perspective).

0   15   30   60   120
SCALE IN FEET

East court.
(Sculptor: Hubert
Dalwood.
Photographer:
Balthazar Korab.)

Mall showing plantings and lighting.
(Photographer: Balthazar Korab.)

Entry court.
(Sculptor: Morris Brose.
Photographer: Balthazar Korab.)

Exterior view showing parking area. (Photographer: Daniel Bartush.)

Interior mall. (Photographer: Daniel Bartush.)

SOMERSET MALL
Troy, Michigan

ARCHITECTS: Louis G. Redstone Associates, Inc.

This rather small but highly exclusive fashion mall aims to create an intimate and luxurious atmosphere. The single court is shaped so that, from the narrower entrances on each end (from Saks and from Bonwit-Teller), it widens to the central court featuring a fountain with space-frame skylight above. This plan enables the shopper to see almost the entire center at a glance. The feeling of elegance is achieved by the use of travertine-clad columns and a specially shaped plaster ceiling which envelopes the columns and gives a sculptural effect through variation of the ceiling levels. The same shapes are repeated in the terrazzo floor. The fountain is recessed and is reached from all sides by three travertine steps.

At each end of the court, the entries to the department stores are accented by a large, freestanding sculpture, one in stainless steel and one in bronze. The lighting is subdued by the use of incandescent lights and accentuated by a number of specially designed chandeliers. In addition, the skylights conceal indirect fluorescent lighting which adds to the outdoor night-lighting effects.

The exterior design departs from the many solid, unbroken surfaces of other centers by allowing each store to have a uniform awning-covered show window facing the parking area.

210

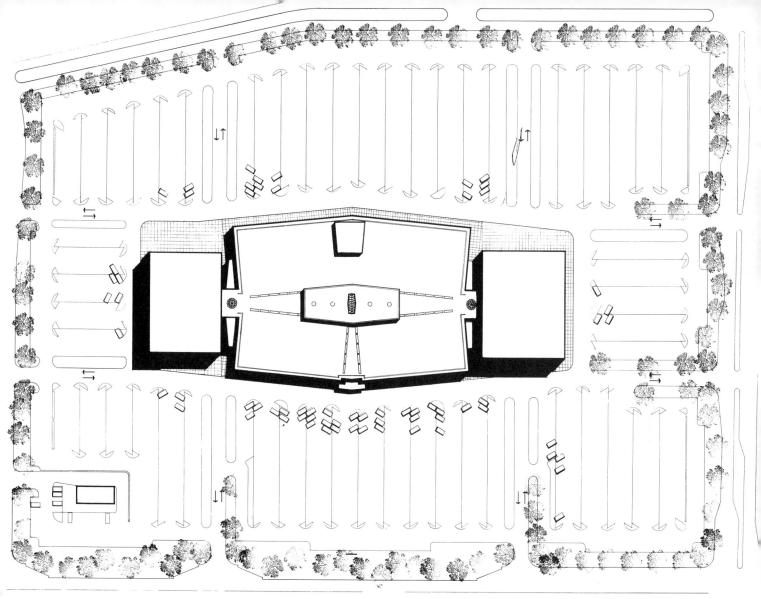

Site plan.

Interior court with fountain.
(Photographer: Daniel Bartush.)

Bronze sculpture facing mall from
Saks Fifth Avenue entrance. (Architect for Saks: Morganelli-Heumann &
Associates. Sculptor: Hannah Stiebel.
Photographer: George Robertson.)

Stainless steel sculpture facing
mall from Bonwit Teller store.
(Sculptor: Jan Peter Stern.
Photographer: George
Robertson.)

ABOVE: *Exterior view of center, ramp, and parking area.* RIGHT: *Center court. (Fountain design: Architect in Charge, A. D. Cole. Photographer: Eric Skewes & Associates.)*

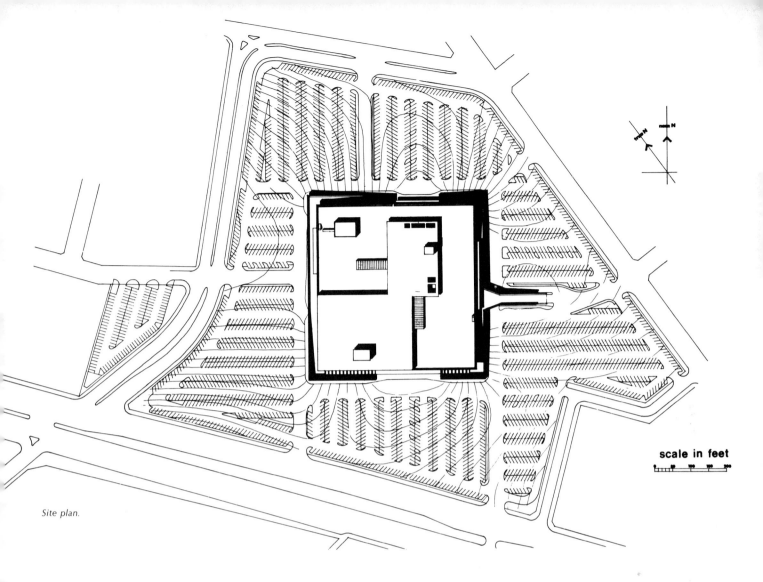

Site plan.

scale in feet

The problems inherent in multilevel centers are, first, achieving easy customer access from car parking to all shopping malls and, second, servicing shops without the expense and complications of planning a number of freight elevators. These problems were solved at Southland by contouring the site to provide direct level access from the parking area to each of the two main shopping levels and by providing a truckway, partly elevated and partly underground, in a complete circuit around the outside of the building. This led to the solution also of a difficult problem in shopping center planning—that of isolating freight handling from customer traffic. The truckway passes under the upper mall entrances and over the lower mall entrances.

As to the interior layout plans, the shops are located mainly at two levels, the Myer store being the only shop to extend to the third level. At each of the shopping levels a pedestrian mall 40 feet wide extends from one side of the building to the other, with a small wing at right angles near the center. At this intersection is a large court common to all three levels. A number of skylights provide extensive visibility between the various parts of the center and introduce daylight into the heart of the building.

Being more remote from the parking area, level three has been developed for those anciliary activities associated with regional shopping centers rather than for retailing itself. Apart from the Myer store at level three, there is an auditorium, a bistro, the center management office, a roof garden covering one acre, and a landscaped area for children's activities, i.e., a Christmas carnival. The bistro's terrace extends into the roof garden and is completely surrounded by water, which meanders through the garden, includes a waterfall, and is crossed at intervals by ornamental bridges. Water for the roof garden, a fountain in the center court, and gardens throughout the site is supplied from a well located on the site.

SOUTHLAND SHOPPING CENTER
Melbourne, Australia
ARCHITECTS: Tompkins, Shaw & Evans

For economy, simplicity in planning, and design continuity there is an extensive amount of standardization. The whole center is planned on a 2-foot 6-inch-square modular grid. The layout of columns, walls, ceilings and floors, and shopfronts and the spacing of lights, sprinklers, and air registers are all based on multiples of this unit. The ceiling tiles, which are 2 feet 6 inches square, and the 1-foot 3-inch-square floor tiles are specially made products. Recurring details such as shop window, sills and wall, ceiling fixtures of well balustrades, shop front glazing, doors, and rolling grilles are standardized. Stairs and skylights are also standardized within this module.

The building is of reinforced concrete construction. External walls are partly reinforced concrete with a white quartz aggregate finish and partly blockwork with split bluestone outer facing. All internal walls are of concrete blockwork. The ceilings throughout the building are inlaid tile on aluminum grid suspension. Floors of malls and courts are terrazzo tile.

Further points of interest are six large ceramic murals by Tom Sanders, a suspended copper fountain in the center court, external wall sculptures at each entrance built up from standard units, fiber glass play sculptures, planting boxes, litter bins, and directory tables by Architect in Charge A. D. Cole.

This center was developed by Myer Shopping Centers, Pty, Ltd.

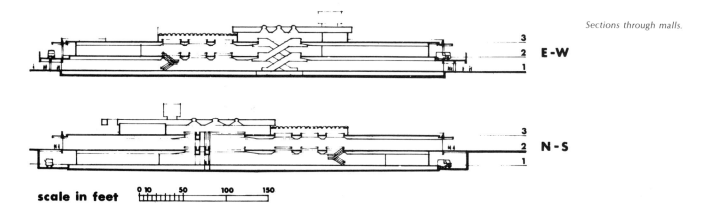

Sections through malls.

LEFT: Exterior view of center showing mall entrance. ABOVE: View of rooftop garden. (Landscape consultant: R. K. Skerritt. Photographer: Eric Skewes & Associates.)

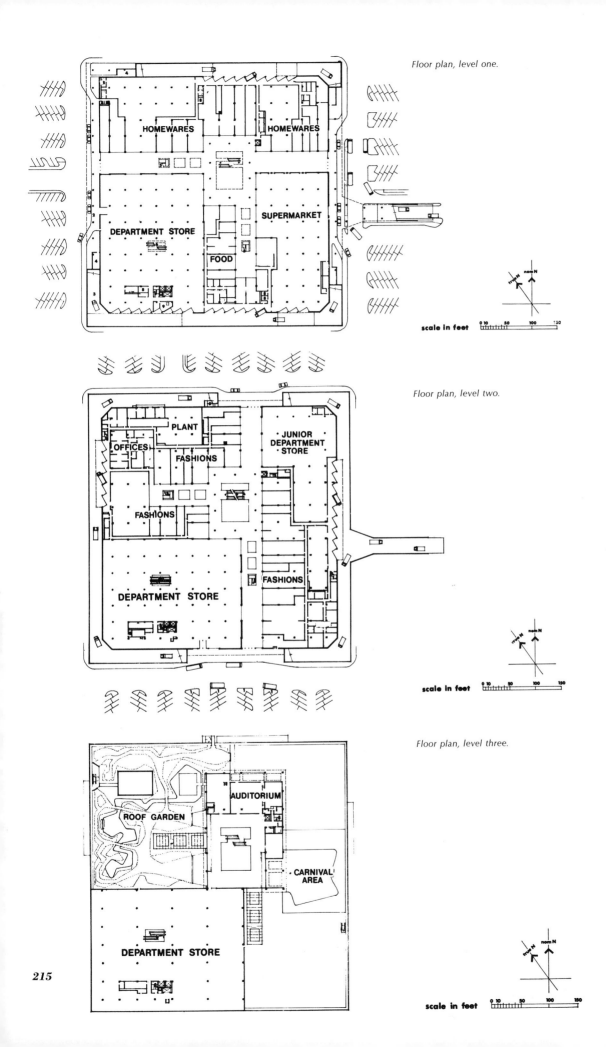

Floor plan, level one.

HOMEWARES

HOMEWARES

DEPARTMENT STORE

SUPERMARKET

FOOD

4

3

true N   nom N

scale in feet   0 10   50   100   150

Floor plan, level two.

PLANT

OFFICES

FASHIONS

JUNIOR DEPARTMENT STORE

FASHIONS

FASHIONS

DEPARTMENT STORE

true N   nom N

scale in feet   0 10   50   100   150

Floor plan, level three.

ROOF GARDEN

AUDITORIUM

CARNIVAL AREA

DEPARTMENT STORE

true N   nom N

scale in feet   0 10   50   100   150

This center near Dallas has a number of interesting innovations. The Y-shaped plan for the three major department stores shortens walking distances. Movement of shoppers is done by ramps, stairways, and escalators. Shoppers may walk a ramp to reach all the shops as they do in a linear mall, but they will choose the shorter, centrifugal ramps that ascend and descend, affording more options and variety. From the center of the mall, two-thirds of the shops of the entire center are visible.

The core area comprises a town bazaar—an element that holds great possibilities for the mall of the future—a place of density and high-level activity offering see-and-do things that generate spectator interest as well as shopping opportunities.

The 20-foot slope of the site permitted design of the shopping area on two levels—three counting a small boutique and snack bar area beneath the central core. This, with a balanced parking-lot configuration, permits several points of entry and tends to equalize the accessibility and visibility of the shop locations. Both levels, then, are main floors of which all doors may be considered main entrances.

Each level at the center has its own shopping sidewalks and direct access from the surrounding parking areas, while the clustering of the stores around an open core results in continuous horizontal and vertical circulation.

The focal point of the central space is a high steel pylon. This steel tube, 5 feet in diameter, is equal to a thirteen-story building in height and is the primary structural support for the central court. Like a tall tent pole, it lifts a fluted white ceiling.

This steel tube also serves as a major air-conditioning and artificial lighting source. At its top, a fifteen-foot-high clerestory skylight emits natural light into the court. Incorporated into its base, 15 feet above floor level, six rear-projection screens provide entertainment combined with sales promotion announcements—a flexible system for whatever use the management finds popular with the customers. A ramp, punctuated with displays, exhibits, and some landscaping, connects the shopping levels.

The roof, which appears to the interior viewer as a lofty canopy, suggestive of circuses and bazaars, is a steel ribbed umbrella of neoprene and plastic, held and made taut by steel cables. Guy cables from the top of the pylon take part of the load from the steel radial beams at their midpoints. Interior cables show like tent rigging.

Skylights pierce the big top, and the pylon penetrates to a clerestory 75 feet high. This glassed-in cone, lighted at night, is visible from afar.

TOWN EAST SHOPPING CENTER
Mesquite, Texas

ARCHITECTS: Omniplan Architects
    Harrell & Hamilton

: *Exterior view showing parking area.*
OVE: *Close-up of center court.* RIGHT:
Center court.

TYSONS CORNER CENTER
Fairfax County, Virginia
ARCHITECT: Lathrop Douglass, FAIA

This center, easily accessible from three major highways, is located on rolling ground on the southwest periphery of the Washington metropolitan area. The project contains three major department stores (Hecht's, Woodward and Lothrop, and Lansburgh's) and an 1,800-foot mall all on one level. The owner states that the length of mall is no handicap, but he wishes that he had provided more satellite space in his program. (Author's note: mall length over 700 to 800 feet is generally not advisable.) The project has a complete basement with a truck tunnel the full length. The basement is all rented, and some of its space contains high-rent offices. A second floor over a portion of the project also contains office space.

There is a large court with natural light in front of each department store and there are also courts halfway down each of the two major legs of the mall. At night, batteries of light on the exterior shine into the skylights, creating distant visibility. Supermarket and service stores are in a separate building.

The center is all electric except for the emergency generating equipment—four units with a capacity of 100 kilovolt-amperes at the central distribution plant plus a 25-kilovolt-ampere generator in each of the department stores. There is no individual metering; tenants pay for utilities on a square-foot basis as provided for in their leases.

Kiosks at the two main entrances to the mall provide high-speed coat-check service for shoppers. By means of motorized, closed-loop coat racks like those used by dry cleaners, attendants in the kiosks are able to press buttons that will bring a particular section of the rack up from a basement storage area in seconds. The developers are Theodore N. Lerner and Isadore Gudelsky.

218

Exterior of Woodward & Lothrop department store.

Exterior of Hecht's department store.

Main mall crossing. Arches faced with red cedar on concrete pedestals textured with exposed aggregate. Other than chandelier, all mall lighting is by concealed light coves. Photographer: Edmund Y. Lee.)

View from East Delta Freeway, foreground; Willamette River in background (perspective). (Photographer: Dudley, Hardin & Yang, Inc.)

This is a single-level two-department-store mall. The interior of the mall reflects the regional character by introducing materials indigenous to this area, i.e., red cedar in the main court and continuous cove in the skylight design. The fountain sculpture by Tom Hardy, a local artist, and the specially designed chandelier give added interest to the interior.

VALLEY RIVER SHOPPING CENTER
Eugene, Oregon
ARCHITECTS: John Graham & Company

Stair to second-floor professional offices and shops. Supporting column is turned wood. (Photographer: Edmund Y. Lee)

Section.

SHOPS   AIR CONDITIONED MALL   SHOPS SCALE 0 25 50

Site plan. (Architects: for J. C. Penny: Williams & Ehmann; for Meier & Frank: Baer, McNeil, Bloodworth & Hawes.)

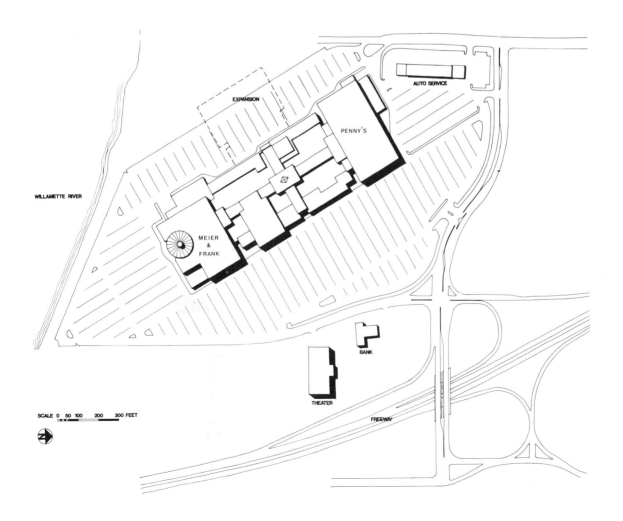

WILLAMETTE RIVER

EXPANSION

AUTO SERVICE

PENNY'S

MEIER & FRANK

BANK

THEATER

FREEWAY

SCALE 0 50 100 200 300 FEET

This center, located halfway between Detroit and Ann Arbor, was developed by Shopping Centers, Inc. It is a one-department-store two-level regional center.

The lower level includes a number of service stores and additional sales area for several major upper-level stores. The display and sales area for a large furniture store is located on this level (30,000 square feet), with the upper level designed as an open-well entry occupying a minimum space (1,600 square feet). Also on the lower level are the administrative offices and service truck tunnel.

The exterior has a unified design which uses two main materials: precast-concrete panels for the entire first story and brick for Hudson's department store. The solid effect of the exterior is softened by extensive use of sidewalk plantings around the entire structure.

A very difficult problem in handling a high water table was solved with a very unique construction technique. The plans called for an underground delivery service and a full lower level. With the existing high water level, it would have been next to impossible to excavate to the required depth without using a very expensive system to prevent the water from interfering with construction operations.

A technique which is often used in the building of seaports was decided upon. In this case it involved the construction of an underground waterproof wall, which enveloped the building complex, approximately 50 feet away from the perimeter of the building. The wall, approximately 30 inches wide and 20 feet deep (the depth of the hard clay layer), was excavated and filled with a liquid bentonite mixture. (Bentonite is a soft, clayish rock that absorbs moisture and, when mixed with water, swells to become watertight.) Once the wall, nearly ½ mile in circumference, was built, it served as a dike. Excavation for the building then began and the trapped water within the "dike" was pumped out by well points, allowing normal construction to proceed without any delays. This solution for the problem of building in areas with high water tables is highly recommended.

WESTLAND SHOPPING CENTER
Westland, Michigan

ARCHITECTS: Gruen Associates
ASSOCIATE ARCHITECTS:
 Louis G. Redstone Associates, Inc.

Digging of slurry trench.

Slurry trench.

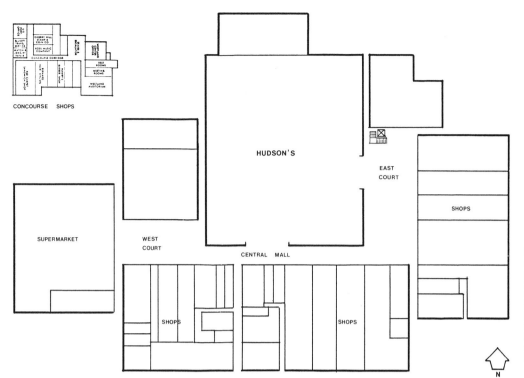

CONCOURSE SHOPS

SUPERMARKET

WEST
COURT

HUDSON'S

EAST
COURT

SHOPS

CENTRAL MALL

SHOPS

SHOPS

N

LEFT: *Floor plans.* BELOW: *Exterior view showing unified design using precast concrete slabs and brickwork for Hudson's department store.* BOTTOM: *East court showing entry to Hudson's department store, glass elevator, play sculpture, and second-floor restaurant. (Landscape architects: Eichstedt & Grissom Associates. Photographer: Balthazar Korab.)*

ABOVE: *East court showing clerestory plantings, special light standards.* ABOVE RIGHT: *Triangle Furniture Store, view from main sales area on lower level showing bridged walk above and main stairway leading to the court above. Note special patterned light design above bridge. (Architect for Winkelman's and Triangle Furniture: Louis G. Redstone Associates, Inc.* RIGHT: *View of balcony restaurant overlooking east court. Note special canvas strips designed to add color and reduce visual ceiling height. (Photographer: Balthazar Korab.)*

The problem was to design a privately financed residential community on a 42-acre site including low-rise multifamily dwelling units, support shopping, and recreation facilities. Ultimate development is planned for 1,200 dwelling units. The commercial facility is a multilevel strip center which contains 55,000 sq. ft. of leasable space for 21 tenants, with living units above shops.

The architect's principal consideration was to plan a viable environment for community life. The primary residential orientation is inward; away from the surrounding high-speed traffic generators. However, the function of the commercial facilities is dual: (a) to provide facilities which are integral to the residential village, and (b) to provide a service node for the surrounding neighborhood.

The open space concept relates to a progression of privacy, from intimate courtyards to landscaped pedestrian malls which form connectors to the large-scale recreation and lake area. The pathways around the man-made lake provide for access from dwelling units to the recreation and shopping facilities. Water, in the form of streams and waterfalls, feeds throughout the entire complex to the lake adding an aural experience to the visual continuity of the project.*

*Reprinted with permission from *The Texas Architect,* September, 1970

WILLOW CREEK
Dallas, Texas

ARCHITECTS: Ralph Kelman & Associates, Inc.
CONSULTING ARCHITECT: Hubert S. Miller, Jr.
LANDSCAPE ARCHITECTS: Naud Burnett Associates and
   Sasaki, Dawson, Demay Associates, Inc.

Shopping plaza with living units above shops.

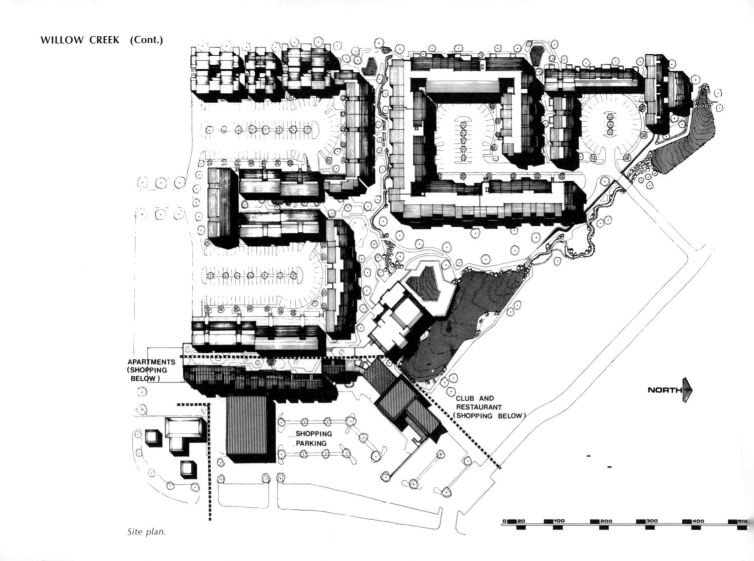

Site plan.

LEFT: *View of shopping area and living units.* BELOW: *View of shopping area.*

APARTMENTS (SHOPPING BELOW)

CLUB AND RESTAURANT (SHOPPING BELOW)

SHOPPING PARKING

NORTH

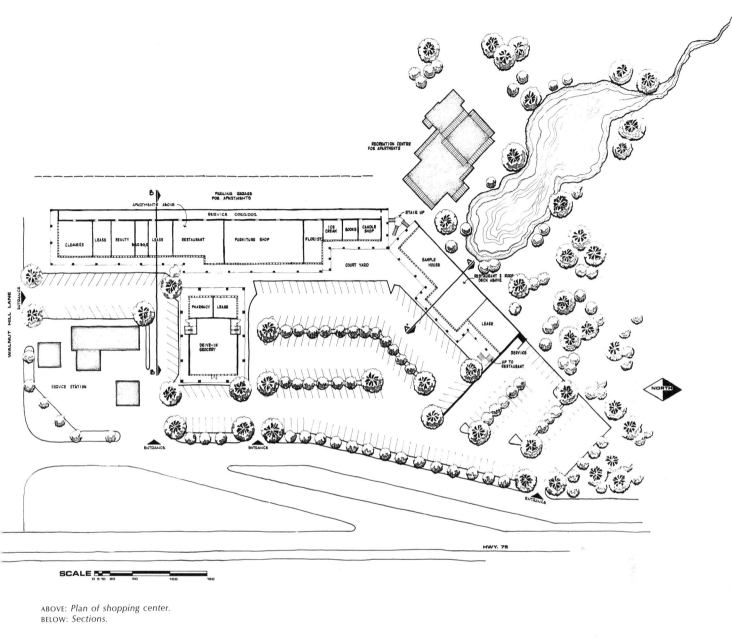

PARKING GARAGE FOR APARTMENTS

APARTMENTS ABOVE

B

SERVICE CORRIDOR

CLEANERS | LEASE | BEAUTY PARLOR | LEASE | RESTAURANT | FURNITURE SHOP | FLORIST | ICE CREAM | BOOKS | CANDLE SHOP

STAIR UP

RECREATION CENTER FOR APARTMENTS

COURT YARD

SAMPLE HOUSE

RESTAURANT & ROOF DECK ABOVE

WALNUT HILL LANE

ENTRANCE

PHARMACY | LEASE

DRIVE-IN GROCERY

B

LEASE

SERVICE

UP TO RESTAURANT

SERVICE STATION

NORTH

ENTRANCE

ENTRANCE

ENTRANCE

HWY. 75

SCALE
0 5 10 20   50   100   150

ABOVE: *Plan of shopping center.*
BELOW: *Sections.*

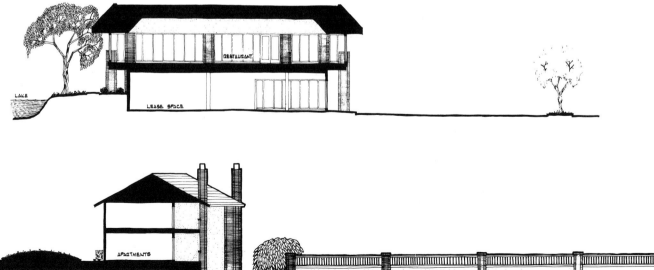

RESTAURANT

LAKE

LEASE SPACE

APARTMENTS

LEASE SPACE

Mall showing ceiling mural.

WILLOWBROOK SHOPPING CENTER

Wayne Township, New Jersey

ARCHITECTS: Welton Becket & Associates

This center mall in northern New Jersey is only 20 miles from midtown Manhattan and has a market potential for approximately 900,000 persons.

Each of the four department stores owns its land and has built its respective store. Construction of the first phase commenced with 106 specialty shops arranged in a single level between Bambergers, Sears Roebuck, and Ohrbachs. Second-phase construction began directly after. This addition included Stern Brothers and forty-eight specialty shops arranged on a two-level mall. The highlights of the addition are the entirely carpeted second level, the extensive use of skylights and interior landscaping, and a 300-car parking deck.

The site consists of 120 acres of carefully landscaped ground with some area left for other uses. Proposed long-range plans call for an additional high-rise office building, an inn, and cultural and recreational facilities.

A special feature of the construction is the exterior walls. These are tilt-up, cast-in-place concrete panels with blasted exposed-aggregate finish. Owner-developer of the center is The Rouse Company.

ABOVE, LEFT: *Exterior of Stern Bros.*
ABOVE: *Exterior of Bambergers.* LEFT: *Site plan. (Architects for Ohrbachs: Copeland, Novak, & Israel International. Photographer: Joseph Molitor.)*

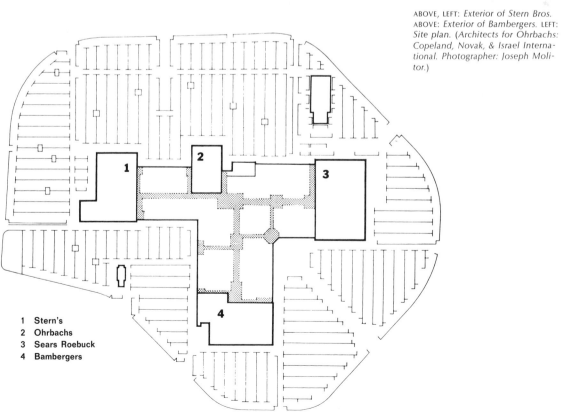

1 Stern's
2 Ohrbachs
3 Sears Roebuck
4 Bambergers

PART FOUR

Store Interiors

In this fast-moving age of changing values in every aspect of our life—social, moral, economic, artistic, and aesthetic—and with the youth seeking new and more stimulating sensory experiences, it is only natural that merchants are compelled to call upon the ingenuity of designers and architects to create new shopping environments. One might say that the traditional guidelines of the past are no longer valid.

For the first time, the designer has assumed complete freedom in using every means at his disposal—a wide range of new materials and innovations in the use of bright colors in strong, contrasting combinations and varied colors for the different departments. The designer is also making use of the variations of floor and ceiling materials and is creating unorthodox fixtures to display all types of merchandise to best advantage.

Peter Copeland of the firm of Copeland, Novak & Israel International, in his comments on future trends of commercial interiors, has this to say:[1]

> The store of the future will have a look that is modern, youthful, and exuberant. . . .
>
> The root causes of the change are, as always, the public's shifting demands and tastes. . . . What will be the changing scene in merchandise and design for the next decade or more? It is clear that it will reflect the influence of youth and of revolutionary art forms and the infinite variety of new materials in textiles, flooring, plastics, and metals. It will also reflect the adoption of modern backgrounds initiated by the style of the boutiques. . . .
>
> Probably the most forceful influence will be the growing acceptance of contemporary design forms on every front—clothes, homes, cars, offices, airports and airlines, TV, theatres, movies—in short everything that comprises the movement and color of our modern life style.
>
> Several merchandise changes have given rise to the new design concept. Obviously the influence of youth has resulted in a virtual upheaval of merchandise. Its predilection for active sports (motorboating, sailing, skiing, biking, motorcycling, camping, surfing) and its love of casual clothes (leather jackets, ponchos, colorful slacks, fake furs) have changed the entire complexion of sports departments. Its interest in recreational goods—cameras, records, transistor radios—and its yen for electrical appliances of every nature and kind have resulted in a tremendous expansion of hard goods. Its liking for the plastic chairs and modern lamps of Italian design and the Scandinavian imports of furniture, rugs, and tableware is beginning to change the look and feeling of home-furnishing departments.
>
> It would be wrong, of course, to assume that future stores will be designed mainly for the young. . . . Merchants recognize the importance of mature customers and will continue to cater to them. But they also recognize the fact that youth now sets the pace and elders follow. . . . The mature man has been so influenced by the colorful garb of youth that men's wear is expanding rapidly in all directions (thus the greatly increased space now required for men's fashions). . . .
>
> Some of the finer specialty shops catering to customers in very high-income brackets may want to cling to period backgrounds with crystal chandeliers and antique furnishings, but these will be few in number. . . .
>
> In the design plan for the interiors, these factors will be of paramount significance.

Significant Factors

> Expanded use of bold, brilliant colors, which have youthful flair and inherent decorating excitement, and of cinematographic and supergraphic art forms. The latter will be of particular importance for clear-cut signing and as striking wall decorations, replacing wallpaper and the use of fabrics for wall coverings.
>
> Elimination of valance treatments in favor of newer, imaginative techniques of hanging merchandise.

[1] Article from *Stores*, December, 1970, copyright 1970, NRMA.

Redesign of traditional islands, both in shape and centered treatment, as well as the redesign of racks and costumers, including molded forms.

Replacement of tables with advanced-design self-selection fixtures.

Introduction of new lighting systems (incorporating greater use of incandescent and quartz vapor lamps which give truer color values to merchandise) and of the European system of flexible light span (this involves a continuous grid for the entire ceiling, permitting the installation of lights and standards at any point in the store).

More intensive use of carpet, plastics, and metals.

Introduction of prefabricated and prefinished wall systems, and of modular prefabricated components of varying heights to subdivide space.

Development of techniques to overcome the growing problem of pilferage. These will include planning space for self-selection merchandise, which is purchased in the open and paid for promptly, as well as planning exits from various departments to make detection control possible.

Creating an Over-all Plan

Perhaps the most powerful weapon in making modern store design adaptable to successful merchandising in today's market is to create an over-all plan that highlights the merchandise to the maximum extent. Such a plan should reflect a use of space that accommodates easily to seasonal and other special exhibit demands and enables the merchandise displays to become a "movable feast." It should also reflect the newly developed and important technique of designing fixtures specifically suited to the merchandise displayed, instead of the outmoded method of accommodating merchandise to fixtures. These fixtures will widen the scope of self-selection without damaging the store's image.

It must be said that in shaping the stores of the future to have a contemporary look as well as a striking beauty and harmony of design, store designers face an enormous challenge. The wide array of materials, the wealth of new fabrics, the ability to utilize numerous avant-garde techniques—all these are wonderful tools. . . .

Needless to say, imagination and daring are essential, but these must be exercised with restraint and finesse so that the effect is one of such taste, wit, and sophistication that the public will find it both exhilarating and satisfying.

The importance of lighting cannot be overemphasized, and it is assuming a greater role in all the concepts being proposed. A few comments are in order at this point. To avoid a drab and monotonous lighting system, a combination of both incandescent and fluorescent lighting should be used. This would help create the necessary accents for special department displays where high-level lighting areas should be provided—all, of course, in conformity with the total concept of the interior store design. The aim, in general, is to eliminate the common objections: glare, reflections, and ballast noise (from fluorescent fixtures). Many of these objections can be overcome by recessing the light sources and shielding them from normal view and by installing as few light fixtures as possible. Another important element in store lighting design is the provision for variable lighting levels by the use of dimmers. These provide proper selling environments for different types of merchandise.

The interior lighting system for each store is determined by the store's interior design, quality, and type of merchandise and by its specific color rendition requirement. A minimum of 60 footcandles is required for general store merchandising, with accent lighting of much higher level for special displays.

This store is a series of three tubes, two of which are oval at different elevations, completely wrapped in carpet. The front, the men's department is off-white with black leather chairs and carpet-wrapped show selectors on the side. The ladies' department, which is in the center, is completely done in red carpet, including the seats. The rear is in silver mylar with different-color cubes and seats.

AGNEW SURPASS STORE
Fairview Shopping Center
Toronto, Canada
**INTERIOR DESIGNERS: Cranfield Stephens
& Associates**

Photographer: Michel Proulx

Decor features in the store are a combination of airport and industrial. The overall color is metallic gray. The airport motif starts at the storefront, of which two-thirds is a cutout of a large plane coming in for a landing. Entrance is through a second cutout at the right representing a billowy cloud.

Inside, the round, chrome-colored wrap desk (called the control tower) has at its back a panel of assorted cockpit instruments. Overhead, a cross of pulsating blue runway lights set on a bias runs the length and width of the store.

Also in the control tower panel is a microphone for a public address system over which "landings and takeoffs" and special sales are announced.

One of the industrial influences is a functional monorail conveyor system, similar to those used in clothing factories to move garments. The system, which runs along three sides of the store, is connected to the back room and is used in moving merchandise into sales position.

On the sales floor, double and triple hanging is used to display such merchandise as pants. Dresses, however, are only single-hung. Many dresses are displayed on S-shaped rods which wind through one side of the store. The S arrangement lets the customer see more of the dresses while at the same time increasing the number that can be displayed.

Charles Johnson, Vice President of Stuart Roberts & Associates comments: The basic merchandising theme behind this store was to find a familiar, everyday item that people are totally aware of and then use it and the elements surrounding it to provide an exciting format. From the very high production and gross sales that this store realizes, it was a very successful result. We have learned that today's shopper wants more than just merchandise. They want to be entertained. In each store we design, this aspect of entertainment is kept constantly in mind. The old approach to retail design—a home-like format with carpet, wood-paneled walls, pictures, moldings, valances, crystal chandeliers, antique chairs, just does not work anymore. The retailer competes for leisure time against other entertainment media, i.e., T.V., radio. He must provide amusement in addition to merchandise.*

AIRPORT BOUTIQUE
Main Place Mall
Buffalo, New York
INTERIOR DESIGNERS: Stuart Roberts
  & Associates

*Designer's comments reprinted by permission from *Chain Store Age,* Executive Edition. Copyright July, 1971, Lebhar-Friedman Inc., 2 Park Avenue, New York, N. Y. 10016.

APOGEE

ARCHITECTS: William Riseman Associates

▼ Newberry Street
Boston, Massachusetts

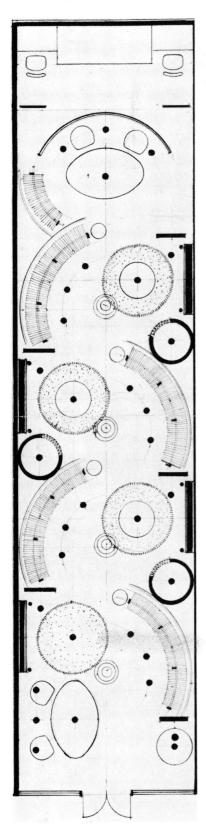

Floor plan.

Entrance and interior.
(Photographer: Leon Kunstenaar.)

The concept for the Apogee shops was conceived by Boston architect William Riseman and his designer wife. Prior to opening any of the shops, Mr. Riseman spent nearly a year developing the philosophy and goals for this new chain, selecting the proper name and symbol, and designing prototype stores that could be readily adapted to any type of location.

The design of the shops, like the symbol itself, is based on a series of expanding circles. There is a circular flow through the interior spaces of the shops implemented by circular racks, dressing rooms, and benches—all of which contribute to the orbital feeling that Apogee strives to convey.

Apogee 1, located at a "launching pad" on Boston's Newbury Street, resembles a rocket ship. Four "space compartments" and a "space caboose" are designed within a 14- by 65-foot area. Transparent fabric, curved walls serve as backgrounds for the fashions. Each compartment has its own cylindrical dressing rooms and large round hassocks on contrasting-colored circles of carpet. The graphic black and silver Apogee trademark, in oversized dimensions, serves as the decor throughout the shop. It also appears on shopping bags and is easily identified.

▼ South Shore Plaza, Braintree, Massachusetts

Sales area. This unique shop, designed to attract the youthful shopper into a traditional store, was inspired by the basic functional beauty of raw construction materials. Here, a hoist pulley strategically displays a kneeling mannequin. The mannequin, in turn, displays merchandise. Ladders and painters' extension planks on pulleys make flexible the movable shelving for mass merchandise. (Photographer: Robert Head Productions.)

BASKIN'S I-BEAM
Champaign, Illinois
INTERIOR DESIGNERS: R. W. Shipley Associates

BONWIT TELLER
Somerset Mall
Troy, Michigan

ARCHITECTS: Louis G. Redstone Associates, Inc.
INTERIOR DESIGNERS: Copeland, Novak & Israel
  International

This store combines traditional with contemporary styling within the framework of the latest techniques of store design, and it embodies in the interior layout—a series of separate spaces—the principle of shop definition. "Bonwit Teller," says Mr. Israel of Copeland, Novak and Israel, interior designers of the store, "represents a very specialized type of store. Its personality is a mixture of snob elegance, aggressiveness, young orientation. Youth—and its complementary ideas—is an important quality. . . ."

The luxurious character of the store is defined when one enters the T-shaped marble entrance hall, designed in the style of the late eighteenth century, where fashion accessories are displayed and sold and from which radiate eight of the twenty-two fashion shops. The focal point of this area is a free-floating glass-walled escalator that rises from a well of foliage. The spectator's eye is drawn irresistibly to the Richard Neas topiary and architectural mural on the background wall rising through to the upper level, the full height of the two floors.

In the transition from traditional to contemporary styles, the store incorporates many ingenious concepts, some of which create shock effects. An example is the Espresso Shop which reflects the young, swinging, far-out fashion point of view. Walls are of mirror squares behind adjustable and removable panels of varied sizes on ceiling tracks. The backs of these panels, painted hot pink or orange, reflect on the mirror walls, resulting in an Op Art effect. Another example is the Safari Shop, where the oak floor continues right up the side walls and is visible when the removable grasscloth-covered panels are relocated elsewhere.

The use of chandeliers, wall murals, oriental screens, period furniture in many areas as well as mod furniture, bar-type counter seats and colorful wall paintings in youth-oriented departments shows a change of pace from one department to another.

Piquenique Bar. This is a "swinging area" in the junior apparel department. Main features are dark-brown lizard-texture tile, contemporary walls with white and brown lacquered trim, contemporary sculpture, lighted panels forming fins which separate merchandise, and modern free-form foam furniture, brightly upholstered. (Photographer: Constance Hope Associates.)

Interior. Total flexibility characterizes Safari Room on atrium floor with natural and brown grasscloth-covered panels which can be eliminated or changed, revealing oak-faced walls and a continuation of floor. Mounted rattan baskets at top of windows simulate blinds. Fur rug is trompe l'oeil by Richard Neas. Yellow in draperies (not shown) is the only accent color. (Photographer: Constance Hope Associates.)

Interior. Shoe salon has pale gray velvet carpeting, English-style architecture, yellow accents in upholstery, and black ground mural adapted from a Chinese famille noire hawthorne pattern porcelain. (Photographer: Constance Hope Associates.)

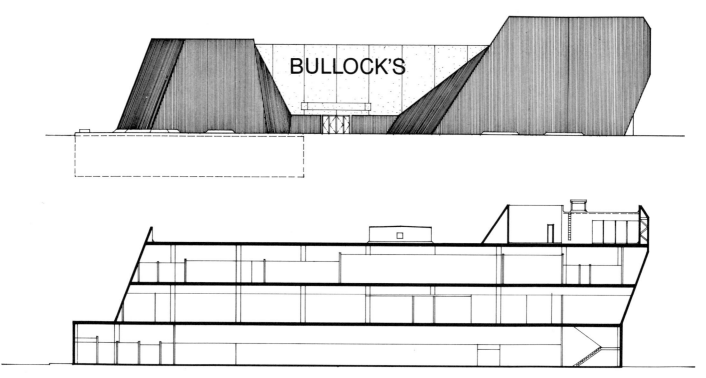

BULLOCK'S

Elevation and section.

BULLOCK'S
Northridge Fashion Center
Northridge, California

ARCHITECTS: Welton Becket & Associates

The design of this department store is a radical departure from the perpendicular and parallel lines usually associated with stores of this type.

According to Charles McReynolds, AIA, director of Becket's Los Angeles office, "the esthetic limitations of the formal box-like design are removed and replaced by the more dynamic sculptured pyramid effect."

On the exterior, earth-colored ceramic paving tiles, each measuring 8 by 16 inches, sweep up the sloped sides of the department store to create two free-form pyramidal volumes.

The store is windowless except for the entrance doors from the outside and from the mall.

Because of the sloping site, the entrance doors are located on the south first level and on the north and east second levels. Made of solar bronze, tempered plate glass, they offer subtle contrasts to the monumental walls. The recessed doorways, seemingly carved out of the walls, help protect the controlled interior lighting environment and provide cover during inclement weather.

The three-level store represents a deliberate break with tradition. In the store's 180,000 square feet of merchandising space, the designers have created a flexible theater lighting system with stage-setting enclosures, bright, vibrant colors and patterns, and simple, custom-designed fixtures.

On each of the three merchandising levels, a brilliantly lighted escalator well serves as the focal point. Tempered glass mirrors line the entire walls and ceiling of the three-story-high well and the sides of each escalator.

Once off the escalator, the shopper moves into spheres of generally subdued lighting with merchandising areas defined by the creative use of incandescent feature lights, bold color, simple abstract forms, large-scale patterned carpeting, carefully positioned fixtures, low partitions, and supergraphics.

Incandescent lighting, set flush into the ceiling, provides a general but minimum light level. But in all areas of the store, the ceiling also contains special feature lights—grids of incandescent light tracks, and each track holds adjustable flood and spotlights. By carefully adjusting the spotlights, the store can emphasize or deemphasize certain areas and easily create differing patterns and colors of light on the walls and merchandise.

To provide a sense of continuity, many areas reflect the exterior design through the use of slanted walls, oblique fixtures, and square, mirror-glass-covered columns set at 45-degree angles. Fixtures throughout the store are simple in design to avoid competing with the merchandise. Custom designed stainless steel and glass display racks in hexagonal shapes are meshed together in various combinations.

Other innovative fixtures include modular glass units, stacked against walls, for towels and linens; recessed wood cubicals, recessed into walls, for slacks; modular cubes of solar gray glass easily assembled in a variety of ways; and tables topped with opaque glass and lighted from within. Most of these fixtures were custom-designed by the architects.

Fixturing and partitions are easily movable to permit the maximum in flexibility when season or style changes require departments to expand or contract in size and scope, especially in the fashion sections. The floor has an electrical grid pattern which allows flexibility for these display changes.

Elevator.

Carpeting helps to identify individual areas of the store, such as the large red and blue square inserts in the Forerunner Shop; a rich golden tan color in the men's areas; patterns of small brown, violet, orange, and red squares in women's clothing; and an oversized chevron pattern in the children's sections.

Supergraphics enliven many of the store's departments and service areas. The art studio is identified by polished chrome letters, the girls' sizes 7 to 14 department by mirror letters, and the collegiate sportswear department by 4-foot-high characters across one wall. Elevators are also identified by supergraphics above the cab and on the door, repeating ELEV and ATOR from floor to ceiling. The V and A contain lighted up and down indicators.

In the first-level beauty salon, women sit in drying stations—twenty-one in all—set on semicircular tiers which gradually descend down to a stage used for demonstrations and small shows. Color television sets are inset in the backs of the chairs for the women's viewing pleasure.

In the silverware shop, the merchandise is displayed in a large carved out section of one wall, a recessed rectangle with curved corners. A sculptured free-form halo effect has been given the inside and outside entrances to the beauty salon and most fitting rooms have slanted, recessed entrances. Cut out wall partitions in the children's shoe department are painted in wide orange, pink, and yellow stripes which, along with bead lights, frame the shoe displays. Children can sit at the foot of the partition on a long black-and-white polka dot lounge.

The architect for the Northridge Fashion Center is Burke Kober Nicolais Archuleta. The developer is Gladstone & Company of Los Angeles.

Coffee shop. Two walls of the coffee shop feature orange, white, blue, yellow, green, and red angled stripes. Over the coffee shop's undulating counter are squares of tin letters, from an authentic old theater marquee, set in selected patterns against an illuminated backdrop.

Optical department.

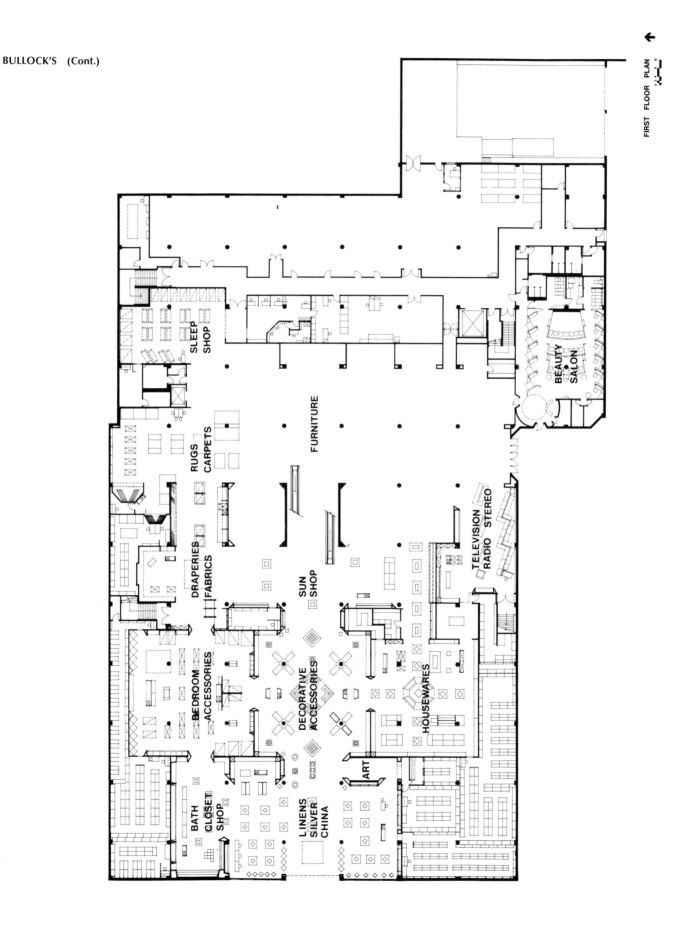

FIRST FLOOR PLAN

SLEEP SHOP

FURNITURE

RUGS CARPETS

BEAUTY SALON

DRAPERIES FABRICS

TELEVISION RADIO STEREO

BEDROOM ACCESSORIES

SUN SHOP

DECORATIVE ACCESSORIES

HOUSEWARES

ART

BATH CLOSET SHOP

LINENS SILVER CHINA

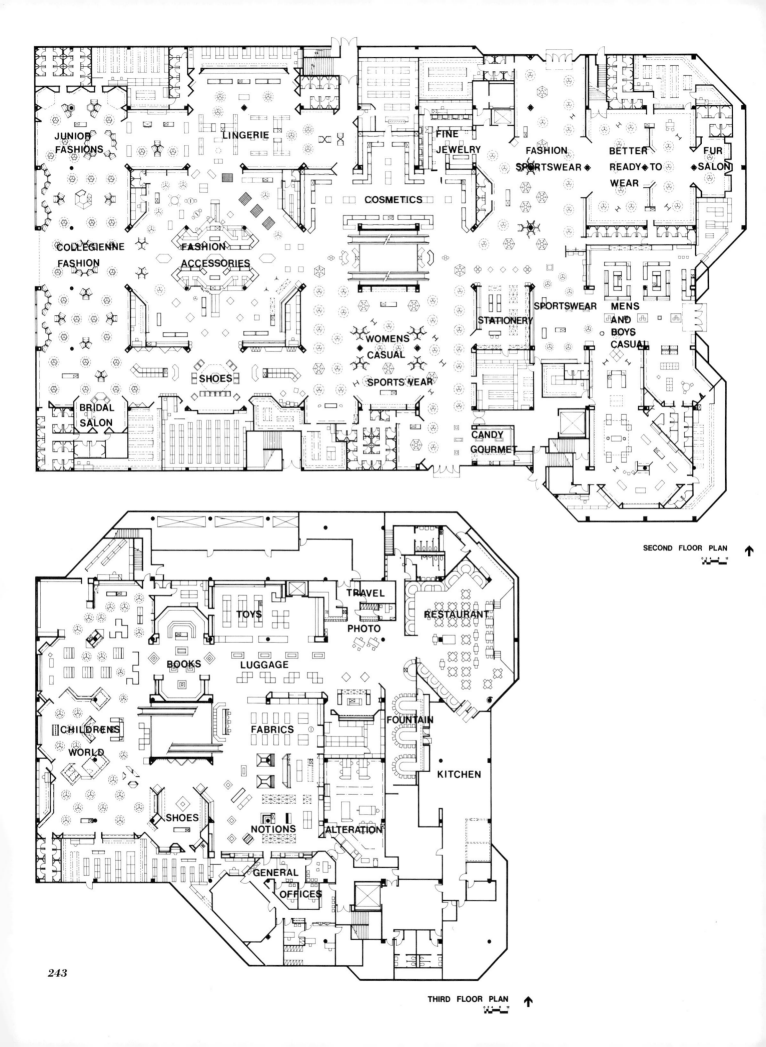

JUNIOR FASHIONS

LINGERIE

FINE JEWELRY

FASHION SPORTSWEAR

BETTER READY TO WEAR

FUR SALON

COSMETICS

COLLEGIENNE FASHION

FASHION ACCESSORIES

SPORTSWEAR

MENS AND BOYS CASUAL

STATIONERY

WOMENS CASUAL SPORTS WEAR

SHOES

BRIDAL SALON

CANDY GOURMET

TRAVEL

TOYS

PHOTO

RESTAURANT

BOOKS

LUGGAGE

CHILDRENS WORLD

FABRICS

FOUNTAIN

KITCHEN

SHOES

NOTIONS

ALTERATION

GENERAL OFFICES

BULLOCK'S (Cont.)

Beauty salon. Flanking the central drying area, the niches in an angled wall configuration are occupied by a total of eleven styling stations for washing and cutting hair.

A ceiling-high mural composed of offset wide squares in orange, white, and yellow dominates the wall behind the stage. Two rows of polished chrome ceiling fixtures holding clusters of clear globe lights help to illuminate the beauty salon.

Walls of the entrance alcove to the beauty salon are a spray-on polyetherene foam, a thick, formless substance that gives the area an intimate, cavelike effect. A rotating, many-faceted, mirrored ball, spotlighted from above, adds elegance to the area as it sends flickering spots of light cascading down the walls.

Decor of the beauty salon is a modern Moroccan, demonstrated by the bright yellow and orange patterned wall coverings and carpeting.

RIGHT: *Women's shoes.*
BELOW: *Bath shop.*

EDGAR CHARBONNEAU JEWELRY STORE

Place Bonaventure
Montreal, Canada

ARCHITECTS: Affleck Desbarats Dimakopoulos Lebensold Sise
INTERIOR DESIGNERS: Cranfield Stephens & Associates

Fascias are of base building oak.
Sliding doors and large panel in
center are of cast metals executed
by Gwen Jones. The wood fascia
runs into the store with a recess
above the central showcase island.
(Photographer: Michel Proulx.)

ABOVE, LEFT: *Parking lot entrance.*
LEFT: *Mall entrance.*
ABOVE: *Gift area. The ceiling is 16 feet high, with Gotham track lighting. The ceiling and walls are custom printed on shiny white vinyl with a design reminiscent of Matisse. The center fixtures are polished chrome and glass set on white formica bases. The perimeter cases are white lacquer and glass. The glass is brown-ribbed to recall color in the jewelry area.* (*Photographer: Leland Y. Lee.*)

The store was originally planned as a prestige jewelry shop. The designers suggested to the client that he add fine china and silver and a medium-priced gift area which would attract more shoppers. This approach worked out very successfully.

Also, since the store has two entrances, people are encouraged to use it as a shortcut from the mall to the parking area.

CHARLES NAYWERT LTD.
JEWELRY GIFT STORE
Desert Inn Fashion Plaza
Palm Springs, California

ARCHITECT: Wendell Veith
INTERIOR DESIGNERS: William Raiser, Arthur Elrod

246

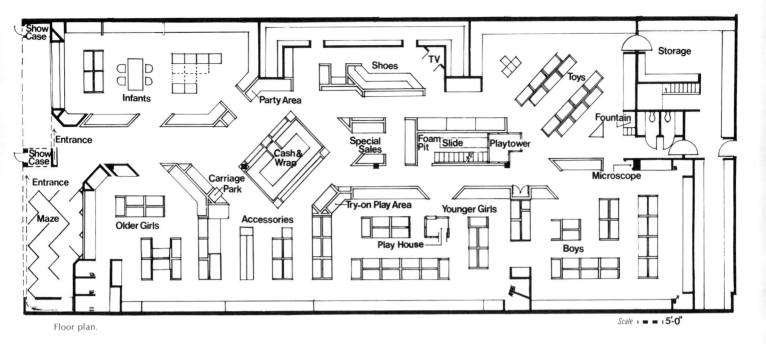

Floor plan.

Scale ⊢ ▬ ▬ ⊣ 5'-0"

The planning for three Children's Place stores (developers, Clinton A. Clark and David Pulver of West Hartford) takes into account "the tastes, physical capabilities, and psychological adjustments of children." According to George Nelson,

Future trends in stores, I think, will show a steady and probably rapid move from permanent installations to mobile interiors. The steadily rising costs are one factor and the acceleration of changing style trends is another. In other words, what I am looking forward to is a store interior which is to some extent expendable after a few years and to a high degree changeable.

According to *Interiors* magazine,

The Children's Place stores live up to their name: they're not just stores selling the whole range of infant and juvenile merchandise—they're fun places, whole mini-worlds replete with divertissements for the little ones. Mother can shop in peace while the kids explore the play house, the slide, and wishing well, the gerbils and goldfish, the fun-house mirrors, the maze, the tunnel. It is OK for children to play with toys set out on yellow island fixtures in the toy department (pilfering and breakage are minimal, and manufacturers are generous with floor samples). Play areas consume about 20 per cent of selling space, and they're worth every square foot of it in come-back appeal to children, the owners say. And much of what merchandising space Nelson gives away to play, he snatches back from the upper air, with overhead displays everywhere of clothing and toys. Colorful banners and hanging cylinders to identify departments further contribute to the carnival spirit.*

*Excerpted from article reproduced by permission from *Interiors*, issue of June, 1971. *Interiors*, article by John Anderson. Copyright 1971, Whitney Publications, Inc.

THE CHILDREN'S PLACE
Willowbrook Center
Wayne Township, New Jersey
INTERIOR DESIGNERS: George Nelson & Company

ABOVE: Wrap and checkout at the store center are housed in an island faced in white Formica. Counter faces are treated with hubcaps and (shown here) convex mirrors that amuse waiting children with a "fun house" device. Abstract-designed fixturing serves for display. (Photographer: Norman McGrath.)

RIGHT: Store entrance. Moving lights and a television screen on which children can see themselves are features of the store entrance. School-bus yellow walls bear the store logo and other graphics as decorative elements. Inside the central column, silver Tovi bulbs on a chaser begin a series of moving lights that continue into the store at ceiling height. To the right is another version of the children's special entrances—this time a Super Tube—an aluminum-sheathed and riveted fuselage. (Photographer: Norman McGrath.)

CRATE & BARREL
Chicago, Illinois

ARCHITECTS: **Richard Acott & Associates**

The problem of designing a retail store for fine glassware and accessories on a 25-foot lot in the old town area of Chicago was solved ingeniously by creating a warm, friendly backdrop for the interior merchandising by introducing special techniques for display, with the objects themselves affording the color and texture.

By clear spanning to masonry side walls with laminated wood beams and decking, a two-story main sales area was created, with an easily identifiable mezzanine area to the rear. Here, upon entering, the customers may readily orient themselves and obtain an idea of overall scope of the merchandise available. The interior space is further emphasized by the low entryway at the stair front.

The side walls on lower portions were paneled with crating lumber to keep the eye low and directed toward the merchandise. The upper portions of the walls are gypsum wallboard, painted white for relief.

The merchandise fixtures were custom-designed, constructed of crating lumber to resemble shipping crates. Fine, thin-stem glassware displayed in a "rough lumber box" creates a strong contrast. Barrels are used for dispensing bulk items.

A wood screen dominates the upper portion of the storefront to shield the two-story glass facade from the morning sun and reduce reflection during the daylight hours, yet it is open enough to permit the two-story structure to read through at night, which is the busiest period. Clear glass globes accent the screen and illuminate the sign, but they are not bright enough to detract from the screen's transparency.

First-floor plan.

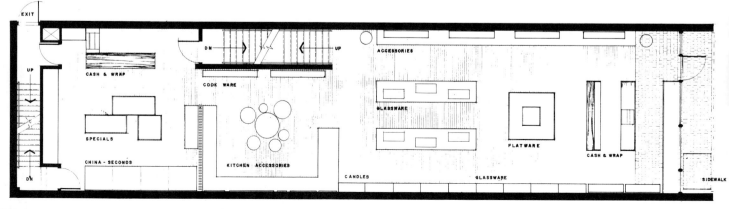

CRATE & BARREL, NORTH
Plaza Del Lago Shopping Center
Wilmette, Illinois

ARCHITECTS: Richard Acott & Associates

Unique features are the suspended fitting rooms with swinging tavern-type doors decorated with supergraphics and suspended dress racks that create an openness at the floor level. The concept also permits a greater range of display techniques, including the hanging of Finnish Marimekko fabrics and Swedish hand-blown wind bells.

In total, this store is a blaze of color ranging from brightly colored fabrics in dresses to a fascinating array of reds, yellows, and blues featured in cooking and dinnerware. These colors are enhanced by the beauty of natural wood.

RIGHT: *Entrance.*
BELOW: *Sales areas.*
(*Photographer: Hedrich-Blessing.*)

249

DESIGN RESEARCH BUILDING
Cambridge, Massachusetts

ARCHITECTS: Benjamin Thompson & Associates, Inc.
ASSOCIATE IN CHARGE: Thomas Green

The Design Research Building is the culmination of a design concept developed by architect Benjamin Thompson over a number of years. This is a five-story glass-enclosed cantilevered building. The basic construction is reinforced concrete. The round-column spacing is 20 by 20 feet and the slabs are cantilevered to about 12 feet.

Throughout the interior the concrete is left unfinished, but the exterior faces of the perimeter beams are sandblasted. The great sheets of glass are set back just 2-½ inches in the perimeter beams so that the horizontal lines are minimized and the building is expressed as a volume, rather than as a structural shape. The glass is ⅜ inch thick, tempered; and set into reglets—1½ by 1½ inches at the sill, deeper (2½ by 1½ inches) at the head for installation. The sheets are clamped to each other by stainless fittings, and the spaces between sheets and at the sill and head are filled with a translucent silicone sealant. . . .

An ingenious method for creating both an interesting ceiling pattern and adjustable lighting was used by creating a 2- by 3-inch grid of natural finish fir connected to 3- by 4-inch plates which are fastened to the underside of the concrete slab.

Lighting is by floodlights, mounted on simple and movable metal brackets hung from the tops of the fins, and served by cable set in spaces routed out of the top surface of the fins. The resulting system is not only inexpensive, but handsome. . . .

In most stores and shops you are primarily aware of displays. At Design Research, you are aware first of what is on sale—the rugs, the furniture; your eye directed by the use of lighting, or a huge panel of fabric, or the color of a rack of dresses. Then you are aware of the architectural background—the plane of the ceiling or the great walls of glass. Then especially above ground level, you become aware of the street and the city beyond; for just as the displays inside give the exterior its color, the views to the outside are a critical part, a critical impression, of the essence of the building. . . .

There are 27,000 square feet of floor space on seven levels (though there are essentially four floors above grade and a sunken ground level visible and accessible from the street). The reception area is a story-and-a-half high, offering glimpses into the display areas both above and below. This flow of space and color continues through the building, as shoppers move up and down the open stairwells. . . .

The shape of the building, with its bays and insets, is used effectively to create roomlike groupings of furniture set off with panels of colorful fabrics, lamps, and accessories.

The upper two floors are office space, reached by elevator from either the reception area or the rear courtyard.

Interior walls are unfinished concrete block; floors are variously brick, hexagonal ceramic tile, cork, or sisal matting. All hardware is stainless steel or chrome-finished.

The merchandise displays were designed by the architect. For example, much of the clothing is hung from stainless steel hoops suspended by simple brackets from the ceiling fins; and many of the racks for fabrics, hats, pillows, and the like are of the same fir as the ceiling and are integrated with it. Finally, much of the furniture on sale was designed by Benjamin Thompson (the building's architect) and built in D/R's workshops.*

*Parts of text are excerpts from *Architectural Record,* May 1970.

Ground and first-floor plans.

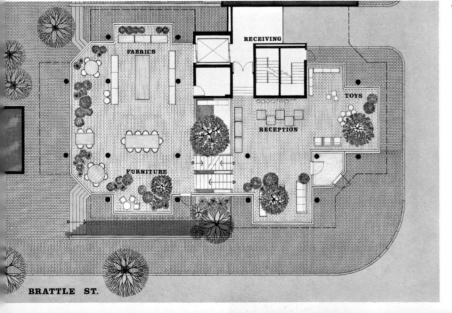

DIRECTLY ABOVE: *Hospitality shop and record department, respectively.*
ABOVE, LEFT: *Silver and china department.*
LEFT: *Gift shop.* (Photographer: Benyas-Kaufman Photographers, Inc.)

Howard Parker, director of interior decoration for Raymond Loewy-William Snaith, has these comments to make on the general trend of this department store design:

This store was planned and designed to meet today's challenges and to seize tomorrow's opportunities.

The department store must retain its role as fashion-setter while meeting the competition of discount stores and other lower-priced outlets. It must therefore reduce costs of selling without loss of prestige through advanced forms of fixturing; at the same time enhancing the sense of theater, the ambiance of overall elegance and status, that is the department store's great point of customer appeal.

The instant theater of the designs places the fixturing in an atmosphere that conveys the traditional attraction of status through colors and forms in the 1970's.

This combination assists the department store to meet the competition of costs; to build and expand its hold on its clientele; to widen the gap between itself and its competition; and to attract the new shoppers entering the market through economic and generational change.

An unusual feature of this department store is the special services provided for the customers: golf school, ski rental shop, driver training school. Other attractive features are three separate areas for cocktails, snacks, and festive dining.

HIGBEE COMPANY
Belden Village Shopping Center
Canton, Ohio
INTERIOR DESIGNERS: Raymond Loewy-William Snaith

Exterior.

Millinery department.

◀ *Juniors' department.*

◀ *Gift department.*

This department store deals in apparel only, and it includes a men's shop. The walls are dry walls, covered with vinyl fabric. Halle's is on one floor covering 50,000 square feet. All areas are carpeted with the exception of some small surfaces in the men's department and the entrances, which are covered in black tile. There is an artificial 20- by 116-foot skylight in the center of the store. Four colors of Plexiglas are presented in a random pattern consisting of an irregularly arranged sequence of rising and falling four-sided pyramids. Incandescent spotlights and sprinklers are arranged between these. For decorative purposes, a number of departments have curtain walls of translucent backlighted decorative glass frieze, brightly colored.

**HALLE BROS.
DEPARTMENT STORE**
Belden Village Shopping Center
Canton, Ohio

INTERIOR DESIGNERS: Gruen Associates

LEFT AND ABOVE: *Sales area.*
(*Photographer: Balthazar Korab.*)

Exterior.
[Photographer: Ezra Stoller (ESTO).]

Interior.
[Photographer: Ezra Stoller (ESTO).]

Interior showing supergraphics.
(Photographer: Hillel Burger.)

◀ **R**obert Alpern, the architect who planned the interiors for the second level of the Hudson Store, comments:

The basic program, initiated by the client, included planning, research, and design of spaces for the following functions: merchandise handling, maintenance and display, general offices and services, special customer services, photo studio, optical studio, beauty salon, restaurant, kitchen and employee dining, interior decoration studio and all sales departments. Furniture, major appliances, music and records, china, lamps and pictures, housewares, piece goods and patterns, toys, drugs, notions, closet shop, bedding and domestics, curtains and drapes, floor coverings, furniture, gift shop, bar shop, linens, bath shop, gourmet and culinary shop, and luggage, constituted the sales areas planned along with supporting stock areas.

The prime directives of this program were total flexibility, ease of altering departmental layout, ease of updating or changing the image of individual departments, and ease of store fixture replacement within a practical budget.

Vertical access and egress to and from this level is accomplished by four stairways, one passenger elevator, and one separate up-escalator located at the South end of the space and one separate down-escalator at the North end of the space. The positioning of the up and down escalators at opposite ends of the floor established a strong customer traffic pattern along the longitudinal axis of the floor. This offered the opportunity of exposure to as many sales departments as possible. All sales departments have been planned and designed as shops and boutiques with their own individual characters.

Color and materials including floor finishes have been selected for each shop and boutique to give the varied customer appeal to each: youthful, elegant, "Oppy," home-like.

J. L. HUDSON COMPANY
Franklin Park Mall Shopping Center
Toledo, Ohio

DESIGNERS FOR STORE AND INTERIOR:
  Raymond Loewy-William Snaith
ASSOCIATE ARCHITECTS:
  Louis G. Redstone Associates, Inc.
INTERIOR ARCHITECTS FOR SECOND LEVEL:
  Levine Alpern & Associates

HUGHES & HATCHER
Birmingham, Michigan

ARCHITECTS:
  Copeland, Novak & Israel International
ASSOCIATE ARCHITECTS:
Louis G. Redstone Associates, Inc.

Interior, showing glass elevator.
(Photographer: Jerry Dempnock.)

Interior.
(*Photographer: Morley Baer.*)

This is a freestanding specialty store in a shopping center. It has all dry-wall surfaces, rubber tile, and carpet on the first floor and carpeting on the second floor. There is a limited skylight over one bay on the second floor above a circular stairway. All lighting is incandescent except for strip lighting over wall fixtures. There are no art objects in the store, but extensive graphic and color treatment is used in specific areas. Plantings are omitted in the interior. The exterior is all light buff brick, white precast concrete, and amber anodized aluminum.

JOSEPH MAGNIN
Stonestown Shopping Center
San Francisco, California
ARCHITECTS FOR INTERIORS: Gruen Associates

256

The interiors of this store are addressed primarily to the young and the very active person with high flair for fashion. The reliance on materials and above all on colors, combined with a very significant use of light in all its available forms, has established an ambience which is characteristic of the Joseph Magnin image. The architects have tried to combine the quiet background with the pronounced accent free-floating within the space.

JOSEPH MAGNIN DEPARTMENT STORE
Fashion Valley Shopping Center
San Diego, California
ARCHITECTS FOR INTERIORS: Gruen Associates

Three interior views.
(Photographer: Marvin Rand Associates.)

JOSEPH MAGNIN STORE
Desert Inn Fashion Plaza
Palm Springs, California

ARCHITECTS AND INTERIOR DESIGNERS:
Skidmore, Owings & Merrill

TOP AND LEFT: *Exterior and interior.*
(*Photographer: Fred Lyon Pictures.*)
BELOW: *Floor plan.*

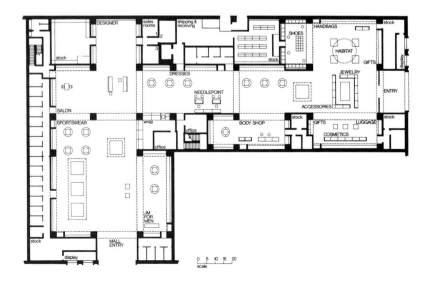

The design solution was to make a departure from the boutique concept of department store layout by utilizing design forms and graphics to define areas as distinguished from display elements.

There's a triangle to step through for sportswear, an oval to enter for shoes, a circle to cross for designer apparel—each rimmed in primary blue and boldly labeled in white.

There are no show windows in this store. All the action is inside, mostly under an orange-finished wood ceiling grid which conceals fluorescent tubes that bounce uniform light off the white ceiling. And at each point of intersection in the grid is a hook for a potential hanging display.

Every fixture in the shop was designed by the architects to be part of the display act: the black and white circular hanging racks with integral lighting in their overhead funnels, white cube and cylinder pedestals, clear glass open shelves, the bright red central raised platform—in which the wrap desk is housed—that can support in style any sort of display, including the live rock group staged there for opening festivities.*

*Excerpted from article reproduced by permission from *Interiors,* issue of March, 1971. *Interiors.* Copyright 1971, Whitney Publications, Inc.

JOSEPH MAGNIN STORE
Fashion Square
La Habra, California

ARCHITECTS AND INTERIOR DESIGNERS:
Skidmore, Owings & Merrill

Interior views.
(*Photographer: Fred Lyon Pictures.*)

Floor plan.

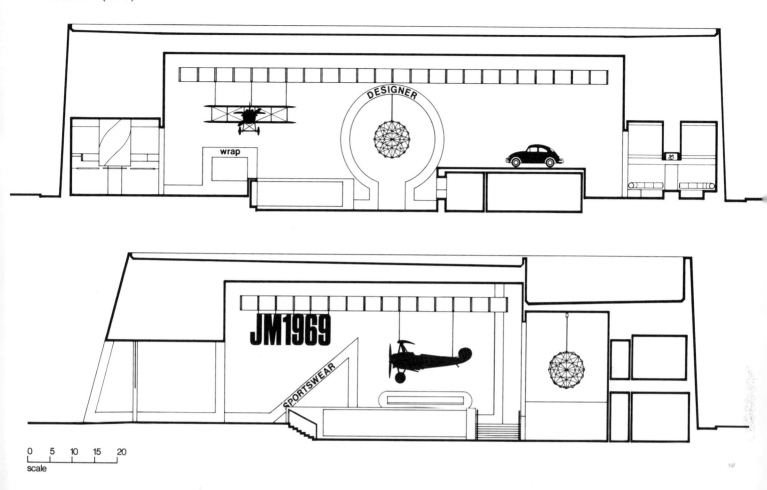

ABOVE: *Section.*
LEFT: *Interior.*

The front of the store accents black granite against white marble with large glass openings and curving forms. On the interior, rich colors and textures make a good backdrop for the leather goods and accessories. Wood parquet floors and custom display tables of teak and chrome are used to sell briefcases, attaché cases, wallets, shoes, and women's purses. Accessory items are prominently displayed in a gazebo set on a raised platform in the center of the store. The gazebo has mirrored walls on the interior to create an impression of more space. Luggage is displayed on a raised area at the rear of the store. This area is carpeted with rich burnt-orange plush-pile carpeting, which is also used on the display platforms. Twelve custom-designed lighting fixtures provide light as well as a decorative effect in this area.

In general, the store design reflects the prestige of a merchandising firm established over a hundred years ago.

MARK CROSS LTD.
Somerset Mall
Troy, Michigan

INTERIOR DESIGNERS: Mayer & Kanner, Architects

Entrance.
(Photographer: A. E. Aperavch.)

Interior sales area.
(Photographer: A. E. Aperavch.)

LEFT: *Exterior. Soft white precast panels. Vertical circulation by central elevators supplemented by corner stairway expressed as part of exterior. Stairways also serve fire stair requirements.* RIGHT: *Entrance to Neiman-Marcus from Collins Avenue; men's clothing to right. Toiletries with mirror-faced showcases directly ahead. Elevators in background. This floor as well as upper floor are both open areas with no partitions between departments, creating expansive feeling.* FAR RIGHT: *Two circular glass elevators located in center of store with skylight above animate vertical circulation between the selling floors. Customers are momentarily on "center stage" and get a glimpse of selling areas on the floors. [Photographer: Ezra Stoller (ESTO).]*

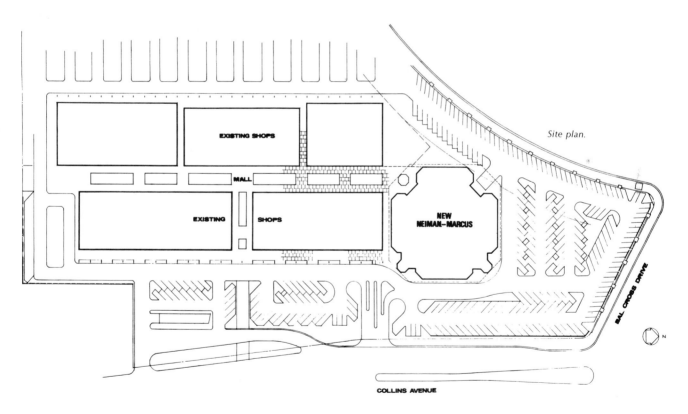

Site plan.

NEIMAN-MARCUS

Bal Harbour Shops
Bal Harbour, Florida

INTERIOR DESIGNER: Eleanor Le Maire
  Associates

In commercial interiors, our point of view is the result of successful design response to changes in our clients' business requirements, flexibility regarding our clients' needs, and programs both present and future which must be integrated with our professional work to achieve a satisfying end result. Trends as such are not a significant tool.*

*Comments by Director of Design Robert Malderez of Eleanor Le Maire Associates.

NEIMAN-MARCUS

Galleria Post Oak
Houston, Texas

ARCHITECTS: Hellmuth, Obata & Kassabaum, Inc.
INTERIOR DESIGNER: Eleanor Le Maire
  Associates

Better apparel shop. This large, semienclosed, and gently curved room serves as the major axis from the bridal salon to the fur salon, making of the three areas a great suite of high fashion across this end of the floor. The specially designed rug and custom furniture express the Neiman-Marcus approach to quality. This department is screened from the traffic aisle by an arched bronze and Carpathian elm fixture displaying fine accessories. The room itself is developed to capture the romantic feeling of eighteenth century Venice with a special carpet in greens designed to suggest the classic geometry of inlaid marble. True reproductions of Italian chairs, sofas, and benches of the period were hand-carved in New York of wood imported from Italy. Four large, hand-carved, gilt Venetian mirrors hang on the walls and offer sparkling contrast to the curved rear wall containing, in individual recesses, the couture collection. A large center display for merchandise presentation also serves as a focal stage for seasonal fashion presentations. [Photographer: Ezra Stoller (ESTO).]

The Nonesuch Shop. The young juniors shop, with glass enclosed entrance, is the only shop in the store so separated. It expresses the age of the young with its own sound and "beat" and "way." Floor is of white polished vinyl; the fixturing is white, low, curved, circular, and outlined with bands of tiny lights. Fitting rooms, opening directly on the shop, are constructed of canvas stretched and laced on white metal frames, printed pattern on pattern, color on color, all stressing the clean-cut impact of white. [Photographer: Ezra Stoller (ESTO).]

LEFT: The blouses and belts gazebo. Area near the main entrance, which is also part of the accessories department, is accented with a white trellislike overhead structure creating a separate identity. [Photography: Ezra Stoller (ESTO).] BELOW: Vertical light and mirror glass sculpture. A 25-foot vertical light and mirror glass sculpture is suspended to define the open escalator well in a bold concept to unite the three floors in with a single visible work of art. [Sculptor: Stanley Landsman. Photographer: Ezra Stoller (ESTO).]

The building, contemporary in design, is of all-white metal sheathing. The metal panels are curved at the corners, top and bottom, over a base of dark reddish-brown split-face concrete brick. Entrances cut into both metal and brick base, form the sculptural motif in the overall design.

The interiors harmonize with the building's facade in design concept. Abstract modern graphics in many colorful designs play an important role in the overall scheme. They are used on walls and ceiling, where they serve not only to identify the individual shops but also as unifying elements and signs of introduction to the interior of the store.

On the lower level of the store, which the shopper enters either from the entrance on the mall or the one on the parking lot, the three major merchandising zones (men's, boys', and girls') are delineated by varied and subtle color themes. Each color theme is established by the carpeting—which is copper in the men's department, a soft blue in the boys' area, and persimmon in the girls' department.

The upper level, devoted wholly to feminine fashions, also has its merchandise zones defined by color themes, but here they are in bold, brilliant colors—hot pink in the area comprising the shops for intimate apparel and shoes, purple in the area where the shops for juniors and young juniors are located, and a sharp lime green in the area devoted to coats, suits, dresses, sportswear, and furs. The accessories form a cross, radiating from a central well to the three entrances. In the center well a specially designed light fixture consisting of twenty-four circular globes is suspended from a polished chrome mirrored ceiling. Since the fixture, with its sculptural quality, is reflected in the ceiling, a striking decorative effect is achieved.

The ceiling lighting is a combination of fluorescent and incandescent, with an extensive use of quartz line incandescent.

OHRBACHS

Woodbridge Center
Woodbridge, New Jersey

ARCHITECTS & INTERIOR DESIGNERS:
Copeland Novak & Israel International

TOP: *Mall entrance.*   ABOVE: *Shoe department.*
(*Photographer: Constance Hope Associates.*)

Interior display.

RCA EXHIBITION HALL
Rockefeller Center, New York

INTERIOR DESIGNERS: Ford & Earl
Design Associates

"The basic requirement," according to the designers, "was to represent RCA succinctly through its diversified corporate activities—which include more than just displaying TV sets. The tie-in factor or theme is information: RCA is an information oriented company."

Exhibit vehicles for the company's products are large graphic displays set into environmental shells. Dedicated TV viewers, however, will see the shapes as the familiar TV tube.

With forty-six graphic panels in all, the total world of RCA, both corporate and consumer, is brightly shown.

Using brilliant shades of hot pink, aqua, fuschia, bright orange, parrot green, and lavender, each shell interior and graphic panel is covered with felt, with plush velvet carpet in a matching color placed on the bottom.

"We used carpet because the material is typical of most residential interiors."

These individual color statements are set off through the use of off-white in the floor tiles on the textured surface of the shell exteriors, and on the walls and louvered ceiling.

The graphics on each panel and in each shell are direct three-dimensional expressions of the total "information" theme while at the same time creating an imaginative and unique setting for the display of RCA products and services.

SAKS FIFTH AVENUE
Somerset Mall
Troy, Michigan

ARCHITECTS: Morganelli-Heumann & Associates
INTERIOR DESIGNERS: Copeland Novak
 & Israel International

ABOVE: *Interior stairway.*
LEFT: *Men's sales area.*
(*Photographer: Constance Hope Associates.*)

Exterior.
(*Photographer:
Yoshio Shiratori.*)

An interesting feature is the supergraphic signs on the exterior and the mirrored effects of the wall designs.*

 *Reprinted with permission from *Japan Interior Design Magazine*, January 1970 issue.

SHU PUB
Takashimaya Shopping Center
Tamagawa, Japan
ARCHITECT: Minoru Takeyama

STREETER & QUARLES WEST SHOP
San Francisco, California

ARCHITECTS: Robert Mittelstadt, Monte S. Bell

The architect utilized a difficult space by introducing a series of platforms that float at varying levels. Entry is via a bridge over the lower sales area, which was created by lowering the ground floor.

The shop's high-impact design message registers at the street: a nylon spinnaker sail with the shop's colors and SQW logo flutters over the sidewalk; a wide-flange structural beam of Plexiglas carries the store name across the shop's 25-foot frontage; broad bands of glossy red and blue with the logo in shiny mylar run straight from the outer east wall through the recessed glass facade and into the shop.

The shop's transparent and reflective-glass shelves and glass-paneled platforms with clear acrylic display trays are suspended by airplane wire.*

*Excerpted from *Architectural Record*, February, 1971. Article by James D. Morgan and excerpted from article reproduced by permission from *Interiors*, issue of March, 1971. *Interiors*. Copyright 1971, Whitney Publications, Inc.

RIGHT: *Entrance.*
BELOW: *Interior.*
(Photographer: Jeremiah O. Bagstad.)

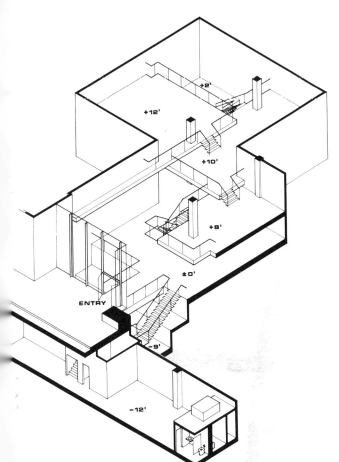

ABOVE: *Section.*
RIGHT: *Street level and mezzanine plan.*

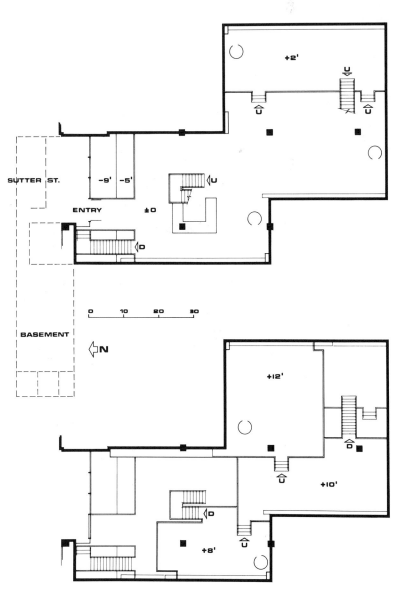

SUTTER ST.

ENTRY

BASEMENT

N

Display and sales area. The store is designed for tight quarters and the style is experimental with a Victorian interior, still an attraction for many shoppers. (Photographer: Alexandre Georges.)

Cash and wrap area.

The Subway is a separate entity in the basement of the Woolf Brothers store in the Plaza. It has its own street-level entrance off the parkway as well as an elevator and stairwell to the men's and women's store above. This central stairwell is enclosed to enable the Subway to have its own background music and hours of operation. The Subway caters to the youth market with its own young men's and women's shoe, clothing, cosmetic, and gift departments as well as a photography department and a "build-your-own" cafeteria.

The modular sales system is of industrial rack piping usually used for cattle pens in the Kansas City area. The ceiling has exposed structure.

According to architect Dr. Justus Dahinden, the purpose of the Swiss Fair is to give, in limited space, an idea of modern Switzerland—her efficiency, capabilities, and quality of workmanship. The idea was to create not merely a cut-and-dried exhibition atmosphere but an animated setting for traditional food and interesting information through eye-catching graphics in a sympathetic and gay atmosphere.

The main entrance on New Coventry Street has the shape of a cubist copper sculpture, like a modern tavern sign. Its structure symbolizes the Swiss mountains and in a sense points to the underlying principle of the unity of the Swiss nation. A special attraction is the pleated, multicolored canopy above the ramp and the colorful designs and heraldic symbols which represent the Swiss communes and federalism. An antique church-tower clock not only gives the exact time but serves as a testimony to one of Switzerland's most important export articles.

The Market Square is situated at a somewhat higher level and four restaurant areas are grouped around it. It is the central forum symbolizing the four distinct regions of the country, each with its own language and culture. The four restaurants, the Chesa, the Locanda, the Taverne, and the Rendez-vous, are so arranged that each one affords a view of the other and all are easy to overlook from the raised platform of the market square.

The Chesa, by its style and atmosphere, recalls famous high-class restaurants in Swiss winter resorts. Suggestive of the ruggedness of the mountains and the architecture of mountain dwellings, as well as the coziness within, is the heavily structured white wall with its nichelike illuminated recesses. The color scheme of the drapes and fittings underlines the character and stark beauty of the region. The antique doorway from the Engadine represents the old handicraft of bygone times.

The Locanda, with its bright awnings and its artistic play of colors, has a sunny atmosphere. The varicolored chairs, lamps, dishes, etc., all combine to create a gay and lively mood.

The Taverne, a wine cellar, is well visible from all sides. Wine, one of the most typical Swiss products, is featured in the architectural design by a ceiling of dangling wine bottles. The impression of a wine cellar is further stressed by weathered wood from old wooden railway sleepers, which is used throughout the interior area.

The Rendez-vous, a cafeteria-type restaurant, features a large mural depicting the driving of cattle to the Alpine pastures in eastern Switzerland. The walls are faced with conventional shutters, from old houses in central Switzerland, through which the light from outside can penetrate. On the other hand, these shutters let the eye wander beyond the limits of the room over the expanses outside.

The Shopping Center, with its Gourmet Corner, has the unconventional atmosphere of a typical Swiss modern drugstore, with woodwork and a rustic wine cellar built of stone and highlighted by a beautiful antique wine press. Three adjoining shops offer typically Swiss articles such as watches, Bally shoes, and Ryf cosmetics. An inside staircase connects the Shopping In Switzerland area with a gallerylike first floor where an elegant perfume shop, a large hairdressing parlor, the Swiss Fair offices, and the showroom of Anglo Swiss Catering Equipment, Ltd., are located.

SWISS CENTER
Leicester Square
London, England

ARCHITECTS:
For Center: David du R. Aberdeen & Partners
For Interior of Shopping and Restaurant Levels:
  Dr. Justus Dahinden

CLOCKWISE, FROM TOP: *Entrance, with copper sculpture. (Sculptor: Sven Knebel.) Chesa Restaurant, with doors from the Engadine. (Designer of inn sign: Margareta Willi-Dubach.) Interior of Taverne Restaurant. Lobby, with Swiss specialty shops.*

UNITED CIGAR STORE

Ville d'Anjou Shopping Center
Montreal, Canada

INTERIOR DESIGNERS: Cranfield Stephens
& Associates

*Island kiosk constructed of oak, shown in closed and open positions.
(Photographer: Michel Proulx.)*

WALTON PIERCE COMPANY

Somerset Mall
Troy, Michigan

ARCHITECTS: Louis G. Redstone Associates, Inc.
INTERIOR DESIGNERS: Ford & Earl
  Design Associates

Elegant understatement serves as a subtle backdrop for optimum display of the collections of Walton-Pierce, an exclusive women's shop located in this high-fashion center.

Located midway between Saks Fifth Avenue and Bonwit Teller, the design criterion established was to maintain the sophistication of the parent store while focusing attention on its heavily trafficked corner location in order to attract the elite clientele the shop is geared to accommodate.

By combining velvets, brocades, wool, and rosewood in a monochromatic color scheme within a very plastic space, elegant tradition is maintained in a contemporary idiom. Using a high ceiling, creating arches, and eliminating corners, the problem of a narrow 40-foot store is solved by blending walls into ceiling and thus creating an impression of infinite space.

A structural column intruding into the space is painted out and employed as an axis for three custom-designed jewelry cases, each highlighted by a chrome stool covered in brandy-color velvet.

The neutral interior with its limited color range and materials, permits the clothing to dominate. The soft contours of the space highlight the fabrics and lines of the clothing.

Sand-finish plaster was selected for the walls, providing textural contrast to the handsome materials of the furnishings. Incandescent lighting, selected for its flattering quality, is recessed into the ceiling and display areas.

The mottled effect of the cut-pile carpeting complements the texture of the crushed velvet chairs. The warm gray of the carpeting is repeated in the upholstery. The same carpeting is used for the bases.

With minor exceptions, all items are custom-designed. Freestanding lighted display cases, designed with rear storage drawers, are covered in brocade, with warm gray suede-vinyl display surfaces, and framed in rosewood. Secondary points of interest are provided by the two large display cases recessed into the south and east walls. Rosewood, used to delineate the glass shelving, is repeated below in the storage unit.

Hats are displayed on simple rosewood cylinders which appear to float from the wall-mounted polished chrome rods. As with all displays, the custom-designed hat bar is wall-recessed to add privacy for the customer. With the exception of the rosewood desks provided for the manager and assistant manager, custom-designed sales desks and chairs are treated to blend in with the background.

272

ABOVE: *Interior.*
LEFT: *Floor plan.*

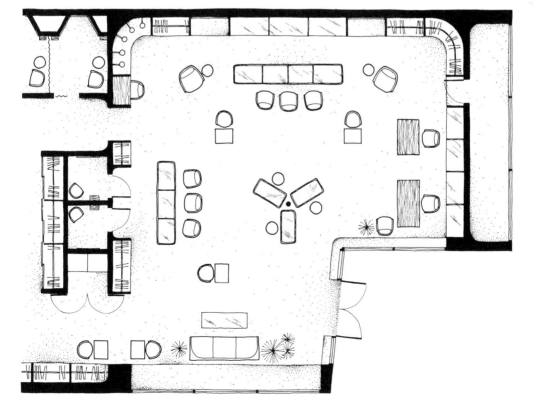

A characteristic inherent in the American way of life is the tendency to discard objects which show signs of wear, old styling, or malfunctioning. This is accompanied by an emotional detachment toward preserving things that relate to almost all phases of present-day living, including the homes we live in, the stores where we shop, and even our communities.

This is much in contrast to the European attitudes on the way of life, which were based on a less demanding standard of living. Urban European families remained in the same neighborhoods for many years only partly because of economic conditions. There has been in the past and still remains a feeling of attachment to their habitat. Through the years, they added improvements which suited their specific needs and reflected their tastes and habits. Economic conditions also compelled them to be frugal. Often the same clothing was worn by a continuous succession of members of a growing family by ingenious recutting and restyling of suits, coats and dresses, frequently turned inside out more than once! Compare this with the average low- or middle-income American family of the present day, where slightly worn or out-of-style clothes are discarded more often than not. And this readiness to discard used things typifies the American attitude toward shelters also. The abandonment of any old or partially deteriorated residential or commercial building, even though it is structurally sound, has been more the rule than the exception in nearly every large American city. It was only at the end of the late 1960s that those leaders and groups interested in historic preservation were able to give a new lease on life to the plans of preserving certain single structures or groups of historic buildings or neighborhoods of entire blocks and streets. Governmental authority to declare these worthy of preservation and reconstruction is now incorporated in the law. The Urban Design and Development Corporation, a nonprofit corporation established by the American Institute of Architects in 1969, has been acting as a catalyst not only in stimulating the preservation of the urban residential community but also in saving the quality and integrity of historic structures. According to Ralph C. Schwarz, president of the Urban Design and Development Corporation, there is a growing trend to rework historic buildings into tourist entertainment attractions, often with the wholehearted endorsement of the preservationists. He warns that there must be a real regard for the original fabric of the structures and a dedication to retaining the identity and quality of antiquity if preservation is to prove an urban asset.

CANAL SQUARE
Washington, D.C.

ARCHITECTS: Arthur Cotton Moore/Associates

This development, by Canal Square Associates, is the preservation of a historic landmark involving complete renovation, new construction of offices and shops, and the creation of a shopping arcade through partially historic row structures. The architect comments:

This project was simply stated: an inexpensive speculative office building, since a market for major office space could not be easily justified economically at the time of planning. Indeed, the few existing area office structures were small and precarious economically.

As part of the design solution commercial and civic aspects were added. The overall evolved mix was 25% mercantile to 75% offices.

Additional program constraints were respect for the neighborhood, historical preservation, design acceptable to the Georgetown Fine Arts Commission, and full realization of the existing high zoning density (meaning the largest project to be constructed in Georgetown in 70 years).

Although the image of northern Georgetown is well established in affluence and prestige, the area south of M Street is largely a blighted industrial slum. In particular, the immediate project area was a discordant mix of a machine shop, a fish dealer, a car wash, a funeral parlor, and a furniture mart interspersed with a sprinkling of residential buildings with a largely transient population.

The site itself was used for low-grade storage, parking, and rubbish collection. The major old landmark warehouse structure, which turned out much later to have an intriguing history as the wellspring of IBM, was on the skids. It had last been used as a greeting card warehouse and then had stood vacant and for sale for two years, suffering continuous vandalism and weather damage. Its tree-lined orientation on the C&O Canal was a notorious gathering point for derelicts. The previous owners felt that the only proper solution was total site clearance for a parking lot. Further site constraints were (1) the presence of two very historic small-scale houses and (2) the problem of designing a structure that would be large enough to be profitable and yet not conflict with the scale and character of Georgetown.

The site was an irregular assemblage of city lots, having for vehicular access only a small section along 31st Street and a narrow ten-foot-wide alley on the north, no access on the west (because of private property), and none on the south because of the C&O Canal.

The decision to keep the old warehouse on the site meant that the site was further constricted and that these structures had to be completely underpinned in order to construct the two floors of underground parking required by zoning. Soil conditions were good and solid rock was encountered only during construction of the sump pump pit. Water was found in the construction of the lowest level but was not excessive, and it remains a minor maintenance problem. Because of the historic nature of the area, many unrecorded underground utilities were found, complicating the construction process.

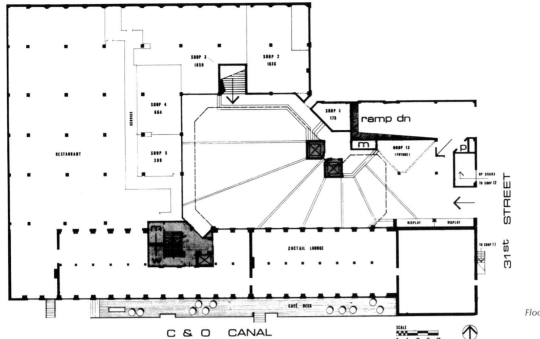

Floor plan, lower level.

SHOP 3
1650

SHOP 2
1836

SHOP 4
664

RESTAURANT

SERVICE

SHOP 5
399

SHOP 6
175

ramp dn

m

SHOP 13
(FUTURE)

p

UP STAIRS
To SHOP 12

31st STREET

DISPLAY   DISPLAY

COCTAIL LOUNGE

To SHOP 11

CAFÉ DECK

C & O   CANAL

SCALE
0 5 10 15 20

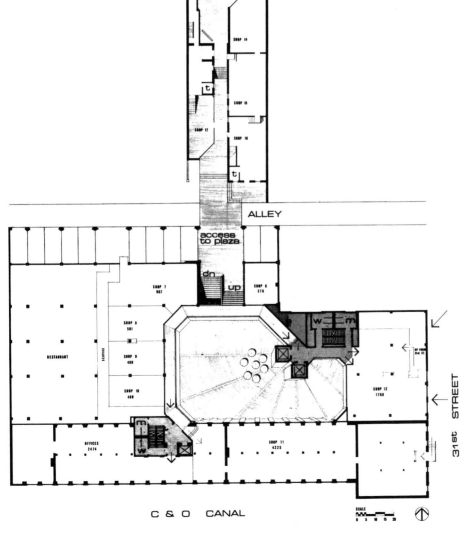

Floor plan, upper level.

M STREET

SHOP 14

t

SHOP 15

SHOP 17

SHOP 16

t

ALLEY

access
to plaza

dn   up

SHOP 7
907

SHOP 6
376

SHOP 8
581

w   m

RESTAURANT

SERVICE

SHOP 9
480

UP FROM
31st ST.

SHOP 10
480

SHOP 12
1768

31st STREET

m

OFFICES
2474

w

SHOP 11
4225

C & O   CANAL

SCALE
0 5 10 15 20

The cost per square foot, which was economical considering the difficult and pioneer nature of the project, was $17. Because of the difficulties involved in underpinning the old building, the necessity of gutting one portion of the old structure for safety, and the general complexity of the project (eight buildings are involved: two old ones for the arcade, three new, and three old warehouses) the final cost ran to $17.20 a foot prior to tenant improvements, the cost of which were largely borne by the tenants as a condition for leasing.

The design solution was to exploit rather than demolish the resource of the old warehouse, particularly its repetitive, industrial, no-nonsense character, and to carry this image around the corner in a new building and up 31st Street in the form of an L, thereby presenting an appropriate scale and character to the public streetscape of Georgetown.

The major bulk area needed to make the project economical was itself shaped into an L, forming Washington's first urban, purely pedestrian square. The square was lengthened and further refined with an introductory square in order to respond to the narrow yet open architecture of the old warehouse, to accommodate the main office core, and to provide a greater visual dimension to the open space itself.

The development of an arcade through to M Street, to give the project exposure to M Street and to tap its important pedestrian circulation, was a major early design decision. Because of the variety in levels, the main square was dished in order to expose the old stone foundation walls of the historic structure. Once opened, this area could respond to the C&O Canal, where a cafe deck has been built. The arcade could thereby have a split-level relationship to the square, resulting in the development of two levels of commercial space.

Although the project began with respect for the old warehouse, the conception of a real town square for Georgetown and for Washington, with a mix of outdoor cafes, shops, offices, post office and public amenities was central to the development of the project. Although a core was provided for the old building, the elevators for the new main buildings were dramatized in order to increase the visual sense of place. Old salvaged elements, sympathetic materials, and extremely spartan metal sash were used throughout to tie in old with new.

Many special features—the drain chain, parking solution, mechanical integration, unique signage, and intimate new-old transitions—although interesting, have been made subordinate and contributory to the overall project.

Accessibility to the handicapped was considered, and there is no main portion of the project which is not available to an unaided person in a wheelchair, via the gentle ramp from 31st Street and elevators, although a few spaces would require a roundabout circulation.

Even though it is important to reiterate that the economic program demanded an inexpensive, speculative office building, through the use of simple detailing, of steel sash and brick, higher rentals were achieved than those in the downtown area.

Having four lobbies, one of which is completely open, and nineteen shop entrances, the complex is not just another makeshift in the landscape with the routine single marbleized entrance lobby, but a human square, a participatory space which fits with good manners into the fabric of Georgetown and the city in general.

Garage entrance.
(*Photographer: Norman McGrath.*)

Outdoor elevator.
(Photographer: Peter Dodge.)

Exterior.
(Photographer: Joshua Freiwald.)

THE CANNERY
San Francisco, California
ARCHITECTS: Joseph Esherick & Assoc.

The old Del Monte Fruit Cannery is a San Francisco landmark that was spared by the 1906 earthquake and fire and stands at the foot of Columbus Avenue overlooking Fisherman's Wharf. The problem to be solved was the conversion of this fine, tough old masonry loft building into a complex of eating, drinking, shopping, and entertainment areas in the middle of the city. Unlike suburban shopping centers which have space to sprawl on one level, this one had to rise vertically. But then, people must know immediately there is an up; people must see other people moving up, and then they must see other people up there.

The center has open arcades on upper levels, an open escalator, many broad, open stairs and an outdoor elevator—all with the idea of making it obvious that a lot is going on at the upper levels.

According to the architect who designed this challenging project and who studied the characteristics of shopping centers in Europe and the Americas, one dominant similarity emerged—the absence of any elaborate explanations or signs. One should see what is being sold. It was decided to adapt this idea of a crowded, open-air market by permitting the architecture to set off the products being sold rather than vice versa.

The architects wanted to retain the rich, exciting feeling of a marketplace which enables a person to go through the place in a clear and obvious way but still gives him the option of getting lost. Thus, there are enough turns, zigzags and corners in the center to offer a hint of a maze.

Inside the center, shoppers on different levels become an integral part of the total scene. The great number and variety of methods of going up and down (there are seven internal and external staircases, two passenger elevators and escalators) all are organized to emphasize the "upness" of the center.

ABOVE AND BELOW: Interior court and open escalator. (Photographer: Joshua Freiwald.)

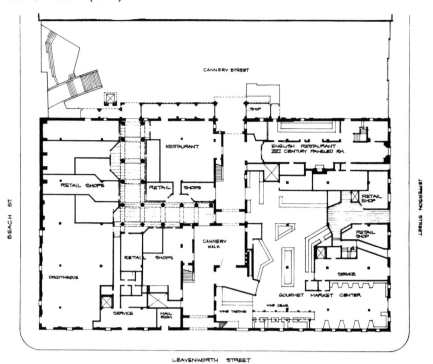

First-level plan.

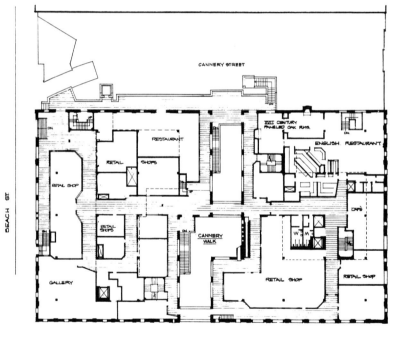

Second-level plan.

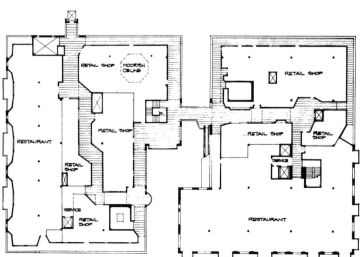

Third-level plan.

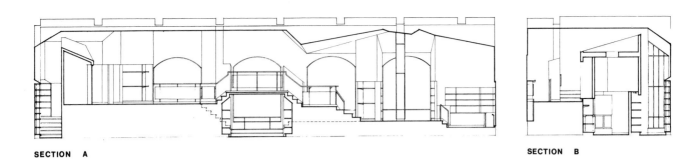

SECTION A

SECTION B

STREET   SIDEWALK

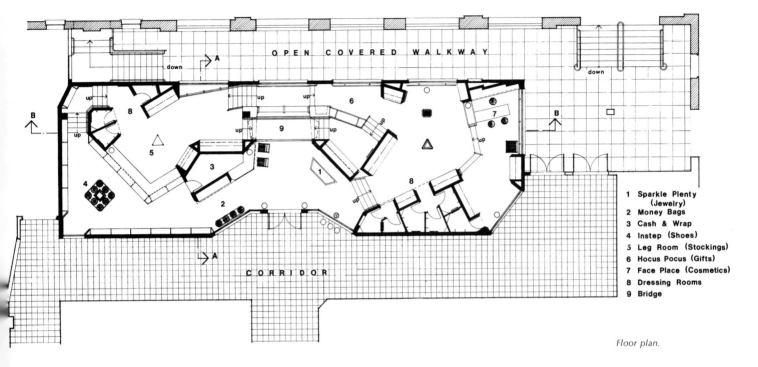

OPEN COVERED WALKWAY

CORRIDOR

1 Sparkle Plenty
    (Jewelry)
2 Money Bags
3 Cash & Wrap
4 Instep (Shoes)
5 Leg Room (Stockings)
6 Hocus Pocus (Gifts)
7 Face Place (Cosmetics)
8 Dressing Rooms
9 Bridge

Floor plan.

This mod fashion shop for young women typifies the gay atmosphere which characterizes the concept of The Cannery.

The main concept of the shop is based on the idea that buying clothes can be an event; that women enjoy the possibilities of role playing and changing roles while trying on clothes; and that they enjoy an audience for this sort of "theater." Thus the shop is arranged to dramatize the process.

It is a long high space with many large windows looking on a main entrance and public walks of The Cannery. Each window frames a place in the shop where various activities or "events" occur, yet all the spaces flow into each other and long vistas are obtained. Levels are arranged reminiscent of a stage to help the dramatization; the circulation doubles back over itself via a glass-sided bridge. Thus the windows really become show windows—not for static display of mannequins and merchandise but for the much more interesting "live" show.

A "now" look is enhanced by the free use of mirrors on walls and ceilings and reflecting chrome elements. All remaining materials are glass, carpet, and painted gypsum board—all in a high-key atmosphere that allows the color to be provided by the clothes and people. A complete stereo sound system throughout the space provides the music enjoyed by the young.

Barbara Stauffacher's striking graphics are painted identically on the outside and inside of the exterior walls as though inlaid clear through, and they are mirrored on solid walls behind the glass on which they are painted.

VERY VERY TERRY JERRY SHOP
The Cannery
San Francisco, California

ARCHITECTS: Joseph Esherick & Assoc.

283

*Exterior. (Graphics: Barbara Stauffacher.
Photographer: Jeremiah Bragstad.)*

LEFT: *After remodeling.*
BELOW, RIGHT: *Original garage structure.*
(*Photographer: Daniel Bartush.*)

DOWNTOWN GARAGE SOUTH
Detroit, Michigan

ARCHITECT: Louis G. Redstone Associates, Inc.
INTERIOR DESIGNER: Peter Duenos

A fifty-year-old garage in the heart of downtown Detroit was remodeled and converted into several uses—upper floor for office use, and part of the first floor and lower level into a restaurant with decor illustrating the sequence of auto models since the automobile's first production in Detroit. The building, located opposite the Cobo Convention Hall, with its new facade and the very popular restaurant called Jim's Garage, is a welcome addition to the new image of downtown Detroit.

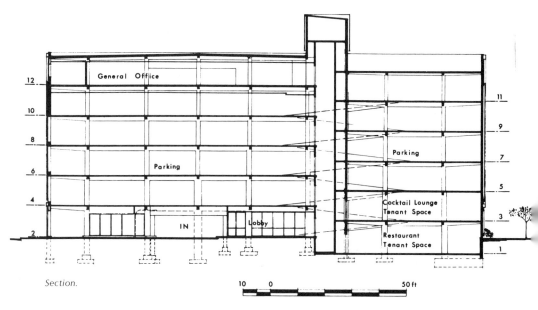

Section.

10   0   50 ft

LEFT: *Interior views of Jim's Garage Restaurant.*
(*Photographer: Daniel Bartush.*)

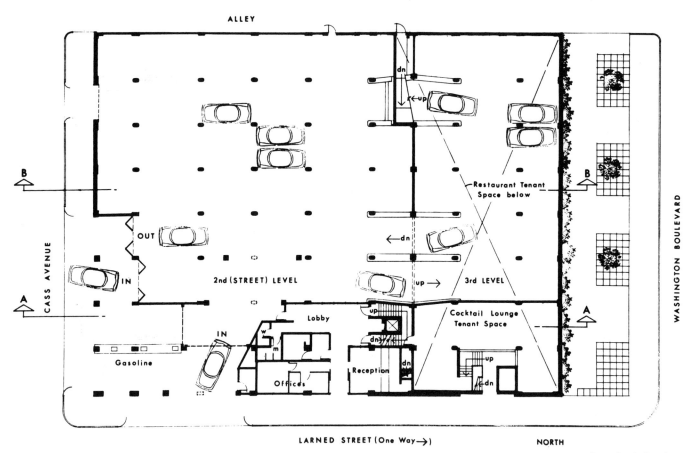

ALLEY

dn
←up

B ⊳——————————— ⊲ B

CASS AVENUE

OUT

IN

A ⊳
————————

Restaurant Tenant
Space below

←dn

2nd (STREET) LEVEL

up →

3rd LEVEL

⊲ B

WASHINGTON BOULEVARD

Lobby

up

Cocktail Lounge
Tenant Space

⊲ A

w
m

IN

Gasoline

dn→

Reception

dn

up

dn

Offices

dn

LARNED STREET (One Way →)

NORTH

ABOVE: *Street-level plan showing restaurant location.*
BELOW: *Upper-floor plan showing new office floor.*

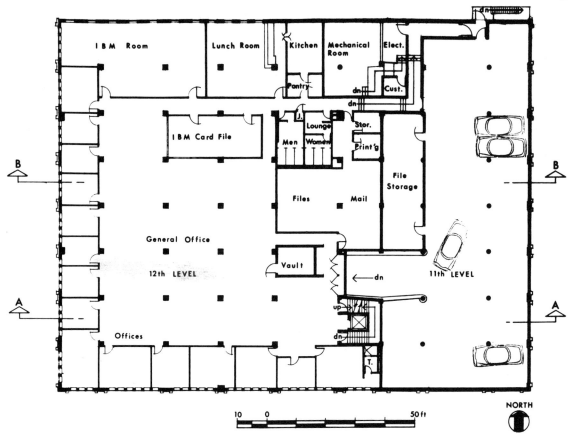

IBM Room

Lunch Room

Kitchen

Mechanical
Room

Elect.

Pantry

dn

Cust.

B ⊳——————————— ⊲ B

IBM Card File

Lounge

Stor.

Men

Women

Print'g

Files

Mail

File
Storage

General Office

12th LEVEL

Vault

←dn

11th LEVEL

A ⊳
————————

up

dn

⊲ A

Offices

T.

10   0   50 ft

NORTH

FORD CITY
Chicago, Illinois
ARCHITECTS: Sidney H. Morris & Associates

Court.

Court interior.

According to architect Sidney Morris, when they wrecked the 1942 Dodge plant, which was used to make airplane motors during World War II, the area between the first and second buildings was allocated for retail and recreation. The area included a bowling alley, billiard parlor, restaurant, twin cinema, post office, and several stores.

The first building was converted into a closed-mall shopping center in the spring of 1963; the second building in the fall of 1963. There were 1,145,000 square feet of area reused in the first building. Both buildings lent themselves well to conversion. Especially helpful was the extra height, which facilitated the installation of mechanical equipment.

The bombprooflike shelter in the lower level was used as a passage for service corridors, meeting rooms, restaurant, and shops. The old ventilating shafts were used for delivery purposes throughout the center. The excellent column arrangement was reused, as were the heating plant, electrical distribution, drainage and storm sewers; but no old walls of the original plant were left standing. The parking area was reused and, where part of the building was wrecked, the floor slab was used for additional parking.

Ford Center is in a thriving community where new apartments and homes are being added. The area is close to good transportation (highway systems) and is supported by a large middle- and lower-middle-income population. Further expansion is anticipated.

Exterior view (perspective).

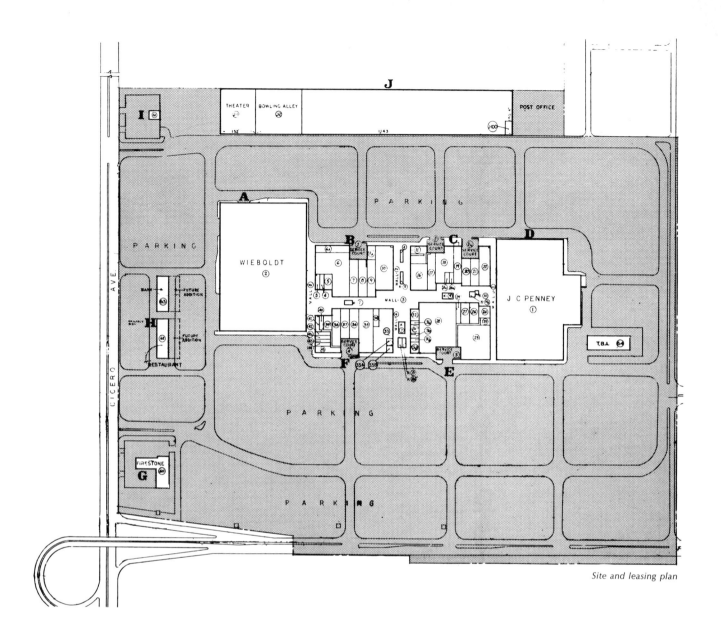

Site and leasing plan

GHIRARDELLI SQUARE
San Francisco, California

ARCHITECTS: Wurster, Bernardi & Emmons, Inc.
LANDSCAPE ARCHITECTS: Lawrence Halprin
 & Associates

Ghirardelli Square, owned and developed by William M. Roth, is a private rehabilitation of an entire city block of historical brick buildings which formerly comprised the Ghirardelli chocolate factory. It is the first major project in the redevelopment of the north waterfront area of the city.

The nineteenth-century atmosphere of the low buildings and the site, which commands spectacular views of San Francisco Bay, determined the design. Old buildings were retained, and new structures, in appropriate materials and forms, were blended with them to create a lively complex of specialty shops and quality restaurants. An interesting series of terraces in the central plaza is created by the stepped floors of the subterranean garage. There are ramps between the terrace levels enabling the handicapped to enjoy the Square.

The owner and the architects agreed in the earliest conception of the Square that full use would be made of the century-old buildings of red brick, but that their restoration would be modern in every sense.

A strict requirement was that any new building would be made fully compatible with the old, through the use of similar materials and forms and not through the simple revival of period details.

As a result, exposed beams, columns, pipes, sprinklers, conduits, footings, brick walls, roof decks, etc., were left intact whenever possible and new elements, such as glass domes, clerestories, gutters, bay windows, were especially designed and crafted.

The Square is virtually a handcrafted project, from the tip of its remodeled Clock Tower at Larkin and North Point Streets, to the bottom of its new 300-car subterranean garage; the great open plaza, kiosk, fountain and gardens, the balconies, terraces, stairs, railings, lights, banners, and cupolas. The "mood" of all these elements in the square block of massive, time-worn structures dating from the early 1860s to 1916, in combination, is one of "a fresh-new-place" and a "nostalgic-old-place," a true Victorian San Francisco mood.

From the start, a seven member Advisory Committee of knowledgeable people helped the owner and the architects to arrive at big and small decisions: the shops, the cafes, restaurants, boutiques, all were to be distinctive operations; the smallest sign had to be tasteful; the contours of the garage tunneled into the slope would determine the planes of the plaza; the huge sign identifying the old Ghirardelli Chocolate Company would remain and would be illuminated.

Of the entire complex of old buildings, the Box Factory, only wooden structure in the first phase of the development, was demolished. A Warehouse Building, a Chocolate Building, a Woolen Mill, and a Power House were incorporated into the complex in the second phase of the overall development.

The buildings initially were sand blasted on the outside and gutted on the inside, to make room for the offices, shops and restaurants.

It is interesting to note that the engineers met the city's earthquake code and yet retained timber frames in an architecturally sensitive manner. Design consultants John Mathias and Barbara Stauffacher and sculptor Beniamino Bufano worked in concert to create colors, symbols and graphics for the 300-car garage so that parking guests would readily know at what level they were leaving their car.

The designers worked also with shop owners on the shape, color, lettering and scale of the signs that would be erected to identify their operations. Each sign, whether for public areas or for shops, was of a special, personalized design.

Ghirardelli Square's footage breaks down to 60,000 sq. ft. of plaza; 106, 450 sq. ft. of garage space, and 54,350 sq. ft. of leasable areas.

"The generous esthetic and recreational considerations implied in these figures," declares architect Emmons, "have paid off economically."*

*Excerpted from *American Journal of Building Design*, March, 1966.

Exterior view.
(Photographer: Ernest Braun.)

Court and fountain.
(Photographer: Roger Sturtevant.)

View from street.
(Photographer: Roger Sturtevant.)

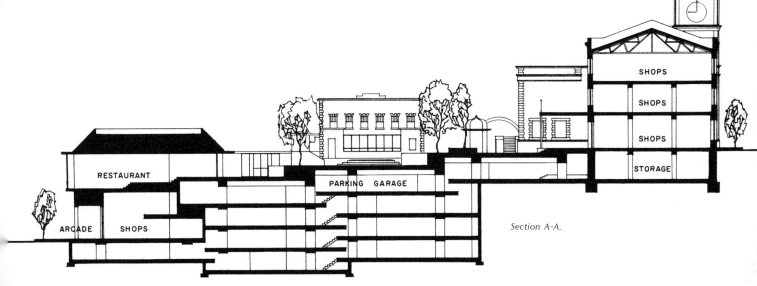

Section A-A.

RESTAURANT

PARKING GARAGE

SHOPS

SHOPS

SHOPS

STORAGE

ARCADE SHOPS

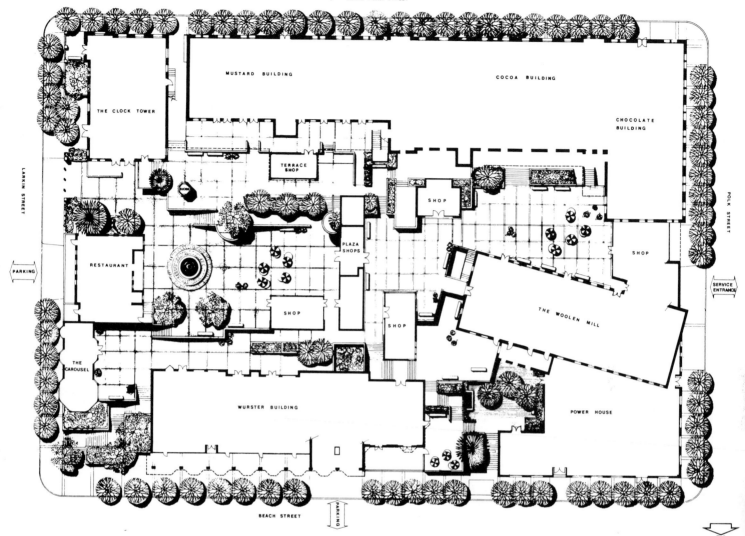

Site plan.

View of restaurant terrace.
(Photographer: Roger Sturtevant.)

According to Benjamin Thompson, the architect for the project,

Faneuil Hall–Quincy Market restoration presents a rare and a genuine opportunity, not only to restore historic buildings, but to bring them back to life authentically as a functioning popular marketplace.

Quincy Market could well point the way for other cities in their replanning not only of major market centers, but of the lively subcenters and exciting streets that future cities need by the hundreds.

The Faneuil Hall Market area of downtown Boston—the Quincy Building, North and South Markets and the streets between—will not only be saved and restored to their condition in the heyday of Boston's central marketplace but the area will also again become a functioning popular market center for food shops, stores, restaurants, cafes, theatres, and such public attractions as parades, puppets, and "people watching."

The plan for the development of the area envisions a true "living market" in the center of Boston. The proposal retains the open street character around the three-block-long buildings, and reserves it for pedestrians in the spirit of a park. It provides sheltering arcades for outdoor vendors and cafes and plans a continuous array of shops and restaurants along both traffic-free streets to create a strong center of activity to serve Boston night and day through the year.

The Marketplace will be operated and maintained as a whole by the Development Corporation. Thus all areas, inside and outside, are programmed continuously as a kind of city bazaar with the variety, balance, and changing activity that is rarely achieved in today's cities. There will be a full range of services, shops, and attractions to create an atmosphere and experience unique to Boston. There will be special emphasis on fresh foods, meats, wine, and cheese to draw area residents on a regular basis.

The key ingredients for a successful operation are these: The Quincy Market (central building) will be operated as a large food-oriented center, with the first floor kept open as a continuous indoor street. Along this street, individual retain concessions will offer meat, fish, produce, dairy goods, cheese, specialty foods and wines. A variety of restaurants and eating places will be stationed along the way, some of them open around the clock.

The present food retailers will be encouraged to remain in the building with the addition of other types of merchants to provide a wide selection of food stores and restaurants.

Under the dome of the Quincy Market, a special focal space will be created by opening the building from first floor to the roof. This Rotunda will have the character of a large lobby or meeting place, where gatherings and informal entertainment will occur continuously.

On balconies around the Rotunda, special food shops and concessions will overlook the activity at this "crossroads" of the marketplace.

Along the outside of the Quincy building on both North and South, a wide clear canopy will extend along the length of the building, creating a covered arcade that may be enclosed by clear panels and heated in winter. Under this canopy, vendors will be able to station their produce wagons throughout the year. Pedestrians may use the shelter of the arcades to travel the length of the marketplace on both North and South Streets. Cafes and eating places will be found along the arcades, with outdoor chairs and tables extending into the street as in a European piazza; these will continue to operate during winter months when the aisles are enclosed and heated, as is common throughout Europe.

North and South Market Buildings at ground level will be reserved for a wide variety of stores, boutiques, services, restaurants, and night clubs. All of these will face toward the traffic-free cobblestone streets, which, with planting, benches, kiosks, play areas and mobile vendors, will become busy pedestrian shopping malls. Major attractions would be positioned at terminal points on sides of the marketplace to assure pedestrian traffic throughout the area.

In selection of tenants, emphasis will be on traditional local restaurants, cafes, and clubs under owner-management, to assure high quality and distinctive character.

The design of all shops, signs, displays, street furniture will be coordinated throughout the marketplace, under the supervision of the architect. Design standards will encourage not uniformity, but consistency and quality, to give the market lively variety, color and visual richness.

The architect's proposal includes the recommendation that the area adjacent to the three market buildings from Faneuil Hall to the Blackstone Block be integrated into the planning of the market complex to assure continuous design of the ground areas to set off Faneuil Hall. If feasible, closing off Clinton Street would allow the creation of "Dock Square Park" as a living gateway between the City Hall area and the market area, as a transition to the waterfront itself. Dock Square Park would be landscaped with benches, flowering trees, seasonal and perennial gardens, and paved walks. On the border of the park would be a semi-transparent Flower Pavilion, filled with cut flowers, plants, and in the winter with Christmas trees for which the market has long been famous.

QUINCY MARKET
Faneuil Hall
Boston, Massachusetts

ARCHITECTS: Benjamin Thompson Assoc.

View from City Hall.
(Photographer: Robert D. Harvey Studio.)

291

Because the Development Corporation has obtained an unusual financing plan, allowing in effect 100% guaranteed financing prior to leasing, it is not obligated to obtain large institutional tenants of adequate rating to move ahead. This freedom creates a number of unique opportunities in the planning of this area as an optimum city marketplace with the scale and magnitude to function again at the center of city life.

To make a successful mixed-use pattern in the Market, the Development Corporation is utilizing a unique concept of variety marketing. Combining merchandising ideas with architectural aims, it hopes to bring the authentic spirit of the market's history to life in contemporary terms by the following means: specific types of stores and shops will be sought as tenants, to assure a genuine balance of offerings and price ranges. Thus, restaurants will range from popular seafood, Italian, and steak specialty houses, to informal soup bars and coffee shops, to elegant first-class club restaurants, and will be located to create maximum variety of activity.

Areas of the Market will be organized into zones, to create strong collective interest and drawing power to different points, and to give visible contrast to the character of various parts of the complex. Thus, a section of the North Market might include a number of small "Discovery Shops," craft, art, and antique shops, while a contrasting section of the South Market would offer a range of quality stores—cameras, jewelry, fashion boutiques, sporting goods, men's and women's wear. Such zoning will add convenience and fun as well as variety and choice to shopping in the Market.

Specific and varied types of tenants would be sought for office and rental areas, to establish a high calibre of occupancy, and to enhance the built-in activity and mix of the Market. Upper floors of the three buildings will be rented to offices, service shops and agencies, clubs, civic and cultural organizations. Special effort will be made to attract tenants who will benefit from the location and the special kinds of space available—such tenants as professional offices, artists, architects, photographers and designers, publishing houses and related agencies, showrooms and import offices. A meeting room, usable as a small theatre, will be provided at the east end of the Quincy building.

Services, clubs, restaurants and amusements will be related to the needs of downtown Boston business and residential areas, to tenants of the market, tourists, and residents of the larger region. Specifically, the leasing plan will attempt to fill commercial and recreational gaps in the area, and to create a genuinely rewarding place for visitors, (instructive, historic, amusing, restful) that will make Boston the place to visit as well as to live.

Outdoor activities and street fairs of many kinds are planned. These would include parades, local musical talent, special festival days, and possibly a Mobile Theatre Unit bringing children's theatre, puppets and special performers in large open-up vans at the end of the malls on Commerce Street.

The street malls and arcades will be made available to all vendors of the Haymarket area who wish to relocate within the market. In areas not occupied by the established schedule of produce vendors, the Corporation will offer space to other kinds of vendors, including artists and craftsmen, special retailers, and a high quality Sunday flea market.

The New Faneuil Market area will provide restrooms, benches, telephones, child play areas, accessible to the public using the outdoor spaces. Throughout the area there will be convenience kiosks providing centralized city information—maps, activity programs, schedules for the market and city. There will also be such outdoor features as individual bookstalls, news and tobacco kiosks, stalls selling balloons, souvenirs, ices and chocolate, and walk-away lunches of sausages, lobsters and crab-on-a-bun.

The malls will be planned and surfaced so that they may be used by service vehicles on a schedule that does not disrupt other activities of the Market. Trash removal, delivery trucks and other vehicles will be able to reach specific service points at designated hours.

After completion of the pedestrian bridge across New Congress Street, connecting City Hall Plaza directly to Dock Square, Boston's historic Walk to the Sea will be able to proceed directly from the Plaza through the Market to the renovated Long Wharf. The open "street" design of the Quincy building provides a direct covered path through the market, as an alternate to the South Street route that walkers may follow.

R. M. Bradley Company of Boston and Van Arkle & Moss, Inc., of Philadelphia are the developers.*

*From *Sunday Boston Globe,* July 4, 1971.

North Market today, view toward City Hall.

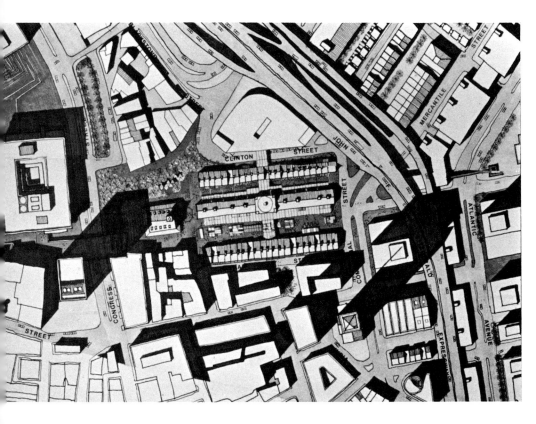

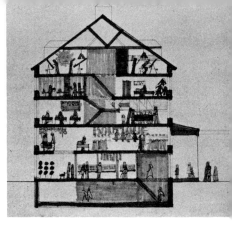

ABOVE: *Section.*
LEFT: *Model of area.*
BELOW: *Sketch showing walk to waterfront through market.*

293

UNDERGROUND ATLANTA
Atlanta, Georgia
ARCHITECTS: Jova Daniels Busby

Underground Atlanta is a restoration project in a long-forgotten, neglected area in downtown Atlanta. Although most Atlantans were aware of the "underground" city's existence, little was done to return the area to active duty until 1967. In that year, a decision was reached to restore the city and create a well-researched mass development plan towards that end. The following year Underground Atlanta, Inc., a private development company, was formed. Operating on an eighteen-month timetable, this company began restoration. The four-block area is under paved-over viaducts which were constructed in the late 1920s as streets to carry local traffic over the train tracks which crossed the downtown area. As a result, the business area, hidden by overhead structures from the main traffic, moved to the upper level and abandoned the old historic street. This area became almost completely deserted and abandoned with the exception of the few derelicts who sought shelter there.

The problem was to create an environment making the best use of the existing historical character of the area. Architect Henri Jova says

> The design tone already exists in this unique area. It becomes a matter of using what is there, of restoring the aesthetic environment that existed during the 1870–1900 period.
>
> We've tried to keep the spirit of the place and revitalize it. We have not attempted an archaeological Williamsburg approach. We've attempted instead, to maintain everything that was there of the period—restoring and freshening it up and we've filled in the blanks in an appropriate way. We're making it a more exciting and swinging neighborhood and we're also introducing a little bit of the 20th century, too. It will be a recreation of that period but brought to life in our day. There will be mod boutiques. We felt these would be proper.

Underground Atlanta currently is a successful business operation for a large number of shops, boutiques, restaurants and bars. This project is an example of historic restoration through economically viable business ventures.

Parking area.

FAR LEFT: Kenney's Alley. This is a
pleasant shopping place for all
members of the family.
Highlighted by old brick,
gaslights, and plantings, it is
lined with interesting and
unique shops and restaurants.
CENTER: Kenney's Alley Plaza as
viewed from upper promenade
deck. The building in the
background is a remodeled old
parking garage. The walkways
and gaslights are all new
construction.   LEFT: The corner
of old Alabama Street and old
Pryor Street, showing the
underside of the reinforced
concrete viaduct that was built
in the twenties. The Corinthian
column marks the original
entrance to the Bentley Hotel.
(Photographer: Clyde May
Photography, Inc.)

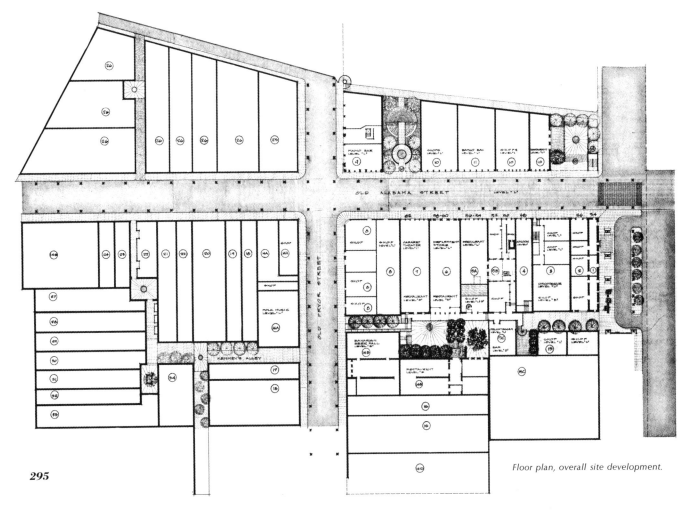

Floor plan, overall site development.

WHARFSIDE

San Francisco, California

ARCHITECTS: Joseph Esherick & Assoc.
DEVELOPER: Abbott Western

Another illustration of the reconversion of a Victorian-style warehouse, built circa 1907, is the Wharfside complex. It is located near Fisherman's Wharf, Ghirardelli Square, and the Cannery.

The upper two floors of the four-story building were transformed into 100,000 square feet of high-class office space. The lower two levels were converted into a commercial complex of fashion shops, restaurants, and a museum of old San Francisco. The open space between one side of the building and The Cannery has been turned into a landscaped mall. Almost all renovated offices feature original brick walls, wood beams, and timbered pillars with the exception of interior offices, where only a few main structural walls are brick. Every effort was made to accentuate the original Victorian flavor of the architecture through design emphasis in furnishings and interior decor to complement the wood and brick.

As with many restorations, Wharfside lent itself to total freedom of office and shop decor that reflected the interests and activities of the tenants. The developers encouraged this individuality. As a result, such interesting effects have been created as a steamship office in turn-of-the century styling, a reception area built around gold-mining relics, a stockbroker's office in early-1900 tradition, and a display of one of the world's largest antique lock collections. These are subtly blended with abundant use of rough-sawn and stained hardwood paneling, luxurious floor covering, and a variety of imaginative lighting techniques. Backdrops are antique brick walls and beams and 250 vintage arched brick windows through which spectacular views of San Francisco Bay, Fisherman's Wharf, and Victoria Park are framed.

The lobby is an exciting invitation with its huge natural-wood pillar, rough-sawn cedar tongue-and-groove paneling, white-painted walls, and two large floor-to-ceiling murals. Lobby and corridors are richly carpeted and entrances to different offices all have wood-paneled doors of different designs, grains, and colors, with some having antique wood-framed glass panes. Many skylights were cut into the roof, creating sun wells in corridors as well as offices on both floors. A large elevator shaft was turned into a light well, creating an atriumlike effect in a third-floor office. Where skylights were not used, large overhead-panel fluorescent lights create the effect of skylighting.

To initiate a successful renovation project, a developer has to have vision and imagination of the potentials. But before any decision is made, a detailed analysis of the economics and the investigation of the condition of the structure must be checked into. Robert Abbott, President of Abbott Western Developers suggests the following guidelines:

> Location for commercial redevelopment should be in an area with potential for traffic and near an area which already attracts people. Most old buildings are in blighted or run-down

Exterior view, renovated building.

locales, and one must be sure that people are willing to enter the area and that it is easily accessible.

Only buildings constructed of natural materials such as brick and stone should be considered. Wood frame structures should be avoided as structural quality of wood is usually poor due to age, and many municipal codes preclude use of wood for public frame buildings.

Determine the market for your building and ascertain if there is a need in the area it will serve. Make certain there is space for ample parking.

Make an engineering study of the building from sub-ground level up before purchase of lease. It will help uncover any hidden or major construction problems that might make the proposed project financially impractical. Take core samples to determine reinforcement and aggregate content if the building is poured concrete. If possible obtain original blueprints of the structure and plans of utility lines from the city. It may save time and help avoid expensive obstructions.

Develop a pro forma financial projection and economic feasibility analysis to confirm initial findings. Make certain that when restoration is completed you have sufficient leasable floor space to realize an 18 to 22% annual return on your capital investment. Determine gross leasable space before taking over a building for restoration work. However, bear in mind that with the relative uncertainties of restoration, you may lose some of your projected leasable space.

Make an attempt to control the project's surrounding environment. This is, of course, dependent on the developer's vision and financial capabilities, but if other developers are involved in adjacent areas, everyone will benefit if plans are coordinated.

Selection and control of tenants is equally vital to successful commercial development. Seek the type of tenants who are looking for an out-of-the-ordinary showcase for their products or services; and plan the tenant mix in advance to attract the community's shoppers and tourists.

A retail complex redevelopment must be a captivating place to visit and talk about and the same holds true for offices.

In a theme development, Mr. Abbott cautions that one shouldn't expect to attract Triple-A retailing organizations or many franchise-type businesses because they fear they may lose their own public identification if they go along with the project's image of uniqueness. On the other hand, Triple-A companies are most desirable for offices complexes as their leases are easily financed and they draw attention to the development.

When redevelopment comprises both office and retail complexes, such as at Wharfside, it is important to soundproof offices from the retail area. The landlord also must control hours, primary use of space in the development and design of interiors and fixtures.

He should also take initiative and control in forming a merchants association to assure unified promotions for which each tenant contributes 1% of his monthly gross. He should control all signs on the property . . . and all common areas, which can become, in many cases, income producers through selling types of merchandise not in conflict with his tenants. . .

The building is a dramatic example of an ever-appealing and exciting work environment that can be created in a historic structure. Wharfside is a good revenue-maker. Rentals average $6.84 and compare favorably with new high-rise office buildings in San Francisco.*

*Reprinted from *Buildings* Magazine, May, 1970.

CLOCKWISE, FROM TOP: *Floor plan, Hyde Street and beach level. Interior of See & Sea Travel Service. (Architects: Andersen & Palmer. Photographer: Craig Sharp.) Interior office of Abbott Western. (Designer: Will Wong. Photographer: Craig Sharp.)*

LEFT: *Courtyard.* (*Photographer: Ian Samson.*)
BELOW: *Courtyard.*

YORK SQUARE
Toronto, Ontario, Canada
ARCHITECTS: A. J. Diamond & Barton Myers

York Square is at the edge of the Village—what once was Yorkville, and is now a part of Toronto as Greenwich Village is of New York or the waterfront is of San Francisco. It is where the action is—but action housed in old buildings—a mixture of new life in old shells.

According to the architects it started with a collection of old buildings, some of which had at one time possessed architectural merit. All had been mutilated beyond the point of restoration to the original. The sites, however, were deep—providing unutilized back yard areas.

A new series of shop fronts were designed. The geometry of the design of the new has been related to the Victorian remains of the old wherever it was worthy of preservation.

There are round and rectangular openings—round windows to look into and focus attention on merchandise, and rectangular openings to walk through. The effect of this focus and separation of shop fronts (as contrasted to the unending, undifferentiated glass shopping mall or to sidewalk storefronts) has been dramatic. One store which was in operation before the renovation now reports a 40 per cent increase in sales.

The supergraphics, done in collaboration with Barrie Briscoe, are designed to enhance the large scale and tie the complex and its signage together, much as the Victorian stringcourse once did. Toronto is rich in such examples of Victoriana.

The irregular backs of the old buildings now form one side of an interior square. A new building, in the form of a U, has been designed to utilize the deep sites and to make a place for pedestrians away from the automobile. A large maple tree dominates the square.

The new building consists of ground-floor shops and a restaurant, a glass-enclosed lunch terrace, open roof coffee terraces, and a small fondue-and-chocolate shop. The back walls of the restaurant and lunch terrace are washed by skylight. Access to the roof level is via corner stairs, making obvious where the access is. The corner spaces are the "dark spots" in a square plan and are hence used for the service cores.

Vidal Sassoon Salon.
(*Photographer: Ian Samson.*)

LEFT: *Aerial view. (Photographer: Ian Samson.)* BELOW: *Rear elevation before renovation. (Photographer: Panda/Croyden Associates.)*

PART SIX

Emerging New Developments in Shopping Environment

At this period of rapid change in every phase of our life structure, which is being affected by economic, social and environmental factors, it is difficult to foresee with substantial accuracy the directions which shopping centers will take. The conflicting opinions of what the future holds directly affect the planning of all centers. It is confusing to read reports by experts on population growth foretelling a doubling of the population near the year 2000 and at the same time to receive comprehensive reports from reliable scientific sources which emphasize the necessity of stabilizing the population and give statistics showing that the birth rate is steadily declining because of the attitude of the younger generation. I personally think that the need for new centers will continue regardless of the lower population estimates.

Social and economic changes will have a major effect on the building of isolated shopping centers which are far removed from the cities and can be reached only by car. There is already and there will continue to be a necessity for using the existing center as a core for a new town. Surrounded by their vast parking areas on land, which is rapidly becoming too expensive to reserve just for parking use, these centers will have to reevaluate their old concepts. It will become more and more evident that from both an economic standpoint and from the standpoint of social and human needs, centers will have to become more than just shopping areas. They will have to be part of a total complex that includes housing, commercial, educational, and recreational facilities. Of utmost importance is the establishment of a long-range master plan scheduling the construction of the new buildings which are most needed. This more intensive use of land will require multilevel parking structures to accommodate the added number of car spaces.

An example of this kind of planning is the Echelon Shopping Center, developed by the Rouse Company. This is a two-level, two-department-store regional center located in the city of Echelon, a twenty-two-minute drive from Philadelphia. Further expansion calls for the addition of two more department stores and a number of other stores and shops. Located on 400 acres, this controlled development will include a school, office buildings, community center, cultural center (theater, library), three dispersed recreational centers (youth oriented), and a village square adjacent to the mall and the lake. Thirty-two acres are allotted for parks, open spaces, and four ponds on the site, making use of the already existing stream. The residential area, including townhouses, garden apartments, and some high-rise buildings, is planned for a population of 10,000.

Another illustration of long-range staged planning is the new town of West Jasper Place near Edmonton, Canada. There the first stage called for the open-mall shopping center. The second stage called for enclosing the mall and utilizing the existing surrounding parking space for office, recreation, high-rise apartments, and low residential buildings, all interconnected with landscaped plazas and walks. Paralleling this stage is the building of facilities for the main mode of transportation, which is planned to be rapid transit. (See pages 304–307.)

Many of the large multilevel centers with three to five major department stores already include theaters, large assembly halls with amphitheaters, skating rinks, and even chapels, all of which indicate the trend for the center to become the hub of a new satellite town connected by rapid transit and other adequate transportation to the nearest major city. One of the forward-looking concepts which illustrates this is shown in plans of the Crossroads Center, Oklahoma City, Oklahoma (page 308).

An example of a European new town core planning is the Nordwestzentrum Center in Germany, which is connected by subway to nearby Frankfurt (page 309); while a key example of phased planning is the Columbia Mall (page 310).

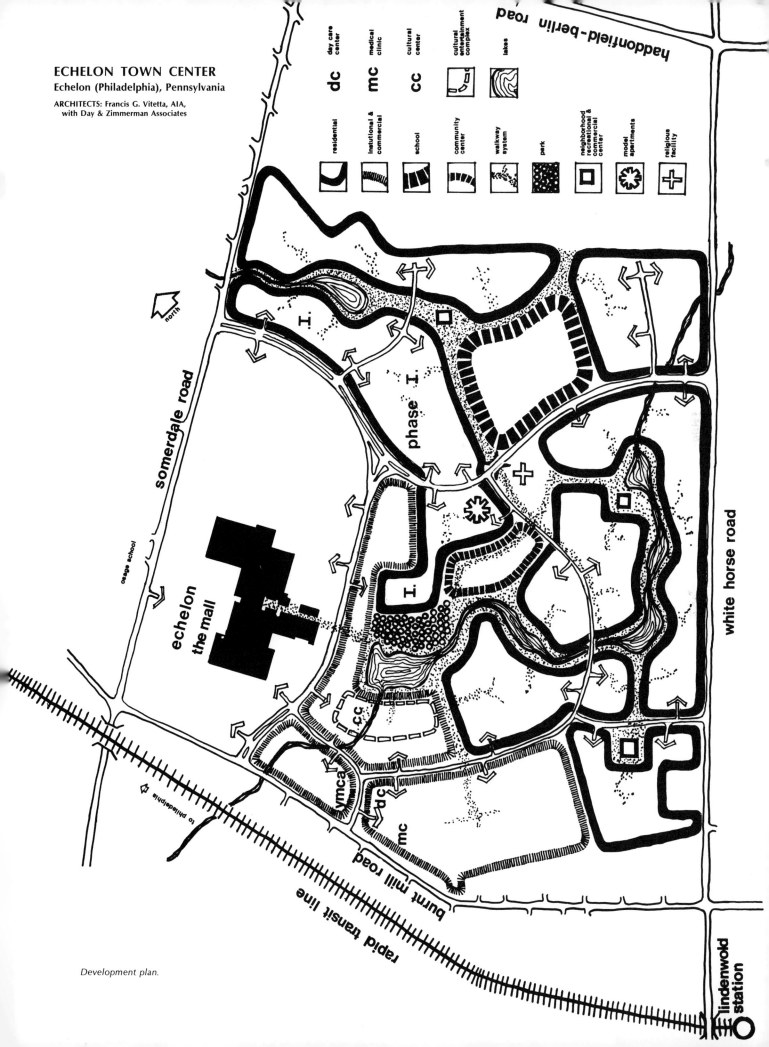

ECHELON TOWN CENTER
Echelon (Philadelphia), Pennsylvania

ARCHITECTS: Francis G. Vitetta, AIA,
with Day & Zimmerman Associates

dc day care center
mc medical clinic
cc cultural center

cultural entertainment complex
lakes

residential
institutional & commercial
school
community center
walkway system
park
neighborhood recreational & commercial center
model apartments
religious facility

haddonfield-berlin road

somerdale road

osage school

echelon the mall

phase I.

white horse road

cc
ymca
dc
mc
burnt mill road

rapid transit line

to philadelphia

north

lindenwold station

Development plan.

WEST JASPER PLACE TOWN CENTRE
Edmonton, Alberta, Canada
ARCHITECT: Peter Hemingway

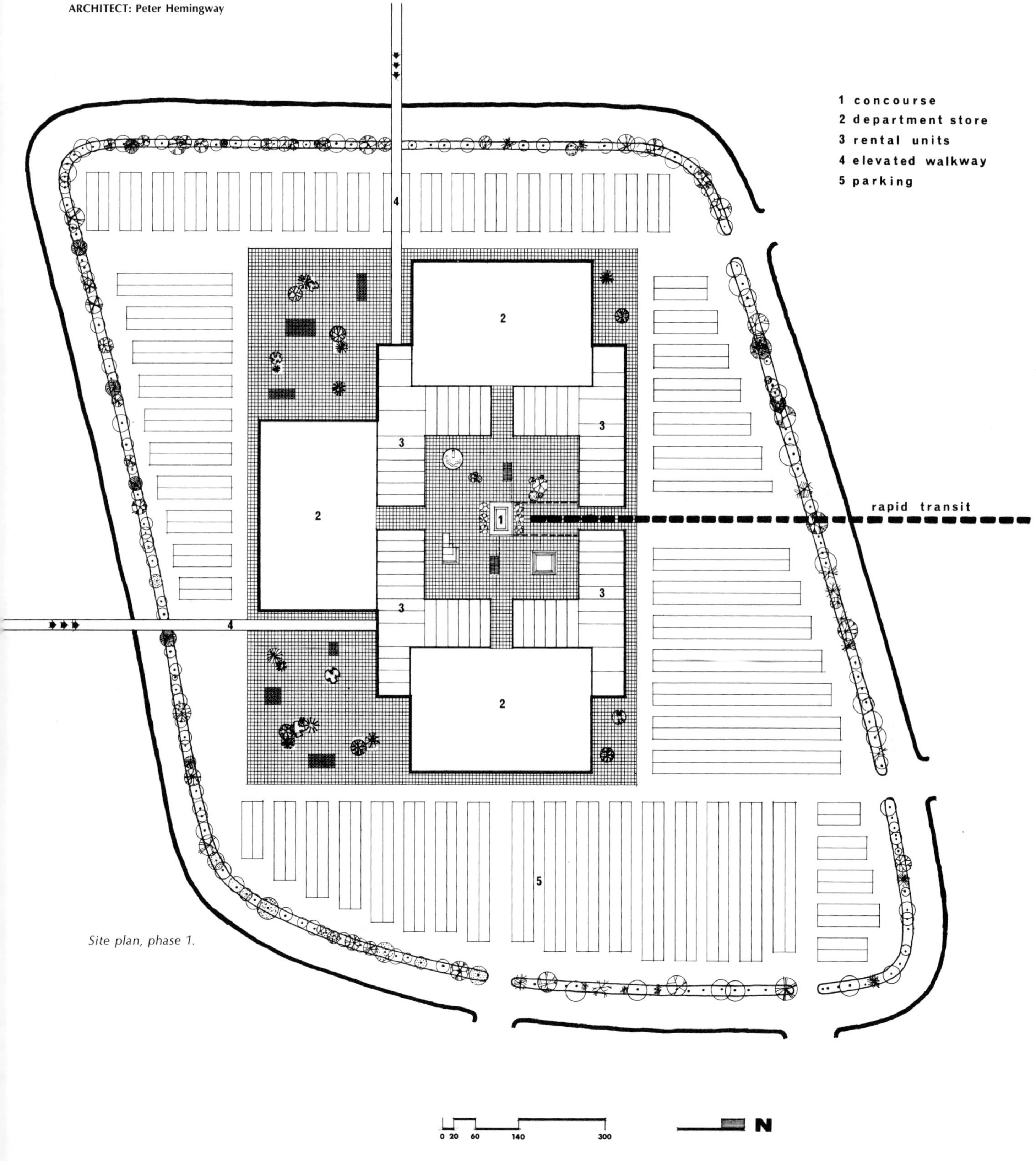

1 concourse
2 department store
3 rental units
4 elevated walkway
5 parking

rapid transit

Site plan, phase 1.

0 20   60   140   300

N

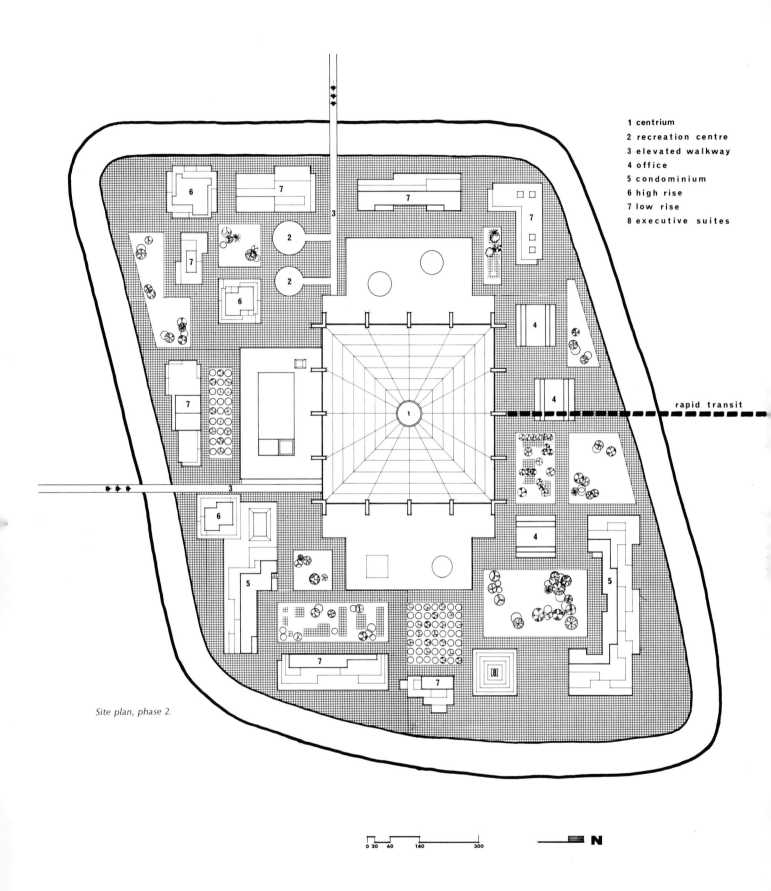

1 centrium
2 recreation centre
3 elevated walkway
4 office
5 condominium
6 high rise
7 low rise
8 executive suites

rapid transit

Site plan, phase 2.

0 20 60 140 300

N

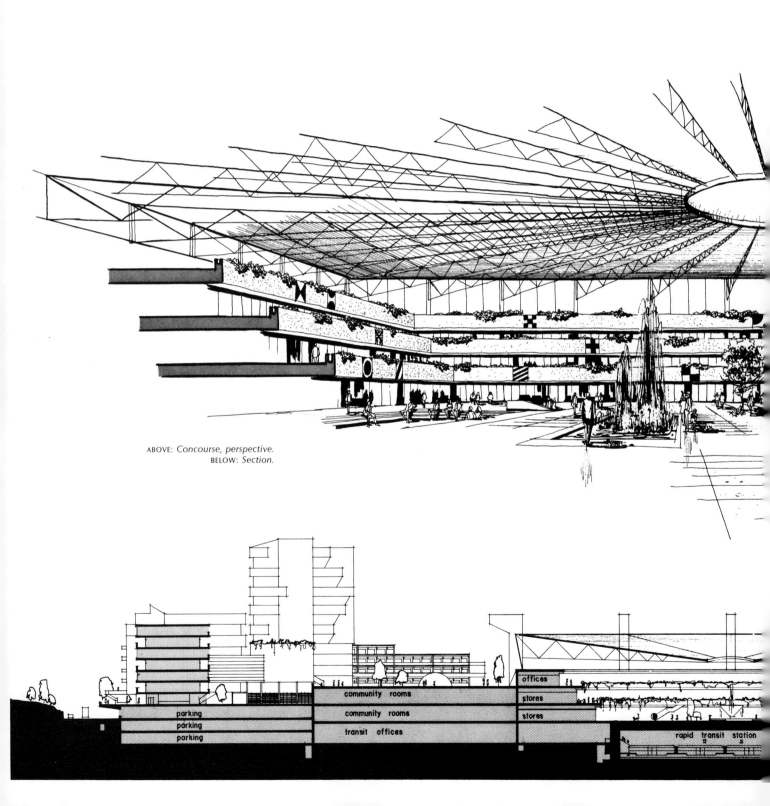

ABOVE: *Concourse, perspective.*
BELOW: *Section.*

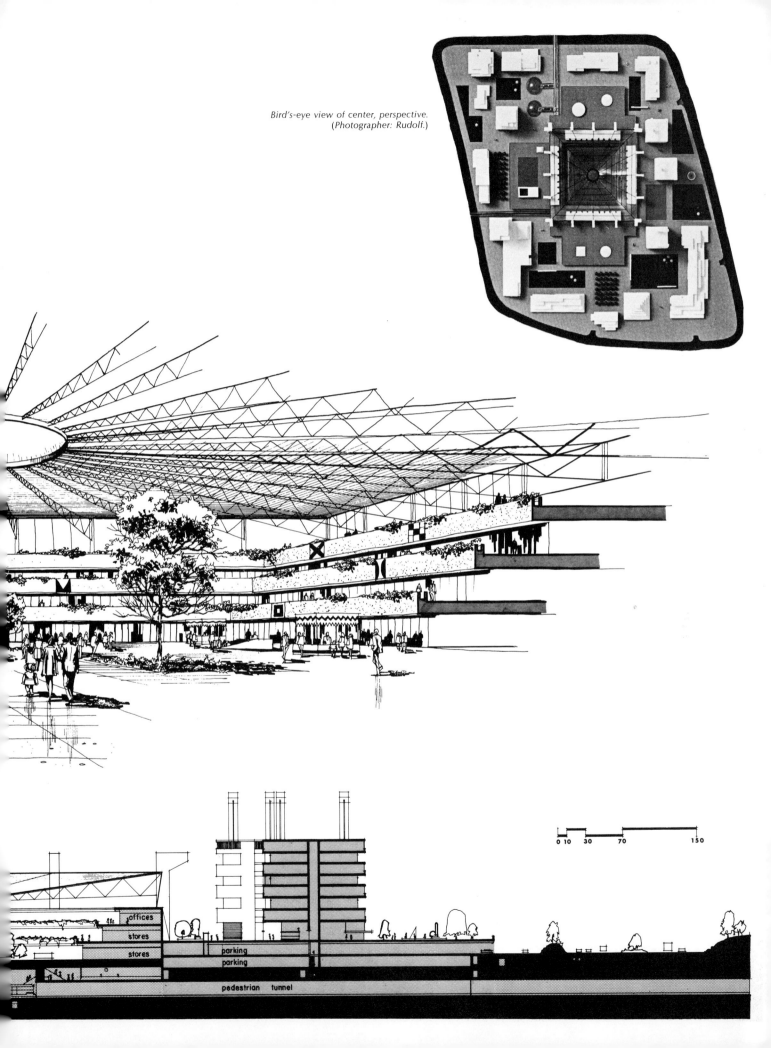

Bird's-eye view of center, perspective.
(Photographer: Rudolf.)

offices

stores

stores

parking

parking

pedestrian tunnel

0 10 30   70   150

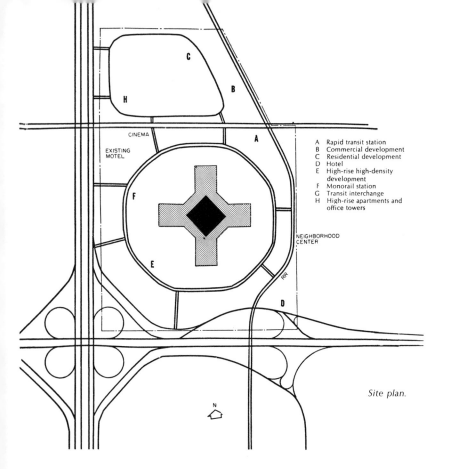

A Rapid transit station
B Commercial development
C Residential development
D Hotel
E High-rise high-density
   development
F Monorail station
G Transit interchange
H High-rise apartments and
   office towers

Site plan.

One of the forward-looking concepts is projected for this center, where the architects have developed an integrated living-working shopping environment. The master plan for the project includes, beside the center itself with its four department stores and various specialty shops, three motor hotels, several office towers, a theater, a high-density residential area including both high-rise apartments and 80 town houses, 50,000 square feet of neighborhood businesses, and a supermarket area for an estimated center total of over 1,640,000 square feet. The role of transportation within the complex was considered of paramount importance and set as one of the goals of total cohesiveness of all facilities via a well-articulated vehicular and pedestrian traffic system. The entire complex is planned to be served by a high-speed belt highway with direct access to all parking areas. Following the path of this highway a monorail is planned, reaching into the housing area and with frequent stops, one of which, it is hoped, will be a link with a projected regional rapid-transit system that would utilize existing railroad tracks bordering the site on one side.

The center was developed by owner Raymond D. Nasser.
Excerpted from *Architectural Record,* March 1970.

CROSSROADS CENTER
Oklahoma City, Oklahoma

ARCHITECTS: Omniplan Architects
  Harrell & Hamilton

Development model.

This interconnected group of buildings covering approximately 19 acres serves as the commercial and cultural center for the core of a new town, which is planned to serve the immediate and regional areas of between 80,000 and 100,000 residents.

The design for the center provides four levels of activities. The lowest level is the subway station connecting the center with outer Frankfurt. Above this is the level for parking (2,056 cars) and for gas stations. The third level is for a bus station, indoor pool, civic and youth center, high school, police station, post office, and storage and delivery facilities. The fourth level provides for attractive pedestrian walks and for additional bus terminals. The design of the center is to accommodate three large department stores, a supermarket, and sixty-eight other shops. There is a medical center, office space, and 175 living units (one to four bedrooms). A public building with two meeting halls—one having a capacity of 900 and the other of 300, as well as several clubrooms—serves also as the cultural center.

NORDWESTZENTRUM
(Shopping center and town complex)
Frankfurt, Germany

ARCHITECTS: Beckert & Becker

View of center.
(Photographer: Werner Berger Fotografie.)

View of center.
(Photographer: Ulfert Beckert.)

Section. (1) subway; (2) parking level; (3) lower pedestrian and service level; (4) main pedestrian level; (5) first floor; (6) ventilation duct of parking level; (7) tree pit; (8) emergency staircases; (9) walkway; (10) service road; (11) stores; (12) retail business; (13) offices; (14) flats; (15) pedestrian bridge; (16) air exhaust of parking level; (17) level of subway gates.

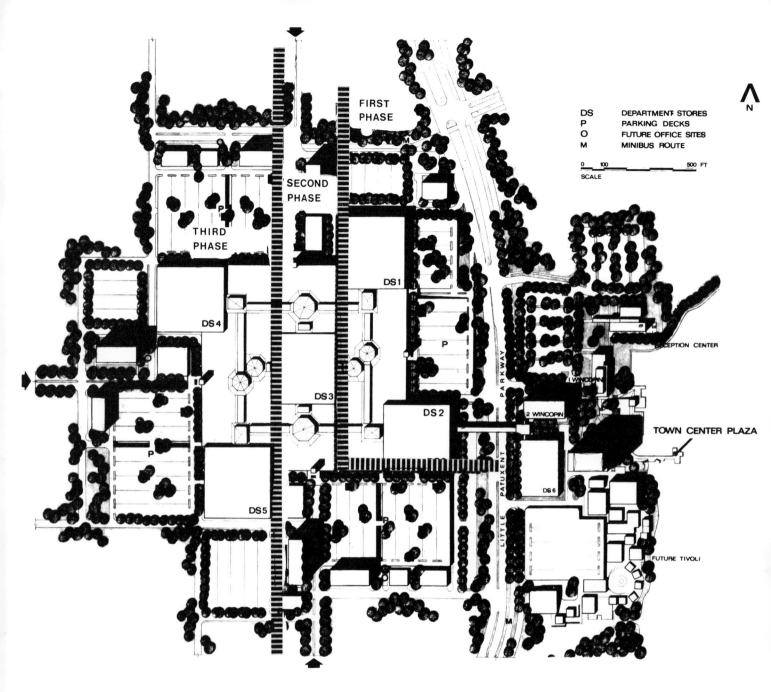

On the site of 70 acres designated upon the general development plan as the core of a town retail center, the program was to design a fully enclosed, air-conditioned, two-level shopping mall to be built in stages up to an ultimate development potential of between 1,800,000 and 2,200,000 square feet of retail selling space. The center would contain, ultimately, five major and one minor department stores and 600,000 square feet of additional shops along with associated public spaces. The latter were to include commercial, display, and garden courts with major shopping facilities around them. Parking at approximately five spaces per 1,000 square feet was to be at grade and on parking decks. The first stage was to consist of two department stores, 300,000 square feet of retail shopping space, and associated public areas. The second stage would add a third department store and 120,000 square feet of retail shopping space. The third would complete the complex and would include deck parking. The center was to be linked with the existing town center plaza and to take note of previous planning decisions establishing highway alignments and entrances and the projected minibus route.

COLUMBIA MALL
Columbia, Maryland
ARCHITECTS: Cope, Linder, Walmsley

The above examples illustrate the ever-increasing recognition that rapid transit will be an essential element in the planning for the new town centers. The fact that Transpo '72 in Washington, D.C., exhibited varied types of rapid transit systems proposed by major automobile and other large corporations foretells the immediacy of people-moving systems.

The new town planning is accelerated by the entrance into this field of a new type of developer. We are familiar with private land developers, department store owners, insurance companies, and property owners as prime initiators in developing commercial centers. The new powerful stimulant is being provided by large industrial corporations like Ford, Chrysler, General Motors, Alcoa, and others. These corporations, through subsidiaries, are in the process of building complete new towns which include shopping centers as well as residential, educational, and recreational facilities. The commercial areas in these new towns will become hubs of cultural and recreational life.

Whether the initiative for the planning comes from private, public, or a combination of both sources, the basic consideration underlying all planning needs to be the creation of an environment in harmony with human requirements.

One important element which will have decisive influence in the planning of both new shopping centers and new town cores is the growing concern for the environmental and ecological factors on the part of the communities involved. The new environmental activists represent a wide range of viewpoints. On the extreme side, some people oppose growth and land development in almost any form. These are frequently the people who view with growing frustration and apprehension the continuing pollution of our environment and desolation of our land. They are convinced that nothing less than a total halt to any kind of growth can save us. They are impatient with the legal property rights that give the owners of vacant, rolling, wooded land the power to use it in any way they please except—or so it seems—in the one way that the protesters see as proper (i.e., leaving undeveloped for public use). They are angry at the frequently disproportionate power of developers and the concomitant insensitivity of local government to the environmental needs of its people.

A more realistic approach is taken by a larger number of concerned citizens, young and old, who are also sensitive to the issues, bright, knowledgeable, and relentless in their pursuit. Their chief hope lies in their determination to ferret out the unpublicized inadequacies in pending developments and in their ability to evolve alternative solutions.

In the smaller communities, opposition also comes from downtown merchants who are distressed by the prospect of a massive new source of competition and from city property owners who wish to prevent a decline in their property values.

It is usually true that the larger developments have the greatest and potentially most harmful impact on the community, so quite naturally these become the prime targets of the environmentalist. Projects most easily identified in this category include public roads, private residential developments and—most obvious and controversial of all—shopping centers. The traditional procedures for obtaining approvals from municipal authorities are being questioned more and more. Whereas in the past the municipalities were only too anxious to have new building complexes which would bring increased taxes, more jobs, and increased land values, the situation now is quite different. The public's deep awareness of additional pollution, ecological imbalance, spoilage of natural terrain, increased traffic and other problems is forcing the municipal authorities and their city planners to study, evaluate, and take into serious consideration the citizens' justifiable demands.

In a recent case in a small midwestern university city, the construction of a large regional suburban shopping center was delayed for several years pending many public hearings and continual bargaining for better ecological solutions. As a result, the developer agreed to contribute financially to the solution of the traffic problems, to subsidize a bus system over a three-year period, to provide space for a day care center to be handled by another organization, and to redesign the parking area so that there would be a number of parking areas separated from each other by a combination of grade levels and dense landscaping. In addition, the developer agreed to provide special turn-off areas and bus shelters.

The shopping center concept also shows its influence in the revitalization of smaller cities and towns throughout the states, especially when they are located close to industries. They seem to be more ready for this change. There is less exodus and the residents are more apt to take pride in the improvement of their "home town." An example from one of the author's recent experiences is that of Northville, Michigan, a city of 6,000 people. Here a progressive city council, with the approval of the constituents, condemned a number of obsolete buildings in the center of town and sold the land to a developer with the proviso that an enclosed shopping mall be built. In this case, the city undertook to provide parking facilities and leased them to the developer on a yearly basis. We see then, whether dealing with large regional centers or constructing small centers within the city, that the citizens' involvement is present in both.

The citizens' concern and their influence on decisions as to location and design of the shopping center may be further strengthened by the current proposal of the American Institute of Architects for positive action. The AIA appointed a National Policy Task Force Committee chaired by Archibald Rogers, FAIA, which proposed that the United States Government immediately allot $5 billion to acquire a million acres in and around sixty urban areas.

It is proposed that the federal government, through the state authorities, would sell or lease individual parcels of this land over the next two to three decades to reliable developers who would follow a master plan for the proposed "new neighborhood growth units" (varying from 500 to 3,000 housing units with attendant services). These "growth units" could be located in the existing cities or be the starting points of new towns.

In addition to the above developments, there will probably be other factors which will emerge to challenge the builders of this decade. All these elements together will have a strong impact on the whole shopping center industry. There will have to be a constant reevaluation and reorientation of thinking to adapt to the fast-changing requirements to improve the quality of our community life and our environment.

Index